Soulful Love

The Search for the Self

By

Deri Joy Ronis Ph.D.

Published by:
Kima Global Publishers,
P.O. Box 374,
Rondebosch
7701
Cape Town
South Africa

ISBN 0-9584261-1-2

First edition February 2002

© 2000 Deri Joy Ronis PhD

World rights Kima Global Publishers. All rights reserved. With the exception of small extracts quoted for review purposes, no part of this publication may be reproduced, translated, adapted, stored in a retrieval system, or transmitted in any form or through any means including electronic, mechanical, photocopying, recording or otherwise without the permission of the publisher.

http://www.kimaglobal.co.za

http://www.DrDeri.com

kima@global.co.za

Cover image: Atmara Rebecca Cloe

Cover design: Alan Fisher

E-mail publisher: kima@global.co.za

E-mail author: DrDeri@aol.com

DEDICATION

This book would not have been made possible without the inspiring heartache by those who unwittingly contributed to its creation.

(Forgive them, Father, for they know not what they do!)

SOULFUL LOVE

Questions are important—they open the mind,
and in our search, we seek and find...
desires come true, find what works well for you
and thus, create life anew.

How did you learn to love?
When someone says they love you, how do you react?
In a romantic relationship, what do you mean when you say, "I love you?"
Does this differ from telling someone you love them universally? How?
Is it easier for you to say "I love you," if you're not romantically involved with that person?
Does the idea of commitment scare you?
What do you need to feel safe to love and be loved?
What is your definition and current understanding of love?
Has it changed over the years, if at all?

Do you allow yourself to unfold in love one day at a time?
How much attention do you give to understand love?
Or do you not think of it at all?
Do you create plans that nurture you and your beloved and share ideas?
Do you allow for growth in space and time?

One aspect of love is surely in a universal sense, without attachment.
Then, of course, there is the way that lovers who are best friends speak to one another.
You desire to share in each others lives and grow...together.

Do you only love from a distance, as if in a dream,
Still searching for your destiny?
Are you afraid to get involved again..
Fearful of what you'll find within?
Practice feeling safe – express your fears

6 Soulful Love : The Search for the Self

And you shall remove the built in stress brought on by the years
Of living in ways that no longer support you, your life or joy..
Many have gone before who feared loves involvement
And yet what would our lives look like without being loved or giving love?
They would be barren waste fields, where we live out only part of our dreams,
Forgotten by the tides of days gone by, it is time to find the love that will renew your soul's ability to fly!

Here are a few ways we love...
We can rise in the morning and bask in the pleasure of our mate's affection,
Moving through the day filled with gratitude, about our connection.. what a gift.
Growing through the rough times and knowing that the greatest challenges bring you much closer, if you allow them to.
Healthy love is being able to love each other inter-dependently, without fear that you'll die without the other or can't be separate or different from them.

There are so many aspects to mature, emotional love,
Sharing in life's journey and the adventures you both create,
It's never too late—to bring newness to your mate..
Never take each other for granted,
Imagine what this feels like?
Communicate what is on your mind that relates to the growth of each of you in kind.
Allow your passion to be expressed in full measure,
Sleeping peacefully with this treasure, warmed by love's presence, this is the essence of soulful love, or is it?

We must allow for spaces in our togetherness,
Without them, our time together may become constrained
With no room left to grow,
and love, without growth, is like a plant waiting to die...

These are but a few attributes of soulful love.
Yet I'm sure I have omitted a few,
Yet necessary for love to grow, it must remain anew.
Consider thoughtfully what your reply might be
To questions of what love implies...

Embrace what you learn
Taking time to think about that for which you yearn
And with answers to guide you, remain consistently true to your feelings..

If you share what you find, it will help empower others to have peace of mind.
Everyone truly wants to know what motivates the heart, mind and soul.
What a way to set your heart free and rediscover anew yet another purpose,
There are none too few.
Does everything you ask of another plant a seed,
Is it based on valid needs?

Release your love from whence it came,
All that unites us is the same.
You are a reflection of what is divine, are you still looking for signs?
Can words ever explain that the soulful search is never in vain?

From the depths of your being desire springs,
It creates the words you long to sing and joining your lives
You create not only perhaps special, precious children,
But works of beauty, as in songs, poetry , books and films, all produced in the mind.
Everything reflects the combination of opposites, male and female,
yin and yang, light and dark, hot and cold, the giver and the receiver...
You need not wait a long time to express yourself unless you think you do!

8 Soulful Love : The Search for the Self

Why not give yourself permission to experience the new?
Of that which you have yearned for – for so long..
Let your intentions be clearly known,
and you will surely reap what you have sown.

Radiate the blessings of shalom
To warm you in winter's melody
And when you think of love.
Let it kindle within your sanctity,
Knowing now — what you do — about your part.
Your intentions will guide you to pass on
the wisdom of your heart.

Deri Joy Ronis
1/31/01

Contents

Dedication 3

Introduction (Comes the Dawn) 11

Chapter 1: Getting Clear – The Odyssey 23

Explains the natural evolution of emotional phases we go through at various points in our lives. The concept of soul-searching is explored as it relates to problem-solving and how to move through the new passages in our journey.

Chapter 2: Overcoming Oppression 47

A discussion of the impact of conflict upon our lives, and how that conflict may have oppressed or suppressed us in some way. Practical approaches for healing the hurts and dysfunctions that people experience due to our cultural mindset of power, domination and control are offered.

Chapter 3: Exploring and Creating Healthy Romantic Relationships 69

Specifically explores our limited views of love in a western context through understanding the concepts of philia, agape and eros. Provides detailed accounts of individuals' issues in relationships, and how they overcame them.

Chapter 4: Beyond Pain: Healing the Heart. 105

Healing the Heart transforms people from trauma to wholeness. It does this by explaining how pain became your experience, and illustrates how to move out of these limiting mindsets into a new cycle of growth. It offers concrete ideas and exercises to accomplish these aims.

Chapter 5: A Discourse on Love 143

Synthesizes various aspects of love from psychology, human sexuality and spirituality. Many perspectives are described in redefining what security is. The concepts of passion, emotion, compassion and trust in relationships are explored.

10 Soulful Love : The Search for the Self

Chapter 6: Everyday Remedies for Self-directed
Well-being 205

This chapter comes directly out of the author's personal experiences over the years as a pastoral counselor, minister, psycho-therapist and mediator. It prescribes simple, everyday methods that people can easily apply to enhance their welfare.

Chapter 7: The Art of Making Peace with Your Life . . 223

A beginning jump-start for readers to employ what they have learned on a very personal level. Concludes with an integrated approach for the ability to attain personal peace, how it is accomplished and maintained through the various stages of life.

Epilogue 241

Bibliography 243

Index 249

INTRODUCTION

Comes The Dawn

"After a while, you learn the subtle difference
between holding a hand and chaining a soul,
And you learn that love doesn't mean leaning
And company doesn't mean security,
And you begin to learn that kisses aren't contracts
And presents aren't promises,
And you begin to accept your defeats
With grace…not the grief of a child,
And learn to build all your roads
On today – because tomorrow's ground
Is too uncertain for plans, and futures have a
Way of falling down in mid-flight.
After a while, you learn that even sunshine
Burns if you get too much.
So you plant your own garden and decorate
Your own soul, instead of waiting
For someone to bring you flowers.
And you learn that you really can endure…
That you really are strong
And you really do have worth.
And you learn and learn…
With every goodbye, you learn."

Veronica A. Shoffstall

~~~

The idea for <u>Soulful Love</u> came about through my own life experiences, as well as the challenges my clients faced. In working with them, we discovered what would help them to move their lives forward, the same way I had chosen to. The title of this book came into being after several changes. Some of those original titles are now reflected as the chapters themselves.

In creating a book, or any other artistic form, it requires one to live, breathe, and think about what they want to express daily. I knew

12 Soulful Love : The Search for the Self

I had to complete this work, for it has haunted me for more than five years. I always believed that my journey would help many people. Writing a purposeful and meaningful book for others is also a way of getting in touch with one's mission and purpose in life. It is also a very practical way to touch the lives of others we don't even know.

The one common thread I encountered was that everyone was involved in a similar search to overcome their more serious challenges. I have never met anyone who didn't want to experience peace of mind, happiness, and the understanding it requires. As a matter of fact, I hear quite often "All I really want is to be happy; I just wish I had peace of mind." Complaints range from not knowing how to handle verbally and emotionally abusive partners to the wide spectrum of dysfunctional behaviors that people grew up with in their families of origin. Perhaps they did not know how to deal with the death of a loved one, be it an adult or a child. Many fears and traumas were borne out of having to adapt to changes, addictions, divorce and self-acceptance. Many of these situations arose by surprise. People were not expecting to be left, to be abused, to be orphaned, alienated or deceived.

I now understand why it has taken me over five years to complete this work. Whether or not I knew it, I was preparing to write the book all the time, because of my own growth through various challenging situations over the years. I have always journaled, which has been very helpful. Processing the changes is equally helpful. In essence, it takes however long it does in order to be able to heal ourselves and make sense of our lives. I couldn't' write about something I was in the midst of living. I had written the chapters throughout the last five years at different points of my journey.

There is a very appropriate saying "Then the time is right, there is no effort, and all the forces in the universe come together to assist in completing the work. The effort was in the preparation, waiting, timing, writing, rewriting, and editing – the overall gestation of that which was awaiting birth all along. In my own search to reconnect with the lost parts of myself, I sought a soulful love. I discovered, however, that peace of mind was tantamount to any other form I wanted to experience with another person. In essence, we all go through searches, and it is ultimately ourselves we must find, come to know and embrace. When someone loses a partner they have been with for a long time, many times they don't want to go on living. These same themes kept repeating themselves in the people I counseled.

Nearly everyone searches outside of themselves for peace of mind, only to discover that it is within themselves. While books and avatars say the same thing, there is nothing that can replace the actual experience. The original title of this work was "The Art of Making Peace With Yourself." I found that "peace of mind" is a byproduct of the soulful search. Everything we expect to find in another that will squelch all of our fears must first be discovered within ourselves. This is not to say that we have to travel the road alone. We are often blessed by those mentors and teachers who inspire us to live a more noble and creative life. To make peace with our lives requires that we first find ourselves. As Socrates espoused centuries ago, "Know thyself."

You must learn to honor all of those situations that challenge you or have caused you pain and disappointment. In actuality, the times filled with the most turmoil force us to grow. Even though some changes are excruciatingly uncomfortable, we create new lives based on the different thinking we had to develop in order to survive. Even Albert Einstein believed that we could not solve a problem at the same level we discovered it. A new element is always necessary. At various points in my own search, I discovered other common themes.

What unites all of our human conflicts is the desire and need to be loved and accepted. Whether working with adults, teenage adolescents, or children, who are in single or dual parent families, divorced or separated, it doesn't make a difference where they work or what their job title is. The same issues invariably show up as a lack of self-love and poor self-esteem. There is often a power imbalance between two or more parties. It is "them" (those other people) versus us, or you versus me. Many conflicts exist due to a limited belief that people have about themselves. Their perception is that they have no control, whether it is over their own lives and circumstances or over the lives of others. It is not surprising that the others with whom people are in conflict rarely ever come to the classes, seminars or counseling sessions. If and when they do, it is usually with an unwillingness at first. As time goes on, however, they start to feel more comfortable because they feel safe, not judged, and become more trusting. That is why it is so important if you are going to invest the time, energy and money in counseling, that you find an honest, ethical, integrity-oriented person, who does not give the profession a bad name. I always advise people that finding a good therapist is like finding a good car salesman. Honesty is critical.

Much of my work focuses on helping others discover what makes them feel better about themselves, which is usually equated with a high regard for the self. Most people are starting to realize that they don't have any control over others. I think what most people want is to learn how to control ourselves and not give their power over to other people. Many problems stem from disharmony in relationship with (but not limited to) the issues of money, loss, career changes, retirement, sadness, depression, multiple addictions, anxiety, family of origin issues, or any of the other difficulties we encounter as human beings. It becomes even more difficult when the conflicts we are having are with non-communicative, significant others. In "The Rules for Being Human," it suggests the following:

We will learn lessons. We may like the lessons or think them irrelevant or stupid. There are not mistakes, only lessons. Growth is a process of experimentation – trial and error. The so-called failed experiments are as much a part of the process as the experiment that ultimately works. A lesson is repeated until learned. It will be presented to you in various forms until you have learned it. When you've learned it, you can go on to the next lessons. If you don't learn easy lessons, they become harder. You will know you've learned a lesson when your actions change....What you create of your life is up to you. You have all the tools and resources you need, what you do with them are up to you. There are three kinds of people: those who make things happen, those who watch what happens, and those who wonder what happened. Take charge of your life, or someone else will. Your answer lies inside you. All you need to do is look, listen, and trust. You will tend to forget all of this.

A long time ago, a very dear older client gave me a gift for my office. It is a framed poster which says, "We go through problems in our lives cleverly disguised as opportunities." This gift was more than just a "gift" to me. Oftentimes, I was faced with the same feelings and challenges about unhealthy relationships and situations which needed to change. These situations could not be sustained without yielding too much self-destruction, confusion, sadness and unhappiness. In my quest, I searched for the answers to some of life's deeper questions by exploring and studying other religious philosophies, and living in different cultures and countries which differed greatly from my own. Although I was not aware of how these experiences would impact my life at the time, I often felt guided. While I didn't always understand what possessed me to do the things I did, and be thought of as "so different" (non-traditional), I became aware as I matured that my life's purpose was being revealed to me one stage at a time. I have long believed that we are given to know what we need to know when it is time and not before then, for what would we do with the information anyway – worry or force things to happen?

Perhaps this is why people are drawn to psychics, or those who claim to predict the future. I have met very few people who are truly gifted in this area, and then there is always our free will. We need to develop our own inner gifts and learn to trust our intuition. We have become far too reliant in our addictive consumption of 900 numbers flashed across TV screens everywhere which promise our answers. Furthermore, our experiences may have led us to believe that numbing our painful feelings and seeking to reduce fear could be addressed through multiple addictions. Addictions have caught nearly everyone in a web, from both affluent families to people we see on skid row. This disease pervades every level of our society, our neighborhood, every school, corporate boardrooms, country clubs and places of worship. It is not a poor person's problem, but a human problem. Addiction, together with the abuse it promulgates, is one of our most severe, current epidemics.

Nearly everyone searches outside of themselves for peace of mind, only to discover that it is within. Because our need to love and be loved is so fundamental, in our desperation, many have looked for love in all the wrong places. Thus, our compulsive consumptions towards sex and other substances provide a temporary relief, and make us forget our unhappiness and our purpose for living. I often wonder what kind of co-dependent world we have built. When we learn to become the masters of our own ships, it is not to say that we can always direct what happens; however, we put our best intentions forth. My Dad used to say it so simply, "Do your best, and God will help you with the rest." Of course, if you are an atheist or agnostic, you need to find a philosophy that works for you. Whatever your belief, there is an invisible power that sustains and animates the universe. It is this power, called the "Ruach Ha Kodesh" in Judaism, and known as the "Holy Spirit" in Christianity, that assists and guides us in accomplishing our goals. Very often, our goals bring about positive changes that effect many people. This is because we live in a reciprocal universe.

A common expression heard in the last few decades is to "follow your bliss." Although this statement may not ring true for you, you are required to find what works best for you. Each one of us is unique and the blueprint for our lives will, consequently, be different. While some are fortunate to know what they want to do with their lives early on, there are those of us who were or are challenged more. It is the proverbial question of "What do I want to do/be when I grow up?" A recent article suggests that it will be highly unlikely for someone to stay in the same profession their whole lifetime. The expected norm in the 21st Century is to have five or six career changes. The former industrial era maintained the belief that you held on to your job for a lifetime. This was a common theme then because the world was much more limited.

This book reflects my present understanding of the evolution of some of our current problems, and the work required of us to move past them. Our many previous systems have failed. We continue to be dominated by fear. Soulful love makes an effort towards the possibility of creating new paths based in love, rather than fear. My approach has always been both spiritual and psychological. Spiritual evolution shifts us from using power to sharing power, both on a personal and political level. And thus, we can embrace the future rather than cling to the old ways of the past.

Raised in traditional Judaism in the turbulent times of the sixties, I found the need to branch out to understand and experience firsthand how other religions and spiritual practices could add more meaning to some of the questions and confusion I experienced in my later teen years. I strongly felt that none of the religious practices of our times were working for the masses of people because of all the war, devastation, and human conflict taking place on our planet. In my search, I studied many of the world's religions, such as Taoism, Catholicism, Hinduism, Islam, Jainism, Baha'i, New Thought (which includes the Science of Mind, founded by Ernest Holmes; and Unity, founded by Charles and Myrtle Fillmore), and the Self-Realization Fellowship principles, founded by Paramahansa Yogananda.

Through my search to understand the dichotomy of life, my interest was sparked to find the answers to other questions like "What is the purpose of life – Why are we here – Where are we going?" Oddly enough, my journey did not culminate in one idea. Rather, it has led me to use an eclectic approach, which I have found to be very useful in my work. As I look back over the last two and a half decades of my life, what has emerged for me is taking the best that each religion has to offer and integrating these precepts into a practical framework for my life. I live a more calm, centered, peaceful life by following some of the recommendations in all disciplines.

The important question for me to always answer is how can I practice what I teach, or as Native Americans might say, "How can I walk my talk?" I have discovered that you don't have to go somewhere to feel God's presence or experience spirituality, although there are certain regions of our planet that promote a more awesome respect for the grandeur of life. I have learned to tune into this presence or access the feeling anywhere, and especially in nature and silence.

This book has culminated in my present understanding of what is involved in the *"work"* that it takes to create a more harmonious, balanced life, especially in today's world. I highlighted the word work, for our lives are an ongoing journey in which much is required of us if we choose to get off the emotional rollercoaster that many of us are on. I believe that change is critical to our personal spiritual growth, social consciousness, organizational health and global and personal security. May this book offer the hope that every child will feel loved by its parents, that you will seek only honest communication as the norm between yourself and others, and social responsibility as the norm in the way business is conducted. May Soulful Love move us into acting out of a conscience that doesn't violate other human beings, and cause you to reflect more on love versus fear, honesty versus lying, nurturing versus pain, generosity versus selfishness, and peace versus violence. Many of us are experiencing the change that is written about here. Once again, you can resist it, watch it happen, or help make it happen.

I wish to thank in particular some of my mentors along the way who have blessed me with their wisdom and kindness. Ottie Sonen was a great gift during some very difficult transitions. She skillfully guided me through many unresolved issues to become a whole, complete adult! I want to also thank Steve Wilson, another "angel" (former therapist) placed in my path, who helped me to deal with issues I was facing years before I ever met Ottie. I have discovered that whenever we go through another life phase, we usually have some kind of challenge, which Gaily Sheehy so eloquently wrote about in her book, Passages. There is help available to all of us, if we will only give ourselves permission to reach out and ask.

Another very significant teacher and influence in my life is the very talented minister, Barbara Lunde, from the Science of Mind Center. She many a time assisted me in overcoming an emotional hurdle, reminding me always to focus on the truth about who I am – a living, growing, loving expression of the Infinite. We actually would joke years later about a seemingly difficult time, and at the time it was difficult! The joke was "Put that in the book as well!"

In addition, I owe a great deal of gratitude to all of the people I have been privileged to work with over the years, including my clients who have also taught me what they wanted to learn for themselves. The same is true about all the various groups of people I have worked with in both organizations and corporations. Dr. Arny Mindell, from the Process-Oriented Institute, taught me a lot about working in conflicted groups. I have great respect for the ground breaking work he pioneered in healing deep wounds surrounding trauma caused by illness, war, and personal devastation. The same is true of the late Danaan Parry, the founder of the Holyearth

Foundation, who first taught me the art of releasing fear and becoming a warrioress of the heart. I also wish to thank those dear departed souls whose words still live on and inspire such as Paramahansa Yogananda, the founder of the Self-Realization Fellowship, Mahatma Ghandi, Martin Luther King, and any of the many others who have taught us about the importance of inner peace and spiritual discipline.

It has been said that when life gives you lemons, make lemonade. While this book explores the art of doing so in a creative, practical way, it also provides insight into many conditions we find ourselves in. Thus, I appreciate having had the opportunity to work in the field of domestic violence, because seeing some of the men and women who chose to change their lives for the better was so rewarding.

I am also very blessed to have a great support system in my family and friends, and you know who you are! Other experiences for which I am grateful include the many wonderful colleagues I have met in the conflict resolution/peacemaking arena, and in the programs and seminars that I both attended and given. I specifically want to acknowledge the work being done by the Men's International Peace Exchange, with which I have worked closely. I would like to acknowledge Paul Kivel for encouraging me in my work. I also want to thank Susannah Bishin for her typing efforts at transcribing tapes from classes years ago, and my former assistant, Virginia Santoro, without whose help, a lot of this would not have been accomplished. Furthermore, I am indebted to Mandy Freedman for her painstaking diligence and patience in helping me complete this work. Last but not least, I am grateful to my publisher, Robin Beck, of Kima Global Publishers who inspired me to finish the book and believed so strongly in its message.

The above people, along with all of my experiences, have brought me to the juncture where I am now. Similarly, you may notice the same to be true for you depending on where you are in your life at different times. Consider what Anais Nin wrote many years ago, and see if any of it rings true for you:

"The woman of the future who is really being born today will be a woman completely free of guilt for creating and for her self-development. She will be a woman in harmony with her own strength, not necessarily called masculine, or eccentric or something unnatural. I imagine she will be very tranquil about her strength and her serenity, a woman who will know how to talk to children and to the men and women who sometimes fear her. Man has been uneasy about this self-evolution of woman, but he need not be, because instead of having a dependent, he will have a partner. He will have someone who will not make him feel that every day he has to go into battle against the world to support a wife and child, or a child-like wife. The woman of the future will never try to live vicariously through the man, and urge and push him to despair, to fulfill something that she should be doing herself.

...She is not aggressive, she is serene, she is sure, she is confident, she is able to develop her skills and she is able to ask for space for herself. The day that woman admits what we call her masculine qualities, and man admits his so-called feminine qualities, will mean that we admit we are androgynous, that we have many personalities to fulfill."

Just as Anais Nin wrote the above as an expression of what she saw coming in the future, my interpretation of what she wrote was also in the hope of transforming our culture. Similarly, others have written with a focus on rethinking masculinity. As a matter of fact, "Rethinking Masculinity" is a chapter in a book entitled <u>Changing Men: New Directions in Research on Men and Masculinity</u>. Michael Kimmel wrote:

"Men are changing....New role models for men have not replaced older ones, but have grown alongside them, creating a dynamic tension between ambitious breadwinner and compassionate father, between macho seducer and loving companion, between Rambo and Phil Donohue. Men today are doing far more housework and spending more time with their children, yet the proportion of domestic time is still skewed heavily toward women. Men are today exploring new options in their work environments, and paying more attention to their physical and emotional health....Men are today developing a wider repertoire of emotions, seeking to express their feelings more deeply and with a wider range of women and men....

The women's movement has suggested that the traditional enactments of masculinity are in desperate need of overhaul. For some men, these critiques have prompted a terrified retreat to traditional constructions; to others, it has inspired a serious re-evaluation of traditional world views."

As <u>Soulful Love</u> implies, the search for the self is critical to the growth of an individual, as well as in seeking partnership. There is a mathematical equation that one times one equals one, and a half times a half equals a quarter. Thus, science presents the truth that half of something is diminished by half of something else, and the whole of something is enhanced by the whole of something else. When we translate this equation to human beings, we have all experienced the disappointment we suffer when we expect others to fix us or make us whole. Many illusions have been shattered throughout the years because of the thinking, songs and literature of the past century, which suggested many dichotomies. "You're nobody 'till somebody loves you." "You're all I need to get by." "I can't live without your love." These are just a few of the millions of messages we have grown through. I am not denying our natural tendency to seek companionship; however, it is, as Thomas Moore wrote so eloquently in <u>Soul Mates</u>:

"A soulful relationship offers two difficult challenges: one, to come to know oneself...and two, to get to know the deep, often-subtle richness in the soul of the other....As you get to know the other deeply, you will discover much about yourself, especially in moments of conflict and maybe even despair, being open to the demands of a relationship can provide an extraordinary opportunity for self-knowledge. It provides an occasion to glimpse your own soul, and notice its longings and its fears. And as you get to know yourself, you can be more accepting and understanding of the other's depth of soul."

So, once again, the work is not easy. The question is whether you are up to the task, or thinking that you can jump from one thing to another without examining the wake of destruction you leave behind you. As Melody Beattie points out:

"Just as nature shifts and moves into new shapes and forms, so do we. Sometimes our shifts happen suddenly. Other times, they take place over years, beginning almost imperceptibly. As we move into increased self-awareness, we will become more aware of these shifts.

We'll know, see and feel when they're taking place. We may not know where they're leading, but we'll know something's afoot. The more we value and trust life, the more we can count on these shifts to lead us forward and trust the new shape being formed in our lives. The more flexible we become, the more we allow for these shifts and work with them, instead of against them, the easier they will be."

I have learned to practice a philosophy based on the affirmation of truth. It reaffirms my hopes, wishes, beliefs and dreams as a reality. It's what happens in the meantime along the road to fruition that can be challenging. May your own search be soulful as you seek to find your "self," and may it be done in love.

CHAPTER ONE

Getting Clear: The Odyssey

Let your life be an exploration.

Let people and places be a part of your life and experience each and every unique situation with a sense of wonder and delight. Look in all directions to seek out the answers you long to know, and discover the secrets that keep questioning your heart.

Be willing to make changes and be ready to face the challenges. Accept the opportunities that present themselves, and endure and cope with the difficulties that can arise from time to time.

Remember that there is no one way to live your life, but a thousand different ways for each of us to be.

Make your life the way you want it to be and create a lifestyle that brings you happiness. Search for your true meaning in life by devoting yourself to your ideals, and enjoy your wonderful adventure through time by making every day special."

~~~

Have you ever felt stuck? This is a common question we ask ourselves at various points throughout life. Sometimes we hope the feelings will just go away, but they don't. Several years ago, I experienced overwhelming feelings of discontent that had been welling up deep within me for a long time. No matter how I tried to ignore or deny these feelings, I was forced to go within and make the arduous journey that would bring me peace of mind. "Peace of Mind" is one of the major themes that I have heard throughout my years in practice. Centuries ago, Socrates philosophized that "The unexamined life is not worth living." Too often, many try to hide from this truth and seek relief in drugs, alcohol, gambling, sex, or any of the other many addictions our age is fraught with.

Soul searching is both a difficult and fascinating process. My niece taught me what an epiphany is; I always called these "aha" moments. You know those times when you really feel you're on the right path. This is not necessarily because you want to take the path, but so often life gives us "situations" which force us to change and grow. We all know too well these moments. You lose your job, your husband or wife leaves you, you have to move, someone you love commits suicide or becomes terminally ill and dies. Other events occur which decide for you that you must do something different to stay alive. I don't mean to just exist, but to really embrace your life and enjoy it, to be the best you can and make use of your abilities. Before my beloved father's death over five years ago, he shared with me that "life is a gift and we should never take it for granted." While I had come to believe this as an adult, I sometimes wondered if "the search" would ever end; meaning how can we appreciate life as a gift when we're mired down with problems.

Problems lead to change, and change brings us to new passages, even if we have to go kicking and screaming. In time, the messages become increasingly clear so that you actually do something different. Insanity has been described as doing the same thing over and over, and wondering why nothing has changed. Or when you always do what you have always done, you will always get what you always got. And then, one day, when you feel like you just can't take it any more, when you reach your breaking point, your spirit finally breaks free from the constraints you imposed upon it.

In my own life, I had allowed myself to live in dysfunctional relationships, which eventually taught me that I didn't have to punish myself anymore. In retrospect, the only reason I can think of as to why I allowed myself to go through those difficult and unhappy relationships for far too long was so that eventually I could share this information with others. Back then, I never knew that I would feel compelled to write a book that would help others identify with their own painful experiences. It is crucial to share information and knowledge that will empower people to live better, healthier and happier lives. Otherwise, why bother having the experience at all? Iyanla Vanzant addresses these issues by using the metaphor of a house and its different floors for defining the various aspects of the evolution of healthy loving:

"Some people jump into the relationship arena, pass go, collect the two hundred bucks, and are never seen or heard from again. Then there are those of us who have been engaged eighteen times and never made it to the altar. There are also those of us who have done our spiritual work, who have created a meaningful life, those who have waded through the stuff, cleaned it up, and still cannot find or maintain a loving, committed relationship. There are no guarantees!

"There is no guarantee that at the end of the day, after all of the work you have done, you are either going to get a partner, have a relationship, or save the relationship you are in. The thing about the third floor is that those concerns are no longer critical for you. Having a relationship or being in love is no longer a critical or key aspect of living. This does not mean you do not want a relationship. It means you will not lose sleep over not having one. What's critical for you on the third floor is healing yourself in order to serve and support as many people as you can, in any way that you can. You have shifted out of the basement's physical attraction, needy, clingy, I got to have you, ooh, baby, baby stuff into love is here all the time…. On the third floor, what you are working toward is how to deal with every situation that comes up, until you really find that one partnership that makes you more than you already are….

"You cannot move toward finding yourself, loving yourself, just for the sake of finding and loving someone else. You must do it for the sake of doing it. You must love, honor, and respect you for the sake of it – no strings attached. This would have made absolutely no sense to you anywhere but on the third floor. At the lower levels, you were still dealing with too much stuff. Now you are ready. Ready to make the shift from conditional love to unconditional love. You are now ready to be with yourself rather than by yourself. You have been through a meantime process in which you have become self-aware and self-reflective in order to make the necessary changes or shifts that will result in spiritual transformation. You are no longer in search of physical, emotional or sexual satisfaction only. You want the true, full experience of love. If this is what you are going for, this is what you will get."

Great learning came out of my own experiences, which taught me that all the time I was living in emotional pain I was really growing. They say that hindsight is foresight, or if I knew then what I know now I wouldn't have allowed myself to go through that. Reviewing the chapters of my life, rather than cast blame on the men I attracted to learn lessons, I grew to take responsibility for my thinking, which permitted me to suffer way beyond what I needed to. Much of my unhappiness was due to the unconscious choices I made because I didn't know about such things as psychological personality disorders or codependency. It was years later when I entered counseling and started to read books that I began to understand the complex issues that my parents' generation didn't have names for.

For example, when I was a teenager and young adult and on into my thirties, I never knew what it meant to be an adult child of an alcoholic or violent family. I didn't grow up in that kind of an environment. These situations were not talked about openly a half century ago. If you don't know what ACOA (Adult Children of Alcoholic Families), CODA (Codependents Anonymous), GA (Gamblers Anonymous) or SLAA (Sex Love Addicts Anonymous) means, you don't know what you're dealing with. Furthermore, if you never know that chemical imbalances in the brain influence behavior, you would be at a loss as to how to handle these situations, other than feeling that you were going out of your mind. Years ago, people would say "He/she has a screw loose!" Now, thank God, we have been able to identify and name the maladies, syndromes and disorders that we have lived with for centuries. We are slowly becoming more enlightened. I am so pleased that many more younger people, even in their teens and twenties, are coming into counseling to understand why they are experiencing what they are. They aren't waiting until they're in their forties or fifties. I feel very fortunate to be in a position of seeing their wonderful growth as they move on and make the necessary changes early on, without having to live lives of quiet desperation for so many years.

We all have a story. Our histories form our stories – the tapestries we consciously or unconsciously weave form our lives. I sincerely hope that my journey into the cause of my former unhappiness helps you to find that which will free you to explore your next realm. May you come to the place where you desire to live your life from a sacred, heartfelt space, and in good mental health. Here is part of my story.

Through a series of circumstances, similar to Redfield's description in The Celestine Prophecy, I was led to meet certain people who helped me make sense out of what was happening in my life. I called it a mid-life crisis, never having gone through one before. My unhappiness and emotional pain forced me to really examine what I wanted in and out of my life. These feelings however, were not totally foreign to me. I had gone through a divorce over twenty years ago, and several other long-term relationships that resulted in dead-ends in that same time period. Now, my experience is completely different. I wanted these cycles of wrong choices to end. I was so afraid that I wouldn't have a chance to explore my unknown dreams. I felt stuck between two trapezes – one that I was hesitant to let go of to explore my dreams, while holding on so tightly in fear of the unknown. The other trapeze approached, but it was still too far out of reach, that I didn't quite know what opportunities would come or what would happen. Do we ever really know?

During these times of metamorphosis, I found myself involved in relationships with men who were not ready to make the spiritual commitment I wanted. My desire was to yield to something much larger than both of us. I had to honestly face our differences, and I came to accept that no matter how much time we would have tried to work on our "stuff," we would never be compatible. I became so frustrated and drained trying to make it work, when the commitment was never there in the first place. It is even more difficult when your partner can't break free of his or her own self-imposed constraints and limitations that come out of their family of origin issues. For example, if someone grows up in a family that is extremely poor, always being admonished about money, and never work through these limitations, no matter how much money they have, they cannot be generous. They might take issue with the kind of gifts you receive, or why you like to do the things you do when they don't. Or perhaps they feel they have to divide and measure every amount of money spent, even down to the cents. Mind you, these situations are not necessarily negative. It just takes two consenting adults who choose to live this way. In other words, you both get the chance to talk about what your values are, what's important to you, what you need and want in a relationship, and what you expect. If these attributes are miles apart, I guarantee that the relationship cannot survive.

In my own experience, I was tired of being with men who measured everything. Although we gave each other many gifts throughout the course of the relationship (and I don't mean only material presents), these gifts could not sustain an emotionally mature, long-term, committed relationship. While we tried to be supportive of each other, it became very evident that the time had come to once again let go and reach out. All of a sudden, you feel like you can't get out of your skin. You feel uncomfortable in your own body, and you have strange feelings within your body that don't let you rest. All of these hormonal imbalances come about because you are mentally and spiritually out of balance. So no matter how difficult it is to let go, if you don't, you might get sick or die. In my own relationships, both parties knew that we had to let go, although we didn't necessarily know this at the same time. This is quite common amongst couples. Some hold on for months, some for years. It becomes more difficult to stay together and be unhappy than to be alone and face the unknown. We all come to a place where we ask ourselves what other opportunities lie waiting for their purpose to be fulfilled. I want to emphasize here that I am, in no way, suggesting that people end their relationships haphazardly. I always recommend that they find a good counselor who can really help them examine the origins of their problems. Then, after choosing to do everything they can to see if the relationship will work, if it can't, do the honorable thing, which would be to separate in the best interests of not only themselves, but if there are children, them as well.

This reminds me of a time when I heard Deepak Chopra speak at a lecture. He told a story about how important it was for him to remind his children at a very young age that they should only be concerned with what their purpose in life is. He encouraged them to ask this question continually, and assured them that uncovering the answer would assure their success. The success he refers to is not just material. It is mental harmony and spiritual peace of mind. So if we enter into relationships more aware of who we are and what our purpose is, then maybe we will experience less hurt. This is similar to the questions that Robert Muller recommended in his curriculum for children. Imagine how different your life might have turned out if you were asked in elementary school the following: What is your purpose? Where are you going? Why are you here? Imagine what the world will look like if your children are encouraged to think this way.

Although we have been working on these ideas for a few decades now, Scott Peck reminds us in his book <u>The Road Less Traveled</u>, that "**life is difficult**." Knowing this and choosing to surmount your difficulties is what is necessary. This is not to say that life is difficult all the time, but more so at different junctures in your journey. Most life altering changes yield emotional pain for all people. Although you may make light of it or deny it, I've never met anyone who hasn't gone through their own dark night of the soul at some point in their life. Maybe they medicated their pain so much that they can't remember. Perhaps in your own experience, anger was the fuel that caused you to make a change. In my own story, I realized that while anger served a purpose, it also masked the fear and pain of having to make the decision to separate. The anger was a gift in that it let me know that something needed to be changed. Anger is always a gift when seen in this light. No matter how many books we read which indicate that change doesn't have to be painful, the reality of living in this physical world is that sometimes pain is a necessary ingredient on the road to self-realization.

I recall the first time I read that "life is difficult." It didn't sit well with me at all. And how could it, when I had programmed myself to believe that life is a wonderful journey. However, included in that wonderment is the stark reality we all know too well. Life is fraught with overcoming obstacles and other difficulties at various points. I have heard that "obstacles" are nothing more than opportunities in disguise. While it has been said that we are spiritual beings having a human experience, eventually we get to the place where we have to take responsibility for our actions, thoughts and what we truly want. When we lie to ourselves and we live in the lie, our relationships become a reflection of this dishonesty. Psychologist Paul Dunion

offers an interesting insight as to what he refers to as the "burden of the lie." Basically, the lie indicates that some of what we have been taught is not true. He disagrees
with the dictum that life is understandable and predictable: "Ancient wisdom tells us that life is mysterious, insecure and unpredictable. There are a number of profound implications to a life guided by this truth. The first and foremost is that the principle task of being alive is to make peace with life's mystery and insecurity. The deeper the peace we make with the mystery, the more we are able to let go of unnecessary feelings of inadequacy and shame since the state of unknowing becomes so appropriate. It is also fitting to experience fear in the light of life's abiding insecurity. Also, needing and cherishing the loyalty and commitment of others becomes so important in the wake of life's fragility.

The concepts of loyalty and commitment share a common, ancient meaning: A faithfulness that help and protection are a constant."

Basically, what Dr. Dunion is advising is that the more we understand the nature of existence, we won't have unreasonable expectations of our partners, especially if they share this view. We may become so complacent and desperate when we hang onto the belief that life is secure and predictable that we are terrified of any change. Ask yourself if you are waiting to die or living your life to its fullest expression.

In Viktor Frankl's book, <u>Man's Search for Meaning</u>, he recounts his horrifying experiences as a prisoner at Auschwitz and other Nazi death camps. Out of his experience, he developed a revolutionary approach to treating patients called "logotherapy." Central to his theory is that what enables a human being to endure and rise above even the worst conditions imaginable is the awareness of the spiritual truth that one's life has meaning. He believes that meaning can be discovered in three basic ways: "by creating a work or doing a deed; by experiencing something or encountering someone; and by the attitude we take toward unavoidable suffering." In the death camps, he concluded that no one survived who believed that life was not worth living.

Consequently, we can all choose to turn our own form of suffering into a personal growth experience that encourages us to seek out our gifts and use them. If you learn to grow from the pain, it will actually help you to move away from the destructive behavior which weakens your resolve to embrace a new pattern to discover your strength and demonstrate your integrity. Our time here is brief, although to some it can seem an eternity because of the "hell" in which they live. It is a luxury to recognize that time is precious and need not be wasted. When you are suffering, it is difficult to think this way. The truth is if we take more time to assess what we are getting into before we do, we are in the process of doing everything in our power to avoid repetitious self-defeating behaviors and argumentative struggles with others. I have a sign on my desk that is a great reminder, not only to myself, but my clients that "An argument is an exchange of ignorance and a discussion is an exchange of knowledge."

One way I chose to grow through my pain was when I entered a two-year intensive counseling mentorship with a gifted elder therapist who really helped me to help myself. I always find that I meet the right people at the right time. I was fortunate to meet her through a personal referral. I believe in the expression that when the student is ready, the teacher appears. It is quite appropriate. It is a good practice to under- stand why you do what you do. The goal of good therapy sets the patient free to live his or her life with the wisdom they have gained so they do not become continuously dependent on someone else.

In the 1980's and on into the present, the word "co- dependency" became a common buzzword in the recovery community. One example of codependent behavior is seen when a person continuously creates situations of enticement, excitement and exhaustion. These are known as the three E's. These experiences, in turn, create the many dramas we invite into our lives. We may become so obsessed with people or situations that we can't focus on anything else in our life other than that. This is a serious problem that has been known to cause life-threatening consequences if we continue on a self-destructive path. When you have lived on the edge of the emotionally turbulent roller coaster, you may think that you aren't alive unless you have a "drama" going on. What would your life look like without these self-created dramas or the need for them? My own journey led me to rescue myself from my worst fears and examine where they came from. In order to get myself off this emotional roller coaster, I needed to understand the originating cause of why I created these dramas in the first place.

Some psychologists suggest that codependency borders on addictive behavior. Therefore, they recommend that you have to remove the substance of your addiction, which can be a person, place or thing. And while twelve-step programs help people to stay mentally healthy, they don't always get at the root cause of an addiction, nor do they prevent the frequent relapses people have. Some of my clients indicated that they had to be in so much pain before they wanted to change. This is when they had their "spiritual awakening" or that "aha" moment.

In <u>The Celestine Prophecy</u>, Redfield describes similar behavior as control dramas. We all learn our behavior in our families of origin, and that behavior is not always healthy, to say the least. At some point, your psyche, otherwise known as your higher, intuitive self, desires more mature, conscious, loving interactions with people you care about.

There is always a universal principle at work in our lives, and while we don't always see or believe it, it is known as the law of cause and effect. The saying that you can't pour old wine into new wineskins is found in the principle of letting go of what no longer serves you to create something more meaningful. A well-known author and metaphysician, Catherine Ponder, believes that a vacuum must first be created (if only in our minds) to begin with, so that new opportunities can appear. From these, we can then make enlightened choices. The truth is that everything is first created in our minds even if we aren't conscious of this. We need to be careful with the thoughts that we think and what we allow ourselves to dwell upon. Following are some examples of behavioral patterns that I discovered in working on my own issues and those of the clients who came to me for assistance. They were all a gift, for while I helped to awaken them to uncover the real truth about their worth after they had been taught the opposite, I also learned so much about who I am and how we all help each other. Both the student and teacher benefit and learn from each other.

In the recent film *Good Will Hunting*, this is clearly depicted in Robin Williams' role as the Psychologist who is asked to help Will Hunting. In the final analysis, his patient helps him just as much to grow into a new life that he, himself, was afraid to embrace. See if you can relate to any of the following examples. If you can, I hope they will inspire you to make changes you want. Recognize your unhealthy patterns and consistently strive to do something different until you find what works. Happy Hunting!

Transactional Analysis (Case Studies)

This model was introduced by Eric Bernes. It is characterized by three ego states, which include the parent, child, and adult. These three states of mind produce unique behaviors to their individual characters, which can be operative at any particular time in the psyche. The key is to recognize which role you are acting out of because this recognition is a very powerful tool to work with to help you overcome your negative behavioral patterns. For example, when you act out of your parental state of mind, you can be either controlling, critical or nurturing. The adult state models the healthiest behavior of all three ego states, that of an emotionally mature person. The child state learns to adapt according to his/her environment.

In control dramas, very often there is a pattern of triangulation in which three players are involved. One usually plays the role of the persecutor, another the rescuer, and the third is the victim. There is a similarity in the roles of the persecutor and the rescuer. They convey the message that they are more okay than the victim. Consequently, the victim always ends up feeling like he/she is not okay. When you stay a victim, you feel like you have to justify your position. To change this behavior, each person needs to know what they want.

One of the power plays that emerge in triangulation is the need to make someone wrong or convince them that they are not okay. In reality, it is not a matter of being okay or right. It is okay to be different. When we give up the struggle of having to make others wrong or right, then we can just be who we are and not allow ourselves to get into defensive positions in the first place. This takes awareness, and I believe it is the first real step in creating more harmony with others. The gift is in acceptance. I have never met anyone who didn't want to be accepted. The problem comes when we try to change the other person rather than letting them change themselves, if they so desire. This frees us to move forward with our own lives. On the humorous side, there is a joke about codependency. Before you're about to die, someone else's life flashes before your eyes.

When you are an adult and your adapted child ego steps in, you might tell your children or your partner "You fix the problem." You may do this out of habit, because you expect other people to solve all of your problems or find the answers to all of your questions. This behavior is a very sneaky way that people get and keep you involved in their personal dramas. By not participating in this behavior, you afford them the opportunity to figure out what they must do for themselves.

The dysfunctional dynamics in couples can show up when one of them acts out from their adapted child state. They may have gotten the message that they had to work hard to keep things together. So, it becomes easier for someone who acts out of the ego child state to stay stuck in situations they constantly put themselves into. In doing this, they delay taking care of themselves because they believe it is their job to fix the other person's problem. It's important to notice how the adapted child state in either partner conveys the message "you fix me," because it fits right into the controlling parent ego state of their partner's personality. So rather than have a partner, you have a parent who reminds you of the parent you grew up with, where these buttons were originally installed. No matter how old you are, it is these very issues you need to heal and work through to be able to move forward in your life.

Perhaps you grew up in a family where your own mother's adapted child ego state functioned being scared most of the time. She put that fear into you, which encouraged your dependency. If you scare a child enough, even in adulthood they will be too afraid to step out on their own, which is where healthy individuation and separation occur for the child to grow into being a healthy adult. Add to this a father who was over protective and too reactive, and you get a child who is taught to fear taking risks and fights an internal battle with their own inner child whose natural urge is to spread their wings and grow. As Kahlil Gibran says in <u>The Prophet</u> on children, "Your children are not your children. They are the sons and daughters of life's longing for itself. They come through you but not from you, and though they are with you, yet they belong not to you....You are the bows from which your children, as living arrows, are sent forth." As Gibran points out, it is detrimental to stifle your child's growth, or attempt to cut it off. Thus, trying to make your child feel guilty doesn't resolve anything. When the child becomes an adult, they may discover that they don't have to accept the guilt that anyone attempts to give them. Hopefully they will realize it is not their job to take away their parents' fears. However, this can be very damaging to little children who think they have to take care of mommy or daddy emotionally.

In Dr. Kenneth Adams' book, <u>Silently Seduced</u>, he identifies a behavior known as covert incest, which is not directly related to sexuality. It occurs when there are inappropriate boundaries between parents and children, because the child is never really seen by the parent as a uniquely separate individual. The parent has difficulty acknowledging the fact that significant others in their lives have their own needs. Additionally, covert incest victims blame themselves if they can't find a spouse. They have an inordinate sense of failure because of being emotionally abandoned in the toxic relationship with the parent. They become extremely needy for love. In essence, covert incest confines the child, makes unreasonable demands upon the child, and is very intrusive in their child's life. Due to the fact that they do not have the emotional connection with their spouse, they expect their children to fulfill the nurturing aspect that their spouse should be filling.

Just imagine how you would feel if, after you're married, you discover that your partner re-enacts the same behavior of either your parent(s) or their own. Our lesson is to know that no one can ever grow for us, and we must each learn how to confront the source of our own insecurities and heal them.

Another potential problem occurs when your significant other mirrors one of your biological parent's fears. For example, you choose a partner who behaves the same way one of your parents did. This behavior may deprive the two of you from sharing quality, fun times together. We are all too familiar with the fact that money and sex issues cause the greatest division amongst couples. If one person in the marriage is angry at their partner, they may punish them by not spending time with them. If they had to spend a lot of time alone as children and they were lonely, they may re-experience the pain of loneliness.

One client, who lived with a man for many years, suffered in this relationship because of her low self-esteem and being unable to take care of herself. Her partner chose not to communicate with her for days at a time when he became angry. She stated that she was so unhappy, but was terrified to be without him because she believed she couldn't take care of herself. Although she supported herself financially with him in their living arrangement, and he continued to "punish" her by not talking to her, she depended on his help for her physical problems. His inability to communicate when he was angry came out of a pattern of dysfunctional communication that he experienced with his father throughout his life. Because no one learned how to change their behavior, it repeated itself. It also gave him a feeling of being in control. Of course, we always have other options; however, our fears may so consume us that they prevent us from taking action. We continue to suffer and believe that we have to suffer. Remember that pain, at times, is inevitable, but suffering is optional. These unhealthy mindsets and behavioral interactions last as long as we allow them to. If you find that you cannot control yourself, even after intensive therapy, you may need to assess your need for medication. The days of hurting yourself and other people are over when you decide to end them.

You may have learned to survive as a child by being angry, even if you couldn't express your anger due to the repercussions you feared. As an adult, your adapted child ego state expresses itself by being angry or afraid most of the time. You may have learned to hide this from others and managed your anger by attempting to control them. Your parental ego state expressed itself in your attempt to control others, which relates back to your inability to nurture those closest to you. Maybe you could only nurture when you got your own way. If you don't know how to ask for what you want, you may get nurtured by becoming sick and hoping others will feel sorry for you.

You might have had a parent whose controlling parental ego state told you, "You're too sensitive and you take things too seriously. Don't have such hurt feelings!" This might be the same exact message you give to your present partner; not because you want to, but because you don't know how to do it any differently. Until you learn more, either through effective therapy or reading about human behavior and understand why you act the way you do, this problem will continue. Each person's adult ego state is capable of thinking. When they can't think for themselves, their critical parental ego state tells their child ego state not to think. What this means, very often is that you, as an adult, can't express your thoughts for the fear you experienced as a child growing up when you attempted to do so. These behaviors are, unfort- unately, quite common amongst couples. However, it is encouraging to know they can change by working on the issues.

I recall in the film, *Reversal of Fortune*, the line where Glenn Close says something similar to "It's easier to love someone than it is to live with them. Living requires work and the problem is that most people are lazy and don't want to do the work and when you don't work out the problems, love goes out the window."

A child learns to adapt to his/her environment by way of rote, learned habits and feelings. The child can identify and express real feelings, needs and wants in a safe environment. Children have a natural inclin- ation to express themselves creatively unless they are taught to repress it. Although we are taught to think, many of us weren't taught how to solve problems. Hopefully, as adults, we learn to think about things before we make decisions. However, if we still operate from the adapted child's ego state as an adult, we may become confused and avoid expressing ourselves for fear of being labeled as dumb or stupid.

The healthy adult ego state is not afraid to ask questions, get information and assess options. The key is to consistently check your feelings out when significant others, including those who remind you of your parental figures, give you mixed messages. This may not be purposely, since behavior can be both unconscious and conscious. However, you want to get to the point where you recognize and accept that **"You don't need to torture yourself any more with the same stuff!"** If you are always dealing with the same issues month after month and year after year, it is time to change the recording unless you enjoy suffering.

When you have identified what you want and need as an adult, you can ask for it. Most of us need and want acceptance, love, time, space and support. At the central core of a healthy adult ego is love, which is unconditional love for yourself as a growing being. At the same time, you need to be attentive to your inner child's state of being and the reality of what he/she feels at any given moment. Who amongst us has never felt scared or so alone? Most of us don't like feeling this way, and so we think we have to speed up the process of growing up. When we short change this crucial step in our growth towards adulthood, we are incomplete.

Eventually, we must learn to re-parent ourselves and create new "moms and dads" in us that can help to heal whatever may be incomplete so we can take care of ourselves. The idea is not to cast blame, but rather, to be able to give to ourselves what we couldn't get. So, if your mother or father did the best they could with what they knew and it still wasn't enough, then you can actually place this new image of your idealized parent, who can take care of you whenever you feel like a scared child who is all alone. Think how much healthier your relationships will be without having to ask your friend, wife, husband, child or employer to parent you.

When you need to make a decision, remember that you always have choices. If you grew up with a nurturing parent versus a controlling parent, your road to resolving questions might be different. For example, if you adapted to your environment over explaining your actions, the wordiness could have cut off the feelings you had, as if you could talk them away. Children are naturally spontaneous, and usually don't cut off their feelings, unless they are told not to feel the way they do. That's when the words get in the way. You can only activate your adult by expressing what you feel. For example, say "I am not comfortable with why you want this information," or whatever the situation may be. In so doing, you create safe boundaries for yourself.

As we continue to grow and evolve, we learn to differentiate between what we think we know through blind trust as opposed to believing in our "gut" feelings and following through with our intuitive wisdom. We need to learn how to trust ourselves so completely that we know when to **trust and not to trust others.** This wise discernment helps us give up clutching and holding on to unhealthy situations with fear.

For example, male and female children are acculturated differently. If a girl receives messages from her father that she should find a "good man" to marry who will take care of her, and the mother simultaneously gives messages for her to be responsible for herself, this girl might be very confused. Would the girl try to hurry up and become a woman? Will she be able to emotionally handle being with a man if she thinks she has to be responsible for herself?

What would happen if we taught our young boys and girls how to be emotionally responsible for themselves as adults? Would we have less divorce if more mentally healthy people were attracting each other? Dr. Laura Schlessinger believes that it would be wise for men and women to wait until they are in their early- to mid-thirties before marrying. I agree with this idea because it gives us a chance to know ourselves better. The world is not the same as it was. Young adults, both male and female, may desire to try out different careers, or to live out some of their dreams. In so doing, by the time they decide to marry, if that is their choice, they won't expect their husband or wife to be the be all and end all of their existence. That's an awful lot of power to give to someone. It's important that we learn how to be interdependent in our relationships. History has not taught us to think this way. I discuss this in greater depth in the chapter on Exploring and Creating Healthy Romantic Relationships.

Some of us learn to survive by believing that we need to be perfect at everything. The values and rules we live by create our experiences. One reason many people whine or complain is due to their fear of not getting their needs met. If you grew up believing that you have to have all the answers and cover every base, you might overload yourself and other people due to the way you survived by over-dramatizing your life or their lives. These dramatic events prevent you from focusing on what is important. Rodger Stevens reminds us that life is a drama, and we play our roles. Problems arise when we have forgotten that we are not our roles. We are really the actors playing those roles. Can you ever be too smart? I don't think so, but I do believe we need to be compassionate to others whose shoes we have not walked in. Learn to honor yourself for the experiences you've had, know what it means to be free and understand your responsibility to use this freedom wisely. A good way to deal with change is to live in the here and now. "Today well lived creates tomorrow." Take time before you make any concrete decisions. The more information you have, and the more time you have to check things out realistically, will assist you in making wise decisions.

Recognize that your inner child has her / his own wants, needs, feelings and fantasies, which may or may not agree with what you were taught to believe about life. You may find yourself experiencing internal conflict, also known as the war within yourself. Is it any wonder why things don't always turn out the way you expect them to? This is serendipity at work in your life, whether or not you believe it. In order to let go of control and not force issues that are not unfolding the way you want them to, allow your higher guidance to lead you to that which is better for you. In Judaism, we are taught that some things are "Ba'shert," or meant to be. Other philosophies and religions teach a similar treatise.

However, when your ego gets in the way, it sure causes a lot of crises. You see evidence of this by having to unlearn what was taught to you if it no longer works. This is a parallel idea of how men and women are acculturated into their roles. If you don't live in the box, you end up thinking something is wrong with you. This thinking is contrary to the statement "live and let live," which suggests that what is "normal" for you may be different for others. There is nothing wrong with this picture as long as it doesn't hurt anyone.

Have you ever thought about or experienced the following scenarios?

- Can you handle separation and honor being alone for a while if it will help the situation? (Many have told me they never had

the chance to live alone, and consequently they fear being left alone or think the worst of being on their own.)
- Would you be okay without being with someone by your own choice or not by your choice?
- Did you ever experience a feeling of freedom and ease in your body when you finally let go of an old idea that no longer served you?
- Can you experience peace of mind alone, instead of struggling to stay in a relationship that you have to work so hard at? (It's better to be alone and feel lonely than to be with someone and feel lonely with them.) Of course, in a perfect world you would know that it's okay to be "with yourself" versus the thinking "by yourself." In the interim, learn to take care of yourself and enjoy your time alone. Find out what nurtures you and makes you feel good.
- How would you feel if you received total acceptance and were understood by those closest to you in your growth process?

Many people today have been both married and/or divorced at least once. When you can identify your patterns and choices in selecting partners, you may realize your selection process was unconscious in choosing a partner who represented either of your parents. The theory is we make these choices to resolve our unfinished issues from childhood. Both people must do a lot of internal work to get beyond their negative behavioral tendencies. Eventually, if you don't deal with the "problem stuff" you had with your parents (even if they aren't alive any longer or have chosen not to remain in contact with you), you can still validate what you feel by writing letters even if you never send them. It is the art of writing what you feel that is cathartic. Many people hesitate to do this exercise, for fear of what it will bring up, or believing that it won't make a difference. You may get to the place where you want to send a letter, and you must monitor the way you express yourself in it. Many have claimed this exercise helps them release their hold on the past. Sometimes, when both parties are willing, it is very helpful to meet with a qualified therapist or mediator. I often recommend that you do a few drafts of a letter before you ever send it. This kind of writing is a process where you get to express most of your rage and anger or sadness in your first letter in inappropriate ways, to the final result of a letter that doesn't focus on casting blame; rather, it expresses in your own feelings what you experienced as a result of unhealthy behavior.

My own experience led me into a marriage when I was ill-prepared for one in my early twenties. I now know that choosing the man I married then was greatly influenced by the domination and control I felt from my Mother during my teenager years and early adulthood. As many women do, I sought refuge and escape from parental situations in my marriage that reminded me of why I left in the first place. It was an issue of trust. It was not until many years later that I was able to fully understand why I did what I did. I didn't know how to take care of myself back then. In order for me not to feel controlled by my Mother any longer, I did what most people do – I rebelled. However, it was really myself I was rebelling against, since I did not know then what I know now! Funny how we do the very things we are told not to do to make a point. We think we are taking control of our lives and making intelligent decisions when in reality we are acting out deep-seated internal conflicts. As I matured, my relationship with my Mother became much closer, because we were both able to express our feelings. We didn't agree on things most of the times because we were two very different people. It was after my Father passed away that my Mother began to go through a very difficult time because she had been with him for over half a century. It was at this time that I suggested we really get to know each other as people, as women, not just the roles we were cast into as mother and daughter. I recommend you do the same with your parents. Find out who they are as people and not who you wish them to be.

Negative behavioral patterns that you don't resolve with your early caregivers only perpetuate the struggles that were set up long before. When I finally got divorced a decade later, I discovered I had many other options. I had closed myself off for years, afraid to follow my dreams because of my parental influences. There were many unresolved issues I still harbored. I had not yet figured out what I wanted for my life. While I was afraid of stepping out and being on my own, I still had a lot of learning to do. We all do. I attracted people who taught me the lessons I needed to learn. I regard those who came into my life at very difficult times as catalysts for my growth. I call them "angels in disguise." Have you ever noticed that when you are going through a very difficult time, you attract someone or new people who help move you forward on your path? I now know that putting my life back together after enduring some very difficult traumas has helped me make peace with myself. I have finally come to accept who I am today. It matters not how long ago you got divorced, separated or broke up; what matters is what you are doing in the meantime.

A book entitled <u>2010,</u> written by Thea Alexander, suggested that in the twenty-first century we wouldn't have to endure painful relationships. Her theory was that we would naturally attract our right partners for a certain time period, and then we would automatically be introduced to our next partner for our new growth when the lessons were learned. The partings would not be painful; rather, they would be filled with joy and gratitude for the time you had together. She espoused that our individual and collective growth would be assured by learning to let go of pain and those situations in which we couldn't grow anymore. We wouldn't have to search. Our next mate would appear! I imagine this idea might create a lot of controversy. It's a great topic for a discussion group! I would be curious to hear your thoughts on this possibility.

To understand what it means to be really loved, practice being emotionally available, reliable, stable, caring and allowing for spaces between you and your loved one. Committed love is not meant to possess another, but to help release the imprisoned splendor that sets you both free. There are also times when you will need to practice "tough love" if your partner violates your boundaries. Realize that your needs, expectations and desires change as you grow. Conscious communication keeps a relationship alive and healthy. Stagnation causes conflict. So does behavior which we now know to be verbally and emotionally abusive. If either of you curse, scream, lie, intimidate, threaten the other person, or seek to embarrass them in public, this is totally unacceptable behavior. Many people have told me they thought this was normal. It is very frustrating when you feel hurt and confused by your partner's behavior. You don't understand why they do what they do. Somehow, they don't either. You must acknowledge and validate each other's feelings. If someone is so out of touch with themselves, and they have never done any inner process work, they will naturally be problematic. You can't expect someone to respond or react in a certain way if they have never learned how.

We are reminded that we all have the power of choice. Accept responsibility and allow yourself to continue to feel what you feel, whether it is uncomfortable or not. While you can continue to blame these feelings on another, it doesn't solve the problem. Both people have the opportunity to state their needs as adults. If this behavior is not reciprocated, then you need to honestly ask yourself why you stay in such a relationship. Many say they stay for financial reasons. Basically, the situations you find yourself in come down to what you can live with, how much you respect yourself, and how you feel about yourself when you see your reflection in the mirror. In mature relationships, you and your partner are for one another and with one another. You are both aware of the fact that at different times each of you will play another role. For instance, if either of you acts out of your child ego state and expresses extreme neediness by vying for attention, this places a lot of stress on the relationship. Instead of having two adults who communicate about their insecurities, you have two child-like adults acting as children. Not healthy! Remember, your partner can't fix you. Only you can.

Situations also develop when a parent makes a child feel guilty after the child asserts its needs and wants. This happens in adults as well. It is wise to learn why you want to instill guilt. More good comes from being loving, kind and nurturing. Everyone desires this. Obviously, there will be times when you can't be loving and kind. However, you can learn to be diplomatic and honest, even in the way you express your anger. Each of us must learn to mirror healthy responses by being very clear and specific in our communications. This takes practice. We have all felt the effects of the unfortunate aspect of destructive psychological game playing. We learned this behavior in order to survive. What often happens as we mature into adulthood is we go back and use our early survival methods. We are slowly learning to transform the need to punish others for our own errors. Many people believe they have to suffer and/or they developed the habit of suffering unconsciously, and then they create scenarios where they don't get their needs met. This behavior reinforces what is known as a "racket," which is counterproductive to positive mental health and happiness. Every time a disturbance occurs, more calamity is created and on and on the cycle goes. In order to advance and grow, we are at any given point being asked to make new decisions which I call "re-decisions." The choice to re-decide an issue is based on accessing our "adult," and simultaneously honoring the feelings that our inner child may be having.

Some parents act out their control dramas because they resent that the other parent is not around as much due to work schedules or custody situations. If they feel guilty, they may try to make up for the lost time with their child in one way or another. Then the child grows up with all the negative rules, beliefs and values of either parent. Unless this behavior is dealt with at a conscious level, it will trigger more stress in their adult life. They may never feel safe to ask for what they need due to the fear of being abandoned. This is why it is critical for parents to come to consensus on child-rearing practices and discipline procedures. Otherwise, the child gets mixed messages, and the parents themselves end up blaming the child for separating them. In previous generations, there were no parenting classes, and much less literature on the subject. This is one of the reasons our society has addressed these problems with mandated classes and counseling to help people understand what is happening and how their behavior contributes to maintaining the problems.

The more we learn to act as an adult, the more focused and clear we become. Ask for what you need. You may not get it, but you validate what is important for yourself. If someone can't give you what you need, give it to yourself. There is a saying which implies that rather than waiting for someone to bring you flowers, plant your own garden. You can also affirm for another person what you think may be in their best interest. However, the final determination is up to them. Learn to communicate without a hidden agenda. If someone continually complains without taking action to change what they are complaining about, inform them that you fully support them to get the help they need. Suggest that they do something different. Simply state, "It's time for you to _____", or "You really deserve to _____," or "I fully support you to get the help that you need to _____." When we allow people to continually complain to us, we are not fostering their growth.

Healthy relationships allow both people time to connect, disconnect, and reconnect. What this means is that neither person fears the time they are without the other. Whether you live with someone or not, it's healthy to take mental space for yourself every now and then. Everyone needs a break. Both people are responsible to create a healthy reality. While you are with and for each other, you are not in the symbiotic place of being like each other, as we usually are in the beginning stage of getting to know one another. John Bradshaw once described this stage as being "out of your gourd." You are so fascinated with the other person in this early phase that you can't see any flaws. We see the other person as ourselves. Healthy relationships are not either "you or me," or "you are me," but reflect an equal partnership of "you and me." It is crucial that both people learn to feel good about themselves in order to be with and for each other. Always support your partner in becoming the best they can. Of course, if you don't feel good about yourself, you wouldn't want to see someone else succeed.

I hope that these scenarios have helped you to understand some of the dynamics that go on in relationships. As you come to know more about the different aspects of your behavior, you may be ready to do something different to change your life and improve it. Knowledge may also reveal that which is unknown. In closing, we are either a part of the problem or the solution. Knowing what will help you to live a more self-actualized life with less pain and more peace is what your odyssey is all about.

CHAPTER TWO

Overcoming Oppression

"...We ask ourselves, who am I to be brilliant, gorgeous, talented and fabulous? Actually, who are you not to be?

You are a child of the universe. Your playing small doesn't serve the world. There is nothing enlightened about shrinking so that other people won't feel insecure around you."

Marilyn Williamson

~~~

This chapter, originally published as an article in the Canadian Peace Research Journal was part of a paper I presented at a conference sponsored by the Consortium on Peace Research, Education and Development in Washington, D.C. in 1997. My focus here is on education, enlightenment and expansion of a very difficult subject. The thought of oppression, in any sense of the word, is extremely uncomfortable. Yet, it may not even occur to most people to define themselves as oppressed.

To be able to utilize the information I offer here in a helpful way is crucial for your self-development. Those closest to us are also effected by the way we interact with them. Consequently, if you use this information in the way it is intended, then the changes that occur for the better in your life will affect those around you. The key is to apply what is useful to you. The goal is to "walk your talk and talk your walk." Whether you are a practitioner who provides service to others, or you are the one who goes for help, you have probably, at least once, been in both roles. Consider the film *Goodwill Hunting*, mentioned earlier, which portrays so well the psychologist and his patient who become equally transformed by the experience of their interaction. Their individual efforts to make radical changes in their personal lives betters both of them.

Conflict is a part of life. To be able to accept the concept of conflict, understand it in a useful way, and learn to move through it, instead of staying stuck as we easily do is challenging to most of us. One of the reasons people remain in destructive conflict for so long is that they don't know how to get out of it. Take, for example, the increased violence in our families, workplaces, and communities. Many believe the reasons for this stem not only from the breakdown in the family unit, but also because of the absence of a soulful quality in our lives. The whole concept of soulful love starts with the self. The late Dr. Carl Rogers first coined the term "unconditional positive regard" for others. We also need to translate this mindset to self-love, which transforms to healthy self esteem. Much of the breakdown we experience today began long ago. The way we were taught to live our lives hasn't been working very well. People are procreating without taking responsibility for their lives and their offspring. People are dying because they can't afford health insurance, and are turned away from hospitals and physicians who want to get paid. Big conglomerates poison our atmosphere, and then we have to take them to trial to make restitution. We have more than enough food in the western world to feed the whole world, yet people starve. Dictatorships continue to thrive, with innocent people suffering, and guilty parties go unpunished. All of these factors are heralding the changes we are making. We are the ones to bring about this transformation. If not now, when? If not you, who? We each have an awesome responsibility ahead of us. It's time we do things differently. Live your life from a wiser perspective. Many teachers have appeared throughout the ages. We see them in each other.

All aspects of our lives are changing, from the way we practice medicine to the way we teach our children. The more holistic approach to medicine combines the best of both Eastern and Western practices. It is one example of availing ourselves of the best care available. Working synergistically, these two perspectives enhance each other. As a matter of fact, Rodale Press has recently published a book entitled <u>Blended Medicine, The Best Choices in Healing</u>. The concept of blended medicine clinics has come about so that medical doctors and doctors of osteopathy can work together with acupuncture physicians, chiropractors, and naturopaths, to name a few. Both fields of science are embracing all forms of healing, from herbal medicine to the most up-to-date pharmaceuticals. More and more people are also starting to take responsibility for their health, and not just relying on practitioners to be healthy. This demonstrates our capacity for working together, even if we differ in our thinking. Whether or not you realize it, your present belief system is influenced from the ancestral legacy that we inherited over 2,000 years ago. Its basis in the western world is found in the various interpretations of the Judeo-Christian writing known as the Bible.

For example, there are many different perspectives which explain how we got where we are, and how these influences affect us individually. In Steve Schlissel's article, <u>Hopelessly Patriarchal</u>, he states that "The Bible is patriarchal at the core, through and through. Like love and marriage, the Christian Bible and patriarchy go together: Any attempt to dismiss the rule of men must begin by dismissing the rule of God....For the scriptures themselves are, in the main, addressed to men. For the male functions as the head in the various covenant spheres, and in addressing them, God makes plain his idea of inclusive language." However, we need to remember that the Bible was recorded by men, whether inspired or not by the Deity, and, during the times the Bible was written, interpreted and reinterpreted, inclusive language was omitted.

There is further evidence that the writings of the Bible have a patriarchal slant. We find that males are often appointed the elders without exception; judges, with one interesting exception; prophets, with few exceptions; and priests and apostles, without exception. In fact, it is difficult to find any visitant angel appearing as female. Schlissel explains:

"Thus, while Eve may have had some sort of subordinate role after the fall, our ethic flows not from the past but from the future....It has been more than one hundred years since Elizabeth Cady Stanton produced 'The Women's Bible,' in which she attempted to demonstrate that Judaism and Orthodox Christianity had to be eliminated if (what would later be called) feminist ideals were to triumph. It was not her intention to make the Bible less 'sexist,' for in her view, this was impossible. Rather, she set out to undermine Biblical authority altogether, focusing on what she regarded as absurdities and contradictions. Contemporary feminist Naomi Goldenberg picks up Stanton's premises, and pitches them to a new generation in her book, The Changing of the Guards....A culture that maintains a masculine image for its highest divinity cannot allow its women to experience themselves as the equals of its men."

Therefore, if we seek to live without oppression, we must engage in the process of dismantling the system that has disappointed us. The propensity for finding a gender neutral language is one identifiable area where the need for change is evident. We see this same phenomena in our current school curricula, which has come to include women's studies. If we look at the way we've been acculturated, we find that much of what we know has its roots in patriarchy. As DuNann states, "It has been defined by many today as Patriarchy." It is not hard to see the effects of the role that stories have played in our lives. As Rabbi Shoni Labowitz says, "When you change the story, you change the whole culture. This is what the patriarchal era did in history, and women have the power now to correct it." It took over several thousand years for our culture to become what it is. We have been forced to embrace the process we are all involved in now. It is creating a culture that makes sense to all of us. I am reminded of this theme everywhere I go. Both men and women from all different backgrounds are asking what can we do to change the culture. This mindset has been revealed at conferences and found in comments such as "How can I feel safe to cry in front of a woman?" "I don't know if I should open a door for a woman." "I don't know how to speak to a man about my feelings."

We ask ourselves if this is about control, or just being able to be oneself without being judged. Does the need for control, which is so prominent in many cultures throughout the world, stem from an outdated model based on power and domination? If it does, then the original model of male/female relationships was based on a dysfunctional system that rendered women incapable of taking care of themselves, especially when they have been viewed as chattel or property. This mindset further complicated the issues of power, domination and control. The underlying assumption is that whoever makes the money (or most of it) controls the decisions. We see this in boardrooms and bedrooms. An article entitled "The Double Standard – A Parable of Ages" explains:

"Once upon a time a Man married a Woman.

Time passed and one day the Man said, 'I love all women. I need a great deal of love.'

And the Woman replied: 'I love all men. I also need a great deal of love.'

Said the man: 'If you talk like that, I will hit you over the head with a club.'

And the woman said, 'Forgive me, Lord and Master.'

Ten thousand years passed and again the man said: 'I love all women. I need a great deal of love.'

And the Woman replied: 'I love all men. I also need a great deal of love.'

Said the Man: 'If you talk like that, I will divorce you and you will find it hard to earn your own living.'

And the Woman said: 'You are a Brute.'

Another hundred years passed, and again the Man said, 'I love all women. I need a great deal of love.'

And the women replied: 'I love all men. I also need a great deal of love. And, as you know, I can earn my own living.'

Said the Man: 'If you talk like that, I shall have to behave myself.'

And the woman said: 'At last.'"

This same principle (abuse of perceived power) was and still is being practiced within a racist context as evidenced in the book The Bell Curve, whose authors suggested that one culture is more intelligent than another. In defining oppression, we must ask ourselves who created these standards. Much of the European white/Anglo-Saxon mentality, which came to America from repressed Eurocentric cultures, was and still is responsible in large part for the violence (abuse) we currently witness. If, for example, individuals and groups continually have unmet needs due to economic oppression, eventually they will rebel. We have witnessed this phenomena more, and see it with what happened in South Africa and other countries who struggle to live in freedom. Gandhi taught that no leader is powerful except for the power that people give that individual to have control over them. Gandhi was referring to political power in this context. However, unfortunately, we see the same as true for those families who believe that only one person can be in control. "It's either my way or the highway." This type of thinking maintains a sense of oppression in those who perceive themselves as victims.

In our families, many of us were taught to fear conflict and we approached it with trepidation. Others thought – why deal with this at all, and swept it under the rug, so to speak. An alarming example of this was depicted in the book and film, <u>The Prince of Tides</u>. The story is about a family whose children lived with a horrible, but true nightmare, which they were told never to repeat. It wasn't until their sister tried to commit suicide that they decided to do something about this untold scar. They were silenced by a mother who was more terrified of the shame that would come upon them if the community knew what happened. This dysfunctional scenario was eventually put to rest when the family had the opportunity to heal the past with the help of therapeutic intervention, which allowed disclosure, honesty and communication in a safe setting.

We have to wonder how many other girls and boys grew up with similar fears, encouraged by families not to talk about the violations and traumas they endured. For example, many a girl grew into a woman who believed that expression of her feelings would result in alienation and/or abandonment. Boys, on the other hand, were encouraged to repress their feelings, resulting in the insecurity they suffered. They were encouraged not to express what they thought only to have repressed feelings intensify during adolescence, which rendered many men emotionally unavailable as they matured. They didn't want to be judged or thought of as being less than what a man should be. I recall my own father saying, after the death of his dad, "My father would kill me if he saw me crying." This is a perfect example of a mentally unhealthy message which many men received. I am proud of the fact that my Dad did give himself permission to grieve and cry when he felt need to express his emotions later on in life.

In the past decade, men such as Robert Bly, Sam Keen, John Bradshaw and Paul Kivel helped to shift ancient mindsets. They herald a cause which states that certain behaviors no longer work.

The unhealthy emotional environments in our families have a very negative affect on our world. The Peace Psychology Bulletin publishes many articles affirming these ideas. Webster's New Collegiate Dictionary suggests that "patriarchy is a social organization marked by the supremacy of the father in the clan or the family." This way of acting has made the journey very difficult. Transforming the issue of non-equality for women and men, in the truest sense of the word, suggests that equality, when seen as a functional aspect of a society that alleges to have respect for all of its people, requires that no one human being be regarded as supreme.

In 1982, The National Organization for Men Against Sexism was created. Their annual conferences and monthly newsletters are geared to help end men's violent acts, such as rape, pornography, and abuse. In addition, the Men's International Peace Exchange in Philadelphia engages men and women in open dialogues about what helps to heal wounds, thereby encouraging individuals to take responsibility for their behavior. It is the task of men and women to help end oppression. The Oakland Men's Project, directed by Paul Kivel, also assists men to change unhealthy behavior through their curriculum and videos.

While we have access to all of the new resources, many people still grapple with the issue of being asked to consider a different value system than the one they were reared in. We see their reactions in the automatic responses of confusion, scorn and fear. It isn't easy to ask people to change the ways in which they were brought up, especially with the belief that the man was indeed the head of the family. You may even have asked yourself how you are being affected by all of these changes. All you have to do is look around and see how many single parent families there are. What contributed to this is the fact that men were taught to be the providers of the family and women were taught to be the homemakers. The economic reality of this system continuing became impossible in the last three decades, unless the man was a highly paid professional. Add to this scenario, men who left their families, and it isn't any wonder why women had to become financially capable and independent so they could take care of themselves and their offspring, especially if child support was not forthcoming. Even though women represent a smaller percentage of those who left their families, deserted husbands also have an equally difficult task of learning how to be homemakers. This is one reason why many men have learned to become more self-reliant when it comes to laundry and cooking. Some have even chosen to be the major caregivers in their families. The same reasons help explain why women have pursued careers that for many years were "off limits" to them. It had to come to this, because the stereotypical boxes we were told to live in didn't work any longer.

There is no easy way to transform centuries-old ways of thinking. The work ahead of both sexes relies on learning how to cooperate because we each need to rethink what role equality plays. Is it any wonder that the struggle for self esteem is a constant challenge of our times? Many are being asked to forfeit their identities, not knowing what their roles are any more. In so doing, some feel alienated because all conventional myths are being challenged.

Being in personal relationships is a real challenge today. Many women and men are no longer willing to put up with the mediocrity or dishonesty that their forebears lived with. More and more people are recognizing that they do have choices and they don't have to suffer. One helpful way to release suffering is to work through your emotions that surface. Don't block them. They are your teachers. We can no longer afford to not take charge of our thinking or avoid the welcome responsibility of transforming our lives. Here are some key points to free yourself. Practice the following:

- Change the way you look at the world and yourself.
- Accept that you no longer need to punish or hurt yourself or others.
- Know that you have the power within yourself to overcome any victimization you may have felt or lived through.
- Give yourself permission to verbalize your feelings. They are neither wrong or right; they just validate you.
- Recognize the common denominator amongst us all is that we are human.
- Practice feeling good about yourself, which in turn leads to a healthy self-esteem and allows you to create emotional safety

by stating what your boundaries are that you won't allow others to violate.

Many have learned helplessness within their family system. John Bradshaw reminds us that many of us split off from ourselves in early childhood out of fear. By numbing ourselves or creating a fantasy world, we can retreat or block our emotions. In so doing, we find ways to protect ourselves. As adults, we have the opportunity to heal past traumas. Never be afraid to get more information when you need it. Learn to speak assertively and give up feeling powerless. It's only natural to mourn the loss of what you had and knew, even if it wasn't necessarily what you would call "good." No comparisons exist to compare hurts. Each person's grief is his/her own teacher.

We all experience consequences on a spiritual level, and may not understand the reason. Have you ever thought of yourself and your actions as a spiritual being having a human experience? In Rabbi Kushner's book <u>When Bad Things Happen to Good People</u>, he states, "When something 'bad' happens that we don't understand, don't ask why, ask 'what;' what am I going to do about this now?" As Ranier Maria Rilke reminded us, we have to learn to live with questions.

Throughout history there have always been women and men who advance human consciousness. In Larry Kaiden's article on "Social Responsibility," he states:

"The responsibility for change lies in each of us taking responsibility for our prejudices and points of view and get away from the idea that 'we' are right and 'others' are wrong... Awareness and acknowledgement are the roads to resolution... What blocks us from resolution is fear... The answers for change lie in our willingness to change... Divisiveness and righteousness must be remolded into cooperation and mutual respect."

As mentioned earlier, changing role identities is causing some of the increased chaos. Many men and women voice their common concern. They don't know how to ask for what they need; nor do they know how to communicate honestly. We say we want honesty, but fear the consequences. Many books, courses and seminars educate and empower children, teenagers, and adults today to be real.

This means being able to reveal your fears, frustrations and anger in a safe environment.

Universal values help us to understand our views and their influence on our past. Examining these influences in democratic classrooms is the wave of the future. In an issue of <u>Gender and Society</u>, Janet Lee reminds us that education of the future will facilitate supportive atmospheres where all students can feel safe and validated by teachers and each other. Specifically, she states: "The classroom can become a place where students can take risks for their own self-growth, as well as practice ways of working together on mutual goals."

Classrooms of the future will be a perfect environment to explore the study of anger. Inter-disciplinary approaches exist in the development of new curricula for Grades K through university. One goal is to reduce the pervasive violence found in our schools, society, and families. Healing oppressive behavior requires that we begin to educate our young children about the psychobiology of their human body. Much anger is misdirected because of the inadequate models we had growing up. Many of us were taught to repress, silence or explode our feelings. As Dr. Tobach points out:

"...We recognize that the life experiences of the genders result in different approaches to social and societal behavior; these differences are related to the experiences of degradation, exploitation and derogation of one gender by the other."

In the last decade, especially in the United States, the issue of domestic violence is being addressed on a large scale. No longer can anyone get away with pushing, shoving, slapping, or hitting. Court-ordered counseling is now mandated. Larry Kaiden offers the idea that partners in a battering relationship are usually motivated by emotions versus rational judgments. He believes these judgments come from the thinking that we adapted to in our childhood. Feelings of helplessness, hurt, fear, abandonment and shame color the way we see our world. He states:

"Unless those wounds are healed, unless the hurts suffered by both men and women who were victimized are addressed, repetition of the situations in which they were hurt is inevitable. Hurt people hurt people. Indeed, any treatment program which does not acknowledge and care for the emotional wounding which is the source of the irrational behavior will be experienced by the client as yet another instance of repeated shame, helplessness, and vulnerability to victimization. Women, also, will feel devalued and disempowered if they are offered support, which indirectly tells them that they should 'know better' than to be involved with abusive partners. The conscious adult in both partners to an abusive relationship is well aware that the pattern of abuse is unacceptable – the helpless, victimized child within each cannot see alternatives unless the experience is transformed."

Another aspect of personal oppression is found in the behavior that was heretofore acceptable. We find, in John Gray's book, <u>What Your Mother Couldn't Tell You and Your Father Didn't Know</u>, the secret many families lived with for centuries – the acceptability of men having mistresses. This idea was originally sanctioned via the earlier European ideals, which were emotionally abusive to women. Because, for centuries, men and women didn't know they had other options, mostly due to economic considerations, they put up with situations that were less than desirable.

One example of the current confusion we see is in the movement towards equality of the sexes. One man thinks it is his job to protect his family and worry about everything. Because of this mindset, he becomes extremely frustrated when he can't fit into this role. He doesn't understand why his wife wants to return to college, instead of being a full-time mother and homemaker. Consequently, the situation at home intensifies because he is very angry and doesn't know what to do with these feelings. He recalls when he had to leave Junior High School to help support his family, because his mother and father were divorced and his father's income was no longer available. He never went on to finish high school, since he didn't believe it was important back then. He was also earning a good salary as an adult. However, years later, when his own marriage was about to end, he realized that he was upset by his wife's decision to complete college, and felt frustrated that he, himself, never went to college. The real issue between them was that, while he really thought he encouraged his wife to be more, he did everything he could to sabotage her efforts. He tried to prevent her return to school by finding one excuse after another of why it wouldn't work. They were giving each other many mixed messages. As a result, the wife finally decided that she no longer needed his approval or permission to do something she had been thinking about for a long time. She wanted to work through the issues with him regarding scheduling because of the children. What came out in therapy was their agreement that they both lacked the necessary skills in knowing how to work together to solve problems. In addition, they never knew how to be honest about their feelings, because of the fear and anger that arose from their judgments about each other. Like so many of us, they never learned how to really listen to each other.

Problems like these can never be solved in families whose rigid beliefs prevent a life of honest expression, especially in people who believe they must be in control. In addition, there are many incidents where chemical brain imbalances further exacerbate mental disturbances. Consequently, if we can't or don't know how to communicate, problems get out of hand. Not knowing how to communicate about the real issues causes so many problems. In my workshops, I often present a model known as "The Anatomy of a Conflict." What always emerges is that what people think is the real issue never is. If we never change what we were taught that is dysfunctional, how will we learn? Many people realize that we are all undergoing a very challenging time in making the transition to understand the relationships we have with ourselves, the opposite sex and with each other. As one man stated in a domestic violence group, "I believe our relationships of the future won't contain the violence that we have lived with for hundreds of years, because of the new information we are finally learning with regards to non-violent relationships and communication skills." His statement is a very enlightening one because it addresses the whole issue of healing oppression. While this chapter focuses on personal oppression more than political oppression, as Joanna Macy once said, "The personal is political." Therefore, the way we express ourselves on a one-to-one basis has an effect on the way we express ourselves in groups and in nations.

Years ago, when and if this information was available, it certainly wasn't used openly for fear that it would dismantle the patriarchal system. Judith Shervin and James Sniechowski point out the following:

"Women and men are the only building blocks we have to form and transform society. Yet our schools do little or nothing to prepare boys and girls to have the skills to communicate with one another with respect and understanding for their differences. We need to rethink what is required before a couple is granted permission to receive a marriage license and procreate ...Mandatory classes dealing with how to negotiate mutually satisfying conflict resolution should be part of every curriculum."

Happily, there is evidence of these changes underway via new legislation, which requires couples to undergo pre-marital counseling for several months. If this counseling helps to create better marriages, there will be less divorce and its aftermath. Similarly, as we learn how to interact with each other with more respect, and learn how to express anger in non-abusive ways, we will continue to advance our individual and collective understanding of what is required to live in a less hostile, angry, sad, guilt-producing world. Have you ever met anyone who didn't want to experience more peace of mind and freedom?

Oppression has been defined as an unjust or cruel exercise of authority or power, and a sense of being weighed down in body or mind. Many books, journals, magazines, curriculum, educational videos, and films exist to help us identify and change unhealthy behavior. The motivation for destructive violence in families, which became known as domestic violence, is not that much different from the destructive violence we witness between people in the same or different cities, countries and cultures on our fragile planet. Three contributing factors at the core of destructive conflict are the need for power, domination and control. Many of the psychological causes are cited in the DSM-5R, the American Psychological Association's Diagnostic Statistical Manual of Mental Disorders.

We can easily identify how people become oppressed in the earliest stages of our development as humans. It is in childhood that we are first taught about the painful but productive experience of not always getting what we want when we want it which is known as delayed gratification. While this has its merits, it becomes destructive in the instance of a helpless baby who needs to be fed and taken care of. In a video entitled *Nature vs. Nurture*, we see what happens to young infants when they are deprived of a mother's or caregiver's love and attention. They go into withdrawal, denial, rage, and repression, which they carry with them throughout their lives unless they deal with it professionally. Their traumatic events are recorded as early as the first 16 to 17 days of their lives. When you add this to the other dysfunctions in a family of origin, it is oft times amazing how many people resurrect their lives from what they were born into. Some of these ideas compel us to ask why people do what they do, especially when oppressive behavior starts in childhood. For example, imagine you are shopping in a store and you see a woman or man hit their children over the head and curse at them. Is this the kind of behavior that will encourage your children to behave differently? We have to wonder what is the long-term impact of these repeated actions on children. How will they turn out? Will they become contributing members of society with high self-esteem? Or will they become pseudo-power-fanatics, seeking to oppress other people through fear and intimidation?

In James Redfield's book, The Celestine Prophecy, he believes that people unconsciously act out their unresolved issues from earlier years. He calls these control dramas. Because of these control dramas, he suggests that people don't get what they want or need because they aren't in control of their own lives. For example, if your answer to a question is "No," show integrity and respect to the other person by explaining the reason for your choice. People who stay with others who don't respect them need to assess how much they respect themselves. It has been suggested that people who persecute others want to be rescued themselves. When you stop responding as a victim to others, you rescue yourself both mentally and physically. You no longer put up with oppressive environments. People who attack others are really asking for help, but they don't know how to get it.

How do you make decisions? If your ultimate objective is to have unity and harmony, then ask yourself what you must do to put up with less oppression. Problems need resolutions that are mindful of not only ourselves but others. Learning to work towards decisions for our mutual good is a dictum of the 21st century. You can't have unity and harmony without justice; and a prerequisite for justice is equality; and you can't have equality without maturity. As we discover what works, we must remember that there is a process we grow through to become mature and act out of integrity.

Some of the following ideas about maturity are quite helpful in learning to heal whatever has oppressed you:

- Maturity is the ability to handle frustration, control, anger and settle differences without violence or destruction.
- Maturity is the capacity to face unpleasantness and disappointment without becoming bitter.
- Maturity is the ability to disagree without being disagreeable.
- Maturity is humility. A mature person is able to say, "I was wrong." He or she is also able to say, "I am sorry." And when he or she is proven right, they don't have to say, "I told you so."
- Maturity is the ability to live in peace with that which we cannot change.
- Maturity means dependability, integrity, keeping one's word. The immature have excuses for everything. They are the chronically tardy, the no-shows, the gutless wonders who fold in the crisis. Their lives are a maze of broken promises, unfinished business, and former friends.

As you can see, the above can be reminders of what we strive towards. There are many situations in life where we have an opportunity to practice empowerment. A common theme noticed throughout adolescence and into adulthood is overprotective parents. A severe result of overprotection may render some children incapable of taking care of themselves emotionally and physically as adults. It is important for caregivers to identify where their overprotective nature comes from. Similarly, families need to learn how to discuss the reasons for their decisions, and invite their children to share their feelings and ideas. The same is true in communications between employers and employees; teachers and children; and any other situations where control is an issue. It is a wise idea to remove yourself from people who try to control everything. However, change is not possible if we can't identify the real problem. Very often, the need for power and control is motivated by fear or loss.

In seeking to heal our oppression, we must understand how the misuse of power was tolerated once upon a time between our ancestors who survived in the jungles. However, as Wilfred Trotter pointed out: "We are driven by primitive, selfish desires to satisfy animal instincts." The difference is that our evolution brings us to a place where we get beyond selfishness. Oppressive environments only exist because people give their power away to others for many reasons. Amongst those reasons are understanding predictors of abusive and violent behaviors. Current research suggests that the levels of the neurotransmitter, Serotonin, can predict violent behavior. We cannot underestimate the important role of brain chemistry and its contribution to violence and violent behaviors. In seeking to understand the psychology of oppression, it is helpful to know that many medications are available which help reduce violent/abusive behavior, such as Prozac, Zoloft, Paxil, Welbutrin and Buspar, to name a few. If oppression breeds violence, then learning more about our body chemistry can only help us. As a matter of fact, Engleberg discovered that: "One of the functions of serotonin in the central nervous system is the suppression of harmful behavioral impulses."

In seeking to understand the evolutionary changes that have taken place, we need to know the similarities and differences about the conflicts that take place in the following scenarios: a gang war in an inner city; between a husband and wife who use violence in the "privacy of their own home"; two angry people in a supermarket or on the interstate who hurl verbal insults at one another; parents and children who physically or emotionally abuse each other; or the destructive wars between any two cultures or countries. Let us consider that we have choices about how we respond to all of the things that we don't like. Gelles and Cornell remind us:

"It is important to keep in mind that what we are experiencing is neither new nor particularly unique to our own society. While we look for causes and solutions in individuals, or families, or even in communities, we should remember that cultural attitudes about women, children, and the elderly, and cultural attitudes about violence as a means of self-expression and solving problems, are at the root of private violence....But we need to consider that people have choices as to how they will respond to stress, crises and unhappiness, and the historical and cultural legacy of violence in the home is a powerful means of influencing what choices people consider appropriate."

To further understand oppression, aggressive behavior is the psychological component of the need for revenge. However, if we are ever to get beyond the "an eye for an eye, a tooth for a tooth" theory, we must shift our way of thinking. As Einstein pointed out, "You cannot solve a problem at the level it was found." If one response to oppression is violence, can it be that oppressed people don't know how to defend themselves from the intentions of those in power? Dr. Mindell says...

"Revenge is a form of spirituality, a sort of spiritual power meant to equalize social injustice....There are many beautiful quotes from God in the Bible, but the divine penchant for vengeance is there, too. Vengeance is central to religious teachings. Confucius tried to compensate for it by advising, 'What you do not want done to yourself, do not do to others.' Buddhists cultivate loving kindness....Nevertheless, when we seek revenge, we are apt to feel we have some sort of divine justification for our actions....Since we have been hurt, we feel we have a right to get back at our persecutors. Abused people have only two choices: either they go numb or they become abusers themselves."

If we compare Kaiden's idea on healing the inner child to Mindell's position that people either go numb or become abusers themselves, we can see why it is crucial for some form of restorative justice and inner healing and action to take place. We have seen the effects of oppression, be it economic, physical, emotional or otherwise. It is one of the primary, underlying causes in the violence that takes place in the microcosm of the family unit and the macrocosm of our planet and its countries.

Some examples of personal oppression are seen in the following scenarios:

- Do you know of anyone who has been threatened with a weapon or some other object?
- Do you know of someone who has been restrained or forced to have sex against his/her will?
- Emotional abuse is defined as the act of being ridiculed, insulted, or shamed in public or in private. Have you ever been told you are stupid, fat, ugly, unfit, or that you don't deserve anything?
- Have you been forbidden to work, or see family and friends?
- Are promises made and continually broken?
- Are your personal, sentimental items destroyed?

One of the effects of the lineage of the patriarchal culture was sanctioned violence or abuse. We went from clubs to knives and guns. In Judith Lewis Herman's book, Trauma and Recovery, she explores the link between victims of political terrorism and those of domestic violence. She asks us to look at "the commonalties between rape survivors and combat veterans, between battered women and political prisoners, between the survivors of vast concentration camps created by tyrants who rule nations and survivors of small, hidden concentration camps created by tyrants who rule their homes." In this same light, Pythia S. Peay quoted therapist Miriam Greenspan, "If we are going to create a world in which less abuse takes place, we literally have to change the world by taking social action. We heal in connection to one another – the world is not separate from us."

There are many ongoing efforts to change the historical negative mindset to one of empowerment and equality. Besides all of the educational outreach mentioned, equally important are the abundant mental health support groups provided to men, women and children, all of whom became "victims" of the various maladies of our times. Some efforts are successful because when people discover new information that works, they pass it on to others and, therefore, the idea grows. One example is found in twelve-step programs and groups that address alcoholism, chemical abuse, gambling, pornography, credit card spending, food disorders, sexual addictions, and the increasing risks associated with all of these dysfunctional behaviors. These support groups are known by the following acronyms: CODA – Codependents Anonymous; ACOA – Adult Children of Alcoholic Families; AA – Alcoholics Anonymous; Alanon; Children in Alcoholic Families; NA – Narcotics Anonymous; SLAA – Sex/Love Addicts Anonymous; GA – Gamblers Anonymous; Incest Survivors. I am sure there are others.

One wonders which came first, the chicken or the egg; the addiction or the environment. To help us solve our current problems, we can draw on the wisdom of some of our former change agents such as the late Dr. Carl Rogers, who pioneered Rogerian Therapy, which helped people listen to each other's stories as an act of love. Iyanla Vanzant, a spiritual counselor, has guided many women and men to creative visualization in helping them imagine the kind of life they are worthy of living. There are many pioneers too numerous to mention who have written books on the post-traumatic effects of oppression in both children and adults. It is interesting and appropriate that history can repeat itself for, as Mahatma Gandhi pointed out, "We cannot dismantle one system without having another in its place." Does this imply that we are "doomed" to repeat the lessons of the past until we learn from them?

The film, <u>The Joy Luck Club</u> offers some answers to this perplexing question. The mothers, aunts and grandmothers began to share their shameful experiences with their daughters, nieces and granddaughters about the years they silently suffered abusive, violent behavior from their spouses. It was then that the next generation chose not to live the same way because of what they had learned. Ideally, all people will have access to the information and opportunities they need to transform oppression into mutually beneficial alliances that heal. If we don't rise to the occasion by changing ourselves and empowering each other, we will reap devastating results that have far-reaching implications.

The idea is simply expressed in a Ba'hai belief: "Each one teaches one." Each person is led to change when they see how that change will benefit them and improve their life. Individually and collectively, we are undergoing a reawakening. The realization is that we don't have to tread the same path we have been down before. The following poem illustrates this point magnificently:

AN AUTOBIOGRAPHY IN FIVE CHAPTERS

Chapter One

I walk down the street.
There is a deep hole in the sidewalk.
I fall in.
I am lost...I am helpless.
It isn't my fault. It takes forever to find a way out.

Chapter Two

I walk down the same street.
There is a deep hole in the sidewalk.
I pretend I don't see it.
I fall in, again.
I can't believe I am in this same place.
But, it isn't my fault.
It still takes a long time to get out.

Chapter Three

I walk down the same street.
There is a deep hole in the sidewalk.
I see it is there.
I fall in...it's a habit...but, my eyes are wide open.
I know where I am.
It is my fault.
I get out immediately.

Chapter Four

I walk down the same street.

There is a deep hole in the sidewalk.

I walk around it.

Chapter Five

I walk down a different street.

Author unknown

This simple and profound thinking is easy to understand. If you believe that old habits die hard, you may never give yourself the chance to make the changes that you know you are capable of. In order to overcome any oppression you have lived with, you must transform the way you think and take informed action.

The organization Men Against Racism and Sexism points this out:

"Oppression is the systematic mistreatment of one group of people by another group of people or by society as a whole; with institutional power as a means of asserting that mistreatment. They postulate that men are oppressed because they are treated as inherently aggressive and violent and as if they do not feel pain or experience the full range of emotions like women. When they get hurt at work or play, they are expected to shrug it off and continue as if nothing happened. Boys and men are not expected to need closeness, reassurance and attention, which is thought to be harmful to their sense of place and importance in the world. If a boy or a man asks for help they are seen as weak, needy and then put down for being like a woman. They indicate that, in truth, every man has always done the best he could to fight the oppression that was placed upon him; even when he acts oppressively towards men or women, he is still fighting against the oppression as hard as he can and as much as he knows how to. Furthermore, they state that all men want, need and require close, loving relationships with men and women. Not seeing this clearly is part of male oppression. Finally, tenderness, closeness and softness are all inherent male traits. It is oppressive to consider that masculinity is only tough, rough and strong, just as it would be sexist to view women only as tender, close and soft creatures. It is one hundred percent feminine for women to be tough, rough and strong."

What they are saying, in essence, is to accept our fragile natures, even in our capacity for strength. Many men and women realize, due to circumstances, that their roles have switched. Adapting to these new circumstances is challenging. Yet, in order for our own evolution to continue, we become the change agents and catalysts for these new situations to develop. If you believe in spirituality, then you might agree you are a reflection of that which created you, and that your actions help bring about change. If the change promotes harmony, integrity and healing in your own life, then these will be the qualities you wish to share with others. That is what overcoming oppression is all about – to not be limited by a past that serves you no longer.

Have you ever experienced what Socrates pondered, that "The unexamined life is not worth living?" When you realize that you are just passing through "here" on your journey, it may catapult you to change what you don't like. How do you want to be remembered? What is the legacy you want to leave? What has brought you to your current juncture? Have you ever thought of yourself as being part of a larger mystery? Every action causes a reaction, and knowing that your actions produce consequences will help you decide how you want to live. Learning to live a more peaceful life requires daily practice. If you find yourself in situations that are burdensome, you are the one who has the power to change it. It might take help. All you have to do is ask, and keep on asking until you find what you need. Very often, the journey leads back to ourselves. Wherever you go, there you are. We always take ourselves with us. I learned a long time ago that you are the only one who will never, ever abandon you. To those who still struggle to overcome what binds them, remember those who came before you and set themselves free.

CHAPTER THREE

Exploring and Creating Healthy Romantic Relationships

In everyday life there are always opportunities to honor both separateness and togetherness...

Something is always stirring in the soul that will have an impact on our relationships.

Tradition teaches that the soul has an important spiritual dimension, so that living soulfully, even in marriage, entails a spiritual life that emerges directly from the relationship...

Marriage is by nature miraculous and magical. We do not understand it and cannot know where it is headed. To care for its soul, it is more important to honor its mystery...If you want to ensure the soulfulness of your marriage, it would be infinitely better to build a shrine to it, find its god or goddess, and tend its image than to follow the "manual" and do it all properly and intelligently.

Thomas Moore

~~~

Have you ever heard, "We teach what we need to learn" and "When the studen is ready, the teacher appears?" Having played the roles of both the teacher and student, has helped me alter the way I think about conflict, gender, and inter-personal relationships. I have remolded my preconceived ideas based on these experiences. The thoughts we rigidly hold onto about the way things 'ought to be' contribute to the common problems many of us suffer through in our romantic relationships, especially today. The reasons are many, yet not having traveled this road before, both men and women grapple with issues that the previous generation never had to. Thus, it's not surprising to find more women than men who attend seminars dealing with this subject. However, I need to emphasize that I've noticed an increase in male attendance at these kinds of workshops.

As a matter of fact, at one conference, we were even asked to "recruit" more men to work on resolving many of the identified problems. The attendance increased from two to eight men amongst thirty-three women. Not a bad start! Yet, what does this tell us?

If we are ever going to achieve more balance between the sexes, we will need the cooperation of both men and women to work together in redefining our roles and purpose. The same is true of same sex relationships, cooperation in the roles we play is essential. The survival of our planet, not to mention our species, depends upon this redefinition. It's important to understand why and if you were ever taught to give away your power. Have you allowed others to determine your happiness? Perhaps, you're not even aware that you've done this or were taught to behave in this manner.

Start to think about what you want in your life. What would you choose or create? Were you ever encouraged to think about what you might want? If not, the mindset of the industrialized era taught that life was a struggle and you had to 'pound the pavement,' (so to speak) to get what you wanted. Compare this thinking to our current western mindset of 'going with the flow' or 'doing what you love and the money will follow.' Ideas change to reflect the needs of the times we live in. As we advance spiritually, hopefully our civilization will do the same. Old structures previously supported by patriarchal beliefs are crumbling. One of the major reasons why so many men and women are confused is because they're operating from these old mindsets while not yet having the tools to change them.

When you follow a recipe, the directions include how much time you need to cook the food and what method is best. Similarly, when you allow yourself to be opened to new ideas which make more sense to you, you'll notice your outlook changing. In following instructions for food preparation, we expect the dish to turn out well. Likewise, we must also give ourselves the time needed to adjust to living by new ideas.

In my seminars, I often ask the following questions. How many have been married before? How many have been divorced? Almost the same amount of hands go up every time. I ask other questions too, such as – how many have ever lived with someone before, still live with someone, decide not to get married, or live alone by choice?

I ask these questions because although, we think of these situations, they are not often verbally articulated.

Just a half century ago, due to 'acceptable societal norms,' of expected arrangements at that time in history, our lifestyle was socially pre-determined. In the patriarchal system, people not only couldn't agree to disagree but they were also expected to conform or otherwise become outcasts. However, in the last two decades, we've moved toward more civility and respect for and with one another. Some would disagree and rightly so because not all have adapted to a more peaceful lifestyle. Many still struggle with the need to control others, which is borne out of a lack of self-control.

To explore healthy, romantic relationships in a new context, we need to understand what dysfunction is and how it contributes negatively to the concept of romance. Being romantic in and of itself is not negative or bad. It is the results suffered by many who misinterpret what romantic love is. Far too much emotional and verbal abuse has been tolerated over the centuries, not to mention the physical and sexual violence that was legally sanctioned in the home before. Many people enter 'romantic' relationships all "gaga" without being aware. They have a set of preconceived ideas about 'this is the way it is supposed to be.' Even John Bradshaw has described this phase of a relationship as being "oceanic." Then, when it doesn't work out, we end up wondering what went wrong. Once upon a time, marriages were pre-arranged. In some countries and cultures, they still are. However, in most of the western world people often pursue one another on their own, and sometimes for the wrong reasons. Let's look at some of them.

There are many contributing factors that create the lifestyles we live. In Paul Kivel's book and video, <u>Men's Work</u>, he asks the viewer to think about the roles men and women were trained to be in, and how they were taught to behave. Some of the common responses I hear when asking people to describe masculine are:

| Macho | Strength | Control | Leader |
| Father | Provider | Intelligent | Ego |

Loser	Perfection	Bossy	Un-com-municative
Double-standard Adherence	Sports-minded	Loving	Sexuality
Possessive	Over-indulgent	Hunter	Jealous

How many of these adjectives are positive? Consider some of the following examples for feminine that I often hear:

Soft	Nurturing	Catty	Loving
Moody	Sensitive	Insecure	Controlling
Bright	Domineering	Creative	Open-minded
Gentle	Kind	Flexible	Mother
Sensual	Peacemaker	Manipulative	Cook
Gullible	Frail	Needy	Wonderful

Do you notice more positive adjectives here? Some of the definitions we have for feminine and masculine are pretty scary. How did our culture and gender identity get us into these little boxes? More so, why have we accepted these definitions? What is gender? The dictionary defines it as:

"sex, or any of two or more classes of words or of forms of words that are usually partly based on sex and that determine agreement with other words or grammatical forms."

These definitions are most confusing because of the significance that gender has now. For example, gender has been construed to be those behavioral traits that we associate as being a 'normal' male or female. What has our society dictated as normal? Don't dress little boys in pink pants; but in blue pants. Who determined that pink is a feminine color? Think of yellow, and ask yourself why that is considered more of a neutral color for both males and females. Another example of the little boxes is seen in schools. Remember kindergarten? Were you thought of as abnormal if you were a girl who wanted to play with the erector set, or you were a boy who wanted to play in the kitchen with the dolls? Who determined that this was wrong? Let's not forget that our own ancestors also came out of this system. Now perhaps we can understand why it's so hard to change. We are dealing with thousands of years of history.

Patriarchy has been described as an ideology that is rooted in the denial of worldly power to women. Patriarchy comprises the history of the world as we have been taught it. While men and women were both given their 'defined roles,' women have generally been omitted from this history. It has been argued that the common root of sexism and the system of war, which is also seen in men's behavior towards women, lies in the attitudes of those patriarchal structures. According to the <u>The Brock Utne Reader</u>, women's oppression through patriarchy has serious consequences for peace and individuals. While some people have viewed women as being peacemakers, the dichotomy is that women, as a group, have been exploited by patriarchy. Just look how long it took for domestic violence laws to be mandated. It's only in the last fifteen years that psycho therapeutic court ordered programs have come about. Did you know it was legal to beat a woman for thousands of years? Now, it's a crime. How far we have come. It was only recently that I came upon two striking examples of the damage that patriarchy has wrought. In Dorothy Bryant's book, <u>Ella Price's Journal</u> originally published in 1972, she describes in detail the journey of a suburban Californian housewife who experiences a deep sense of discontent. What Ella discovers by deciding to attend college for the first time at age 35 forces her to painful but empowering choices. In the afterward, Barbara Horn writes:

"Within the course of a few months, Ella notes aspects of her previously routine suburban life which she now finds annoying and, at times, intolerable. Needing a clear head to read and study, she cannot share martinis every evening with Joe, an activity that used to constitute their most enjoyable moments together...

Before she begins keeping a notebook, Ella does not know why she feels empty and lost, and cannot perceive that she has choices. By the end of the novel, this woman, once fearful of any transgression, has rejected the major institutions in her white, suburban, lower middle class world: family, marriage, motherhood, religion, psychiatry…She has joined what Adrienne Rich calls the "thousands of women asking" 'The Woman Question' in women's voices."

One of the major reasons for this book came out of the author's own experience listening to women weep in her office saying that going to school was the only positive thing in many of their lives. It's not surprising to find in the research done in <u>Women's Ways of Knowing: The Development of Self, Voice, and Mind</u> that many women still feel silenced in their families and schools. Based on in-depth interviews with 135 women across the country, Gloria Steinhem in 1981 suggested:

"that when women talk, their behavior is not compared with men's but is assessed against the standard that holds that women should be seen but not heard. When women deviate from a standard of absolute silence, they are thought to be loquacious and out of line."

Feminist and women's studies have sprung up in the last four decades. Research suggests that "patriarchy may damage and distort women's perspectives as well as those of men and may embrace women as peacemakers – images that reflect and serve the prevailing gender order." Again, this idea confirms the boxes we were taught to live in. And now, centuries later and a history of women being silenced by death in the "witch" burnings at the stake, we still haven't eradicated the old myths.

For example, in our children's fairy tales, we are taught to believe that if you kiss someone they will no longer be a frog, or that you have the power to turn 'him' into Prince Charming, or vice versa, the Prince rescues Cinderella. We've been conditioned to believe that we have the almighty power of making someone's life miserable or happy forevermore. These ideas, generations old, suggest that we need to have someone come along to break the spell. What is the spell? The spell of being alone or the negativity associated with labels like bachelor and spinster? This cultural role model teaches us that if you're not married, there must be something wrong with you. Isn't that true? Do we not assume something is wrong with someone if they aren't married? Even though it was more acceptable for men to stay bachelors; they also suffer for the same stereotypes.

Historically, it was expected that men take care of women, because the prevailing belief was that women couldn't take care of themselves. As a matter of fact, the story of the dowry projected a message that a woman's future husband was being given something in exchange for his agreement to marry her. This same system perpetuated the idea that a women was to take care of others, not herself. It's not difficult to see why so many divorces have ensued. The inequality that we've lived with spawned these challenges.

I am reminded of a couple I saw in counseling. They came from another culture. He was 29 and she was 21. They met when she was fifteen and got married when she was seventeen. They had three children in a short time period. She had tried to commit suicide and he couldn't understand why. She explained to him that she was so unhappy because she wanted to be more than a mother and a wife. She felt trapped and limited; seeing no way out due to the cultural expectations placed upon her. Because they both lacked the skills to communicate effectively about their problems, he had become physically abusive, hoping to keep things the same. A domestic violence arrest forced them into counseling. He believed that she should be happy, since he worked and was financially successful. He really couldn't understand why she wanted to return to school. Consider the films being made in the last decade, "East is East," and "Kadosh," which portray many of the problems we have alluded to.

No matter what sex we are, what culture we're born into, or what our ancestors believed, inherent within each man and woman is the desire for self-realization; to know more, be more and to have the chance to explore all the options available to us. Consequently, if someone you're close to doesn't think the same way you do, there may be severe problems that can't be solved without professional intervention. Furthermore, these differences in thinking are not limited to the culture and gender expectations alone.

If it wasn't for the acceptance of European/Middle Eastern/Asian standards that it's okay for men to have mistresses, one wonders if we would live with less chaos than we do today. When men left wives and didn't support the children they had with them, women had to learn to take care of themselves and their offspring. Thus we have the situations we do today. This is one reason why the courts had to create legislation to enforce some system to ask fathers to be co-responsible to pay part of their children's support. I am often surprised to hear angry men say that they're having to pay child support for a one night stand. Excuse me! Whatever happened to each person taking responsibility for their actions?

There are of course many reasons why people are reluctant to get married again. It is the common fear of going through a similar experience. It is also why more pre-nuptial arrangements have come into being. As one colleague states:

"I guess men are more afraid of intimacy and commitment than they are of our 'wrath' or anything else! The married women I know do not make marriage sound like an enviable state! One woman has no sex in her marriage because, although he is impotent, he won't speak to his doctor and he isn't interested in being affectionate either. Another woman's husband travels a lot in his work, and she doesn't care if he is faithful to her, and when she does have sex with him she says she has to perform! Another woman says her husband is faithful, but gone more and more at work now that the children are gone. The women at work talk about husbands who don't help around the house, and about how glad they are to have them leave to go fishing, hunting or camping.

One man I work with who sees his wife on weekends since they work in different cities says a man will do almost anything for readily available sex. I think women will do almost anything for 'love,' including enduring beatings, unfaithfulness, alcoholism, etc. I don't think either sex has much of a handle on what real love is. The people who usually seem most satisfied in their marriages are people who started out as friends and have stayed friends through their marriage. It is a rare woman who says her husband is her best friend, but I think those are the strongest marriages. I only know one woman who ever told me that."

Knowing now, from the start, that marriage isn't just about romance and starry nights, it takes commitment and work to enjoy the starry and romantic times. More and more people are rethinking what it means to be married. This is an important step if it will help prevent divorce and the emotional trauma that both children and parents endure. Has it only been in the last two decades that we have questioned whether or not everyone is emotionally ready for marriage? Not everyone wants to be married. How do you view marriage? Do you see it as a legal contract, a spiritual commitment to a larger purpose, and/or both views? Do you see it as neither of these, or any idea not mentioned here? Think of all the attorneys who would have to change the focus of their practice if there were no divorces or amicable mediated agreements. We do see this happening more now because of "mandatory" mediation in the courts. This system asks you to take responsibility for your own behavior and choices in determining what is in your best interests and what will be the least damaging to your children. However, mediation doesn't work unless both people are emotionally mature, conscious and not willing to play games. The War of the Roses is a film which depicts the worst possible scenario between two "adults." The current laws in our legal system are flawed. It's not surprising then, that current statistics state 60% of marriages end in divorce.

Surely, our generation is recreating history. It would be extremely wise to create classes in preparation for marriage, so people realize what they are getting into without divorce being such an easy option. Some states are now adopting legislation to mandate couples to attend classes for six months. Some states also require that both parents attend classes on parenting before they are allowed a divorce.

Why do you think it's so difficult for people to stay with one person for fifty years or more today? In a time where everything man-made is replaceable because it is more expensive to repair it, have we not done the same thing with people? Do you give a relationship the time, effort and work it requires before abandoning it? Robert Johnson, in his book, We, states:

"A man is committed to a woman only when he can inwardly affirm that he binds himself to her as an individual, and that he will be with her even when she is no longer in love, even when he and she are no longer afire with passion, and he no longer sees in her his ideal of perfection or the reflection of his soul. When a man can say this inwardly and mean it, then he has touched the essence of commitment. But he should know that he has an inner battle ahead of him. The love potion is strong, the new morality of romance is deeply ingrained in us. It seizes and dominates us when we least expect it. To put the love potion on the correct level, to live it without betraying his human relationships, is the most difficult task of consciousness that any man can undertake in our modern western world...But a commitment to passion is not a substitute for a commitment to a human being... We are all committed to finding passion, we are all committed to being eternally 'in love,' and we imagine that this is the same thing as being committed to a person. But the passion fades, the passion migrates to someone else we feel attracted to. If we are committed only to follow where passion leads, then there can be no true loyalty to an individual person. If it is romance that we seek, it is romance that we shall have – but not commitment and not relationship."

His commentary is interesting to ponder in light of commitment. In the Hebrew calendar, during the month of Adar (Joy), which is usually in the late winter/early spring, we are asked to reflect on love and relationships, including our spiritual connection to God and a sense of our own divinity. There is a Hebrew saying which, when translated into English, means "I am to my beloved as my beloved is to me." Does this statement remind you of anyone? Imagine that the beloved is you, and then ask yourself, "Can I see or feel the beloved within myself?" Do you accept your own divinity? If not, why? What would you have to experience in order to believe this? Some by-products of this are feeling a sense of peace within; that you don't need another person to survive; and the realization that you're a human being having a spiritual experience and vice-versa. What else can you imagine?

In our search for the beloved, we must also learn to love ourselves unconditionally. How can we really love another without experiencing a healthy sense of who we are? You are the only person who will never abandon you. Most people are shocked when they hear this. It doesn't take much to see that many of us were or are plagued with low self-esteem, so if and when we get rejected by someone, we lose ourselves completely because we lose our identity. Many of the songs, books, movies and media, in general, speak of the pain of love. Or is it control? If you were not taught to love yourself, and you were taught that the prince or princess was going to come along and rescue you, then you are still searching for dragons, frogs or witches on whom you can cast your spell. What is the spell you are casting or breaking? What are you being rescued from? Yourself?!

We look to our companions as if they can protect us from the great unknown. So for a while, we experience some peaceful times, coupled with the hills and valleys of life's struggles. We know that whether we are married, cohabiting with someone, living alone or with roommates, we all experience life. Sometimes, it can be a comfort having someone there, and most of us have all gone through the other times of just wanting a little space for ourselves.

No matter how much we attempt to complicate our lives with gadgets or busyness, eventually we'll have to accept that it is healthy to have time alone and learn to enjoy our own company. Simultaneously, it is also healthy to choose not to be alone. However, in our culture that was never really a choice. While it is natural to feel lonely at times, we all have the opportunity not to be terrified by it. I have discovered that the most common fear people seem to have is of death or the unknown. Yet, it seems that if we want to have peace of mind in our lifetime, we will need to make peace with this "ultimate" experience of the unknown. As I understand it, none of us bypasses this event, – at least not in the bodies we're in now!

What is your perception of death? Have you read books on the subject or have you avoided it? I think on some level, death is a continuation of our experience, but only in a different place with a different awareness. My reasoning is based on the contemplative miracle of life. We come through another person when we are born, and then when we lose our physical bodies, our spirit leaves our body. That spirit is our life force. You may ask – where does the life force go? It depends on your belief system. Some believe in reincarnation, or an angelic presence, or finality. Many books exist on the subject. My goal is for you to become more comfortable with what you really believe because it will influence your relationship either negatively or positively with another as well as yourself. Why even mention this subject on a chapter on healthy relationships? If we don't explore our deepest convictions with another as well as formulate our own decisions about such matters, then this too can be a roadblock to true intimacy.

The renowned Persian poet, Rumi, wrote about finding ourselves spiritually in the <u>Search for the Beloved</u>. What is it that attracts you to another person? They say the eyes are the windows of the soul. So beyond a physical attraction, there is also a mystical attraction, or an awareness of soulful recognition. You know this deep level of connection is not possible with everyone you meet for the simple reason that you don't have the time or energy it would take to sustain such intimacy with more than one person. Some people try however. This is why most relationships fail when affairs begin. Unless you complete the lessons with your current partner, chances are you will experience the same scenario in your newly formed dysfunctional relationships.

Many books suggest that we have soulmates. My theory is that there is more than one soulmate for everyone in this lifetime if your experience allows for that opportunity. Much of it depends on circumstances and timing. Biologically speaking, people didn't live as long one hundred years ago as they do today. Back in the 1800's, people often died earlier due to the physical hardships they sustained. If they were married when they were fifteen and died at forty, their marriage was short-lived. Now that we have the capacity to extend life, people live longer. Today, if you live to be ninety or a hundred and you were married at twenty, you'd have sixty or seventy years together.

There are lots of adjustments required along the way. Many people don't have the tools to deal with the problems that longevity produces. I recall John Bradshaw in a video saying, "A blood test is not good grounds for getting married!" Whatever triggers you emotionally lets you know that you've got more work to do. How important it is to you to be happy or right? When expectations are not met, ask for what you need, and recognize that others have limitations too. Can you accept, adapt or adjust to another's behavior? If you can't, as the saying goes, are you willing to plant your own garden, pick your own flowers, and not wait for someone else to do it? This requires a lot of maturity.

Both my paternal and maternal grandparents seemed to be "happily" married for over fifty years before their physical demise in the '70's. I wondered why so many marriages aren't sustainable today. My own parents were married over fifty years when my father passed away in August of 1995. I recall the Rabbi asking my mother about their relationship before the funeral. Mom responded and said, "Sometimes he was my best friend, and other times he was my worst enemy!" How could one not make a statement like that after spending over fifty years together? As stated earlier, many suggestions have come forth to reverse the trend of if the marriage doesn't work out we'll get divorced. Current legislation is looking at making it more difficult to get a marriage license. The same ideas apply for permission to have children. Why should people be able to have children if they can't take care of them. These ideas are not unrealistic in light of the serious problems we face today.

Many people are rethinking the entire concept of marriage and wonder if it is even necessary. This idea is especially true for elders who don't wish to give up their social security, or choose to maintain their own places and/or live together. The same is true for younger people who've been married more than once and are terrified of the financial and emotional burden and backlash they suffered. Some never recover. Today, it is almost impossible for only one partner to work unless they are highly paid professionals. With costs skyrocketing and the fact that there are more single parent families than ever before, problems are almost predictable. Look at the common denominators.

Several centuries ago, when men hunted for food and women did the gathering and preparation, their lives were much simpler because their needs and wants differed from today's world. In John Gray's book, <u>Men Are From Mars and Women Are From Venus</u>, he ponders who is out there hunting for what on our freeways? Unless you choose to live in the Australian outback, Brazilian rainforests, or out on the land somewhere, ancient models are no longer adequate for our survival today. We must wonder if today's drive-by shootings are not indicative of man's need for aggression, having no outlet for it. There are many ways to get rid of your stress today. Can you think of any safe, positive ways to release your anger and stress? Medical studies show the correlation of aerobic exercise to the reduction of stress in our lives. One reason is because your brain chemicals become more balanced through the increased output of the neuro-transmitter, serotonin. This is also the body's way of eliminating negativity through the natural production of endorphins. However, whether the contributing factors to aggression or violence are due to learned behavior and/or to psychobiology, the more we know about ourselves, the more we can control or change our undesirable traits. Meditation, visualization, walking, and other healthy habits create positive mental health. Some medications are also helpful. You have to find what works for you. You need to practice the art of self-control, and take care of your body and mind. This expresses a wholesome positive self regard. Healthy self-esteem is a prerequisite for a good, loving relationship.

In some of my classes, people attempted to define love. The following are their responses. See if you agree, or disagree. Consider what adjectives or descriptions you might use. LOVE IS:

Space to be and let be.

Caring for one another and sharing; accepting as well as giving and experiencing one another.

What you share of yourself with another in a caring, growing, unfolding space; being open to receive; unconditional acceptance, ever-growing and changing.

Love can only be given, not earned, deserved, bought, or swapped for. When I enter a relationship, I am willing to love. The return is up to the other party.

Unconditional acceptance of another person to explore his/her own self-growth. It includes trust, sharing, intimacy and commitment on an equal basis.

Open and truthful communication with "trusting" each other as the most important quality in a man/woman relationship.

A desire to give and receive good things; to give to one's self. My own awareness of how much I care for another person. It involves my acceptance of the other person and what I am willing to sacrifice to maintain that relationship.

When a couple can support and care for each other unconditionally, while allowing each to be themselves.
Allowing your partner to be who they are and accepting them.
Putting him or her first as in caring.
Loving that person as you love God.
Allows for and encourages the other's growth.
Loving the other person when it is not returned.
Caring as much about someone else as I do about myself; seeing someone for who they really are, and not trying to change them.

It's important to examine a multitude of definitions on this complex issue. One meaning of love comes from Charles Fillmore's book, <u>The Twelve Powers in Man</u>:

"Love is the faculty which gives us our ability to know our oneness with all others, and to feel a desire for only good for all....Love is a power which both gives out and attracts; it diffuses itself and expands. It is the principle or law which unifies the great variety of interests and activities in creation into a whole; it is the energy which brings forth and produces."

Compared to charging a neutral battery, the equation looks like $p+n = c(2)$. Negative ions plus positive ions equal a completed circuit. Positive ions lose electrons and negative ions gain electrons. The stored energy contained within a battery is filtered and controlled in a certain direction and forms a complete circuit. Similarly, a prototype for balance in relationships could look like this:

Over-Balanced	Balanced	Under-Balanced
Possessiveness	Acceptance	Hermit/Loner
Dependency	Freedom	Fearful
Jealousy/Greed	Understanding	Unavailable

Would you include different qualities? How does the above chart compare to other definitions of a balanced love relationship? The following list was generated in my course based on a discussion of

other issues that effect our relationships; namely children, no matter how young or old they are.
1. Inability to communicate because of discomfort in what we want to say.
2. Know how to say NO and not feel guilty. Ability to express healthy anger and state boundaries.
3. How you feel about your children's lifestyle if you disagree with it; or the way they raise their children (your grandchildren).
4. Coping with divorce (both the couple and their relatives, parents, offspring).
5. Whether or not you subsidize your offspring if you are in a position to, and how to do it.
6. Coping with children/parents moving away.
7. Apportioning your estate to children living in a foreign country or out of state.
8. What are your own personal issues that you may want to discuss with your children and don't?
9. How do you feel if your children are (child is) mad at you? What role does self-esteem play?
10. What do I need to do for myself in order to get my needs met with my children without manipulation?

In addition to these ideas, what else would you recommend for an open dialogue?

We can see the importance in finding workable answers to those questions. These issues have contributed to the demise or ongoing journey of couples who marry and have children. Imagine what your life would be like if you didn't have any children, goals for self-improvement, humanitarian projects, or dreams/ideas to create something new. Again, you may wonder what this subject is doing in a chapter on healthy relationships. It's another crucial issue that must be discussed.

Exploring and Creating Healthy Romantic Relationships

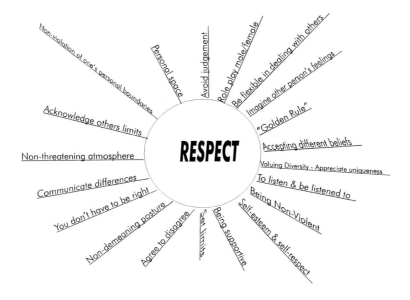

Your "search" for a healthy romantic relationship is similar to discovering what motivates you. What gets you out of bed in the morning? How can you ask another to complete you so wholly without even knowing what you want? Many never even question these ideas because self-actualization is a low priority or they've never thought of it. If you're worried about paying rent or knowing where your next meal is coming from, your focus is different. Let's examine Maslow's Hierarchy of Needs. (See page 109)

We're at a new crossroads in relationships. I've often heard people say, "I want a normal relationship." What constitutes normal? One couple, married for over twenty-five years, says, "There's nothing normal anymore. What you are talking about is traditional, and even that takes a lot of work." People who make commitments to stay together don't always do that, especially when there is abuse of any kind or as co-dependency suggests, if you get ill being with someone because of the stress.

How many people have stayed with alcoholics or those addicted to the many numbing devices I mentioned in Chapter Two? People get sick or in worst-case scenarios, they can get arrested when they attempt to control another. I have seen this happen to parents, children, couples, fathers, sons, mothers and daughters. No one can control another unless they think they can be controlled or want to be. What of the desperate people who are afraid to be alone and remain with someone to their mental and physical demise? As you improve your mental health, you come to realize, as Dr. Lowe stated, "My mental health is the most important thing to me." A profound Co-Dependent Serenity Prayer states:

"God, grant me the serenity to accept the people I cannot change, courage to change the person I can, and wisdom to know that it is me!"

What qualities can you identify that create healthy romantic relationships? No one likes to be criticized or judged, yet we all know too well what pushes our buttons; those irritating behaviors. There are ways to let your partner know what you find annoying without putting him/her down. A healthy statement is, "I love you and I don't like your behavior." Tell them why, what you feel, and what you need instead. Be very specific. If you don't know what you need, you can't expect your partner to know. In addition, while you'd like your mate to contribute to your happiness, very often we assume that it is their job to make us happy. While the notion sounds good, no one can make you happy forever or all of the time. It is not their job!! Ultimately, each person and couple must find what works for them.

Your inner turmoil and struggle are your teachers. You're fortunate to live in an age and time when so much help is available. You need to muster the strength and have the courage to come forth and ask for help when you need it. Dr. Carl Jung identified our "shadow" as being an important part of our nature. We can befriend our shadows, which are nothing more than our fears or those parts of ourselves that we have shunned or dislike. They are waiting to be recognized, embraced, and let go of when you realize what you don't have to hold on to anymore.

In our search for love, once we think we've found it, we then become terrified that we may lose it. This loss is due to fear, mistrust, sickness or death. No matter how much we love another, eventually, we will have to face our aloneness again, if only due to the fact that one of us will die before the other, unless both go together. Everyone has faced this fear at different times in their lives. The search to share your life with another is borne of your desire to add more meaning to your life. No one else can define what is important to you.

If you're not enjoying your life or prospering and learning from and by it, you can change it. Change does not come from outside yourself, although a lot of helpful information is available to make a positive change. You really have to want a different experience. Most people are used to doing "business as usual," meaning that they don't think life can be any different. We usually see things this way because of our upbringing. However, I've always recommended that you re-educate yourself to find what works best for you. Discover what you really believe; not because someone else told you to think a certain way.

In John Bradshaw's books, Healing the Shame That Binds You and The Family, he suggests that we have to go back and heal the wounds of the past so we don't repeat them again nor have them destroy our current relationships. Earlier on, we discussed what happens when you enter into a relationship unconsciously. What this portends is that if you say you're attracted to someone and act on that attraction without getting to know them, you might one day ask yourself what went wrong. It takes time to get to know what goes on inside another person's head. What are their likes and dislikes? Do they reveal themselves? Are they honest? Is there enough in common with similar values to sustain a long-term commitment? We don't get to know someone on a deeply intimate level overnight. Ann Wilson Schaef in her book, When Society Becomes An Addict, suggests that we are trying to fill the void, or the emptiness within. Nothing and no one else can really take that away; no food, no alcohol, drugs or gambling can take away the emptiness permanently.

You need to ask yourself what the emptiness/void comes from. Sex is satisfying but it does not connote compatibility. What gives your life meaning or purpose?

It is not up to another person to provide you with a purpose, although two people together may create a larger purpose for their lives. We all want to have a unique experience, and to feel connected. Some want to make a difference and know that what they do matters. Nelson Mandela, in one of his speeches asks, "Who are you not to accept your divinity?" When you act unconsciously, you wander around aimlessly, forgetting that you live on 'borrowed time.' If you feel that your life lacks meaning, what will you do about it? Do you know where your limitations come from? Do your emotional blocks create problems in your romantic relationships? To answer these questions, we must understand what empowerment is.

Technically, when you empower another you give them the authority to do something. In a non-traditional, literal sense, it also suggests that you can ask for what you need and want. Needs and wants are different. For example, we need oxygen to live, and yet the quality of the air we breathe is different according to where we live. Another example could be that we all need money to live, yet how much money we all want or need is different for everyone. On another level, you can say that you need love to survive, but what kind of love and at what price? I believe we all need love and caring, but we have a choice as to how that gets modeled and whether or not it is acceptable. How often have we heard and seen atrocities committed in the name of love, God or religion? I don't think the Creative Force, Spirit/God, or however you choose to address that which animates and sustains life, would be too pleased with our progress.

Romantic, loving, caring relationships and marriages don't just happen. They are created by the willingness of both people to share power together so that they each respect one another and can understand what is important by listening to each other. I'm not surprised by the comment I often hear from divorced people, that they wouldn't want to marry again. In John Bradshaw's public television series, he so aptly points out that many men and women don't discuss beforehand (before making a commitment) such important issues as who will pay the rent/mortgage, who will pay the car notes and insurance, who will do the grocery shopping. Do you find out how you celebrate the holidays? Do you open gifts on Christmas Eve or Christmas morning? What about expectations when it comes to visiting in-laws, parents, friends? Does this important stuff get discussed, and if so, do you find that the person changes after you marry them? Do you wonder what happened to the things you agreed to? For those who never discussed these things, are you surprised that there are major arguments or that you lack the skills to discuss these issues intelligently without turning them into power struggles?

These are the ordinary day-to-day realities that people need assistance with when they come in for counseling. Addressing these issues now may prevent future generations from making the same mistakes their predecessors did. If you know not what you're doing, is it a mistake or rather, a lack of information? Just as we learn to ride a bike or tie our shoelaces, so must we learn how to communicate effectively without verbal and emotional violence/abuse.

When men and women first meet, traditionally they allow their hormones to determine if they want to know each other better. However, when the lust or sexual attraction fades, as it often does, they have little else to sustain the relationship. Dr. Paul Wanio tellingly comments in his article, "There are No Condoms For the Heart;"

"To isolate or split off the sexual side of your being from the rest of yourself so that you might partake in casual sex, is not only degrading and limiting, it is psychologically unhealthy.

By behaving in an intimate manner without actually being intimate, you create a 'psychic contradiction.' You allow someone to get extremely close to you physically, without being psychologically prepared for the experience. In fact, it is not possible to be prepared... To really know someone is a highly developed skill that does not occur in one week or month, nor is it merely dependent upon time. It requires in-depth awareness, emotional sharing, honest communication, trust and non-defensiveness.

You can place a condom around a penis, but you cannot place one around your mind.... Safety on a human level requires trust, respect, commitment and love.

Remember, there are no condoms for the heart. Mistrust, defensiveness and 'game playing' between the sexes largely takes place because casual sex has become an option.... The harm in casual sex is that the concept itself creates mistrust.... How would you feel if your mate said to you after an affair, 'Hey it was only sex, don't worry.' Would you be relieved? Hardly. Because you'd know that even if the sex was able to be twisted into something impersonal, the intimate aspects of this loving act could potentially arise to further threaten your relationship.... If sex is so casual, it would be as silly to object to an affair as objecting to shaking hands.... Once you develop the ability to find fulfillment in a committed, monogamous relationship, you will wonder how you could settle for anything less. And, you won't."

While sexual attraction and having a fulfilling sex life is important, it is not the be all and end all of your relationship. As a matter of fact, many men and women are shocked to learn that they can be best friends, and still be in love. Many unhappy couples stay together for economic survival or wait until their children are older. You need to ask yourself if your children will suffer more from the tension, unhappiness and fights in the home, than if they had quality time alone with each parent, assuming one parent won't abandon their children as punishment towards their ex-spouse.

I am reminded of a story where a couple was married for over twenty-five years. They had two teenagers at the time they separated. It was many years before the woman had enough courage to leave an emotionally and verbally abusive marriage. She was too afraid to communicate with her husband about his behavior. Every attempt she made to do so was met with more ridicule, denial, scorn and threats. After much thought and planning, she located a job and apartment in another city, and left one day while everyone was away. Prior to taking this drastic action, she had asked him to go with her to counseling for many years and he refused. To this day, one child blames her for leaving and rarely speaks to her. It was only after she left that her spouse was willing to go for help, which is often the case. She had reached the point of no return – too little, too late. This man was a "victim" of his own upbringing and had never dealt with his shadow side.

I've heard many similar stories over the years. The sad thing is that so many divorces could be prevented if people would get counseling beforehand. Many people have had a negative view of counseling, especially due to the many stories that circulated over the years about the 'abuse of power' from psychiatrists. Most aren't even aware of all the differences in today's specialized fields. There are important distinctions such as, licensed clinical psychologists, social workers, marriage and family therapists, addictions professionals, pastoral counselors and mental health counselors. The field had to change to include professionals from many disciplines, because in the past, issues dealing with domestic violence, addictionology or other problems weren't addressed.

Someone once compared relationships to sports, saying "If you like to play tennis and they like to play football, you better find someone who likes to play your sport or accept that the two of you play a different game." As a matter of fact, there is nothing wrong if you each prefer different things, as long as you do enjoy your times together, alone, and have other common interests. When I spoke earlier of empowerment, this included the act of making decisions together versus the patriarchal model which said, "Do this because I said so." That same power play is seen daily amongst children and parents, husbands and wives, and in companies between employers and employees. No matter what a person's age or sex, everyone deserves respect and an explanation of what one finds offensive. Unless we change the patterns, we'll be mere robots, acting out rote behavior or habits. Power imbalances are obvious in many other arenas. They are no longer acceptable since the power/ domination/ control model has caused more problems than it solved.

Earlier on, we took a look at the "boxes" that people have been stereotyped into. These boxes are based on outdated data relevant to the societal norms of yesteryear. These societal norms grew out of the system that believes it is a man's responsibility to handle everything. This idea not only results in many men dying earlier than their spouses, but also creates women who don't know how to survive if their spouse dies because they never wrote a check before, and similarly, it creates men who didn't know how to cook or do laundry. Much of the current younger generation has reversed these trends, however, we're still challenged to develop new mind sets that address previous problems. Finding the answers that will improve our society and individual lives is our current task.

To shift your thinking requires that you become aware of what you do, say, think, and understand the reasons for your behavior.

You don't have to do what anyone else tells you to do if it doesn't work for you. You must also take responsibility for your actions. For example, if you want to be a full-time homemaker, there is nothing wrong with that as long as you let your partner know about it up front and you both agree. A common complaint is, "He/she wasn't like that before we got married." One reason why people usually put their best foot forward in the beginning is because they're afraid to let the truth be known. However, if we don't reveal those secretive parts, as many of you know, you sabotage the relationship from the beginning. Eventually, your partner will leave because they feel deceived and may wonder how they can trust you again. As hard as it is, you owe it to yourself and the other person to be up front about those issues they will find out about any way. When the truth does come out, some couples actually choose to work on their problems versus abandoning the relationship. Both people must feel comfortable enough with each other to surmount many of the predictable phases the relation- ship is bound to go through over time.

We have come a long way historically. A society is made up of men and women and the prevailing social order of the day, which suggests and determines the reasons for changes that have to be made. Society has now accepted that it's okay for fathers to have family leave, and for men who choose to be more involved in their children's lives, to be stay-at-home dads. I saw these changes a lot when I co-facilitated domestic violence groups. Many men who participated came from all different cultures and ethnic backgrounds. They were arrested for what was once considered acceptable behavior for centuries. They were shocked when the police arrived, and were told they had to go to jail. They couldn't understand why they were court ordered to join group therapy dealing with anger and violence for the behavior that was sanctioned for many centuries had now become a crime. This behavior is not limited to the heterosexual community. Many gay and lesbian relationships suffer the same problems as well.

In addition, women who have been subservient for so long are being forced to address their low self-esteem issues. Many still fear for their lives and won't press charges. They are also terrified of supporting themselves, especially if they've never done that before. As we transform our abilities, not making them liabilities, we will discover that we have the capacity to evolve, and thus live a more balanced life. Perhaps, we can then create a more harmonious framework in which our marriages thrive so that a new legacy is one of soulful joy.

More men are also adjusting to a woman's choice to use her maiden name and/or both of their names. I have heard of cultures where women give their female offspring their name and the man gives his sons his last name so that the progeny of both family lines continue. I've also been advised that when a women is wealthier than a man, and she doesn't put his name on the home in a second marriage, he feels emasculated, the same way a woman does when her spouse doesn't put her name on the deed. It is an interesting paradox that the same power imbalances that existed for one sex for so many years is now done to the other sex. History repeats itself. It reminds me of women who are elected or get into positions traditionally held by men where they still use the power/domination/control model. This comes from a lack of training, which if they practiced new techniques, would empower them to do things differently. A lack of trust that begins in our families gets passed on to us, which then gets passed on into our community, and thus, our world. This would include the creation of a trusting work environment, but, how can you trust another human being if you don't trust yourself? One of the reasons we don't trust ourselves is due to our past conditioning. Some may have heard statements like "Who do you think you are? What makes you think you can do that? You'll never amount to anything etc. etc." Many of these messages came from those who themselves never believed they could do more. In order to move forward, we must learn to forgive others and ourselves by not repeating unhealthy behavior. I often ask people, "What is the lesson you are learning from this experience?"

A culture which teaches that a traditional way to get out of a relationship is to lie, have an affair, and betray the trust of the one we propose to love, is unhealthy. Some of the reasons more people seek integrity oriented therapists and counselors are to help them have the courage to be honest, say what is not working, and ask for help. It's often difficult to verbalize your unhappiness about why you don't want to be in the relationship anymore. No one wants to be hurt or hurt another. Yet the motivation for having an affair is brought about by many factors. Loneliness and inattentiveness in the relationship makes us look elsewhere. Many don't want to deal with the economics of the situation because separating assets, cars, a house, and all of the other material trappings that define what you call a marriage or a relationship are a lot more difficult to deal with than a one night affair or an ongoing affair. Yet it happens every day.

It is hypocritical to claim that you're so in love with someone yet be terrified of telling them how unhappy you are in the relationship. Is this love or codependency? To be honest enough to express what it is that you're unhappy about can create monumental positive changes for both of you. All it takes is one person to do things differently. This behavior requires a healthy amount of self-esteem. Being able to ask questions like:
1. What are we going to do about this problem?
2. Will we choose to work through these challenges?
3. Will we give the relationship our best before we say it can't work?
4. Will we take time to heal our emotional wounds.

Brad Blanton, author of <u>Radical Honesty: How to Transform Your Life by Telling the Truth</u> offers some helpful insights:

"Authentic intimate relationships require that we tell the truth about what we feel, what we think and what we are. If we don't tell the truth about what we've done, if we're not willing to tell the other person who we are, then what we have is a relationship in which we are constantly performing...The reason we have a 53% divorce rate is that people are just worn out from performing for each other. And as for the remaining 47%, half of those are terrible relationships. They're miserable, but they are terrified of being alone. So only about 23% of relationships are authentic, intimate relationships where people are actually sharing the way their lives are with each other. And they are powerfully committed to common goals and helping each other achieve them...We don't have to hide anymore."

Guilt doesn't solve problems. It is a part of our collective unconscious as a species which acts as one undercurrent of the prevailing mindset built over centuries. It is habitual; not necessarily helpful. For example, countries won't grant divorces based on irreconcilable differences. They are entrenched in systems dictated by malevolence. Consider that you must hire a private investigator to prove infidelity. Ha! Is there something wrong with this picture? The very people that created this unworkable system are still controlling the ways you can get out of it, and, they're making a lot of money from it!

The book, Sexual Arrangements: Marriage and the Temptation of Infidelity highlights true stories from many of the couples they counseled. They believe that by demolishing the myths of what people believed marriage was supposed to be and do, that men and women may be able to reconcile their fantasies by sharing their views on the role secrecy plays in a marriage. Husbands and wives view affairs very differently. People are taught to see themselves as failures or to be shamed if their relationship doesn't work. Consider what Iyanla Vanzant states in her book, " Acts of Faith,

"Divorce or separation following a long-term relationship creates many feelings. One of the strongest is "something is wrong with me." If your mate becomes involved with another person or gives what you consider an unacceptable reason for moving beyond the relationship, the feelings of inadequacy deepen. Why? What did I do? How could you do this to me?

Somewhere in the process you lose sight of the fact that people have a right to change their minds. You may not want them to do it. You probably won't like it when it happens. But people have a right to change their minds and it has absolutely nothing to do with you."

Our schools do little to prepare us in dealing with personal growth issues. Those who can't read, write or do arithmetic, are at a great disadvantage. But most of us suffer even though we have these skills; we don't know how to listen or communicate. One reason why we have so many classes in these subjects today in the continuing education is because we need help. Our public schools are being asked to use relevant curricula that deal with all of the subjects once considered taboo:date rape, safe sex, sexual abuse, sexually transmitted diseases, alcoholism drug addiction, and divorce, just to name a few of the ills we are bombarded with.

Personal growth and change can't be prevented. We are meant to grow, otherwise we stagnate. Whether you're alone or with someone, the growth continues. You usually don't grow in the same way or at the same rate. This is why it is crucial to maintain an ongoing dialogue with each other about who you are growing into and explain how you are changing. Otherwise, you'll wake up one morning and wonder who the person next to you is. It is both people's responsibility to schedule quality weekly time together. Growth isn't bad. It challenges us to do more and be more. Learn how to value and honor your differences. The diverse ways we express ourselves are not only necessary, but reflect our personality type. Don't ask your partner to be someone they're not nor put them into a box.

Both people must do all they can. Utilize effective counseling, take a temporary separation if needed, and work on your individual family of origin problems before you can truly decide whether or not you'd be better off without each other, unless you enjoy being miserable. You don't have to prolong your suffering. While separating is a very difficult decision to make, prolonging the inevitable will only wreak more havoc on everyone involved. In the larger scheme of things – 'the big picture' – realizing what you're unhappy about and being able to express it won't ensure you'll stay together what it will do is force you both to face the truth. Many would agree that the fear of abandonment prevents us from being honest. Let us not forget the influence of economic concerns. It's hard to practice integrity if you aren't taught about it. However acting with integrity won't necessarily ensure a smooth transition either. Nothing but time makes it any easier.

It's not surprising that many books focus on the interconnection of our mind and body and how they correlate to emotional and physical pain. This can bring on disease, due to the stress, created from being unhappy over a period of time. Do you know people who stay in a marriage where one or both people 'feed off' each others' illness? When one is well, the other is sick, and vice versa. This is a scary way to live because it suggests that unless we get the attention we want, we might choose to get sick. What do you think?

How much longer will it take to see the benefits of integrity and honesty? Living in a culture of denial; it becomes normal to not want to face the 'music' of our choices. Of course, it's mentally healthier not to compromise your values, but honesty requires emotional maturity. It isn't surprising that many people fear true intimacy although they may yearn for it. The energy and time it takes to keep good relationships afloat scares some people off. Lately, it seems to scare a lot more folks! It's easier to complain about someone else and not take responsibility for your actions. To continue on with the way things are versus making decisions about what you'll do if nothing changes is also a choice.

We grew up in a culture where we were taught 'until death do us part'. It hasn't been an easy dictum to live with when many were taught to believe that suffering was their lot in life. Consequently, we wonder what is wrong with me and ask questions such as 'Where did I go wrong'? Or we see things with limited tunnel vision and, perhaps, we don't recognize that both parties didn't heed the warning signs saying "HELP" when the relationship was in trouble. We all must accept responsibility in allowing negative behavior to get us where we are or were.

Many men and women display the characteristics of being overly sensitive and emotionally unavailable. Many tend to stereotype and say men are one way and women act another way. However, both sexes are capable of learning healthy behaviors that work. Operating on primitive hormonal drives doesn't change your consciousness. Ernest Holmes, the founder of the Science of Mind, taught that you can change your life by changing your thinking.

Ask yourself – What works for me? What is my story? How do I fit into this picture? What is important to me and what do I value? In a healthy relationship, it is safe to admit that you don't have all the answers. Both people become "disenfranchised" when either person tends to be a workaholic and believe it is the only way they think they can get recognition. For some people, achievement may signify earning a lot of money. While many men have died premature deaths because of their belief and the stress it produced in trying to "provide" for their families, many professional women today, are experiencing the same problem. Healthy, harmonious living requires that you learn to balance your inner and outer drives. It is a normal desire for both sexes to fulfill their lives. In the pursuit of fulfillment, however, it is important not to forget what you value. Your personal history weaves a tapestry of your life. Telling our stories is helpful because it allows us to talk about our lives and express how we got where we are. A very helpful exercise is to listen to someone while they tell their story for fifteen minutes. Then reverse roles. It's amazing what happens when you really feel like you're being listened to.

Listening as an act of love inspires respect and a profound sense of appreciation for another's journey. Successful listening does not mean that you have to have answers for people. You know how helpful it is after you've told your story. At times, we all need a sounding board. Often just by having the chance to talk, we get our own answers! However, ask the one to whom you're talking if they don't mind being a sounding board for you. Many people assume that their spouses, parents or children can handle hearing all of the emotional turbulence in their lives, and this is not the case. That is why it's helpful to have a mentor, therapist, teacher or really good friend you implicitly trust to help you work through your "stuff." Realize that those closest to you cannot see clearly for that very reason.

We have many common themes among us. One is looking outside ourselves for validation. Many suggest that unconditional love is a goal. However, as Brenda Schaeffer suggests in her book, Is It Love or Is It Addiction?

"They do not seek unconditional love in healthy belonging because in a good love relationship, we no longer crave unconditional love from our partners. The only time we needed that kind of care was in the first eighteen months of our lives. We no longer need it from others because we can grant it to ourselves...."

Our Western notion of love is very limiting at times, and the English language inadequate to describe it. Consider that the Greek language has three words to describe different aspects of love: agape, eros and philia. The romantic and sensual/sexual aspect is eros; agape is the family aspect, and philia is brotherly love. Hopefully, these definitions will contribute to your overall understanding and expression of healthier love. Men and women are becoming their own heroes and heroines. They are less willing to be miserable in a love relationship simply because they realize it is better to be alone and be lonely than to be with someone and feel that way.

Challenges and Suggestions:

Both people have to want to grow and move through the inevitable challenges that will confront them at various stages of their commitment to one another. Some of the obvious challenges we can predict are that we know we are going to lose someone we love to death, or we may die before them. We'll also lose our youth and other predictable losses over the course of a lifetime. These necessary losses present us with the awareness that life is filled with duality. You need to be cognizant of how your perspectives on life add or detract from your mental health. Judith Viorst explains this in detail in her wonderful book, Necessary Losses.

Another common complaint we hear which has never solved anything is the proverbial "nagging." People nag to get attention in the hope of having some need fulfilled. It is also an unhealthy behavior used to gain some control. Once again, you always have other options to use in dealing with uncooperative family members and significant others. All you have to do is STOP being codependent. However, this behavior is hard to change overnight. You can **practice not being codependent whenever it rears its ugly head!** How? You must be ready to use other plans for yourself since you can't control what another person will do. You need to create a 'bottom line,' also known as a boundary, that will not violate you or your values.

If you find there are many other positive qualities in the person you claim to love, then you may choose to be with them; doing things for yourself and accepting what you are capable of doing. Another example of doing things for yourself is if you like to dance and your partner doesn't, you can join a dance group, arrange to go out dancing with friends, or go to establishments where people dance. If you like to go out to the movies, and your partner doesn't, go alone, or go with friends, but do go! The same idea holds true for traveling, the arts, or anything else you enjoy. One common description amongst couples who don't enjoy the same activities is if the other person has an adverse reaction to your partaking in any of these activities. This behavior is clearly a control issue. Remember as Kahlil Gibran advised, to have "spaces in your togetherness."

I've heard many such stories over the last decade. Some folks learned to accept, adapt and adjust to their mates predilections, for the common things they enjoyed together were of value to them and not such a sacrifice. They could also enjoy their own interests. No one person can meet all of your needs all of the time. Dr. Carl Rogers believed that it was possible to connect with someone on about two out of seven levels of togetherness. The seven possible levels of sharing potential compatibility are: aesthetic appreciation, spirituality, common financial goals, habits, sexuality, your culture/ background, physically (as in sports/exercise) and psychologically. To ever expect one person to fulfill all of these levels is totally unrealistic.

You have to know what keeps the two of you choosing to be together versus feeling stuck. If ever you do feel stuck, find out what you can do to feel differently. Join a support group, read a book about your problems, find a good psychotherapist, or take a class. Dr. Eric Butterworth, in his book <u>Discover The Power Within You</u>, recommends asking – "why mortgage your future happiness with the traditional marriage vow of 'until death do us part' when you can create happiness one day at a time in your relationship by renewing your vows daily?" What an idea! It makes me think of the biblical statement of "I die daily." I have always interpreted this statement to mean that we let go of outmoded ways of thinking and behaving that no longer work in our best interests and adopt new attitudes that create a more positive experience.

Did you ever observe plants? They die yet also refurbish themselves. Although you may cut them back, they re-bloom and continue to grow. We are the same way. It is scientifically proven that our skin replenishes itself, as does our hair, nails, and even our brain cells regenerate. Although we can't always see the growth process, we observe the results. Similarly, we need to communicate our mental and emotional changes to the significant people in our lives. Otherwise, we may end up asking each other – What happened

Exploring and Creating Healthy Romantic Relationships 101

to you? Who are you? I don't know who you are anymore! It is when we stop communicating that problems arise if left unchecked.

Did you ever try telling an out-of-control person that you won't accept their behavior, or that you'll talk to them when they calm down? You do not need to subject yourself to others' inappropriate behavior. Living in argumentative environments is not healthy. We are not meant to struggle against the river. Another wonderful Eric Butterworth book, In the Flow of Life, addresses this issue by way of imagery. See yourself not going against the current of a river. You know when you've knocked your head against the wall so much, you have to wonder why you're doing it! Do you enjoy suffering? What would your life look like if you had little to complain about? Life's experiences provide us an ongoing laboratory of learning, and learning is what life is all about. Eventually, you'll have to devise a new road map when the old one is no longer useful.

Indifference doesn't work because apathy sets in. When you've been with your partner a long time, you will find that you're not excited by them all the time; especially when they leave the bathroom door open! You'll discover idiosyncrasies that you'll have to adjust to. You always have a choice though; you can ask for the bathroom door to be closed!

Indifference can also stem from a lack of romantic expression toward the other. Another example is when you have children, you don't date each other, when you're setting up those special times just for the two of you. Have you ever taken a small vacation away from the children? Many couples are totally surprised by these ideas and have never even entertained them because they set up limitations such as, - I feel guilty; I don't have the time; we don't have the money. If you don't have children, ask yourself when was the last time you became creative by calling each other up and inviting him or her out for a date, just like you used to do before you were married.

Exploring the ways in which we create romance with each other in the 21st century requires a renaissance of your own creative spirit. Express what is in your innermost heart and mind. Be playful, and allow your inner child to come out. Remember that boredom sets in due to complacency and if it is one element that will destroy a relationship, it is that, and taking the other person for granted. In the

1800's and early 1900's, masses of people were too busy making a living and struggling to support a family so that the leisure time more of us enjoy today was not as available then. However, in light of the 21st century, this problem is not all together gone. Many families still struggle with the same issues.

One successful factor I see in couples who stay together a long time is their ability to discover new things that interest them both individually and collectively, and their exploration of new avenues to share together. Even if both people work full time, they still schedule quality time to be together for without it, they set up a predictable failure by not communicating and enjoying each other. Several years ago, this condition was labeled ISD, Inhibited Sexual Desire. The APA determined that many people, stressed to the maximum lose interest in sex. It becomes one more thing you have to do. Many couples suffer from sexual frustration which is one reason why both of you must also be willing to be flexible and step out of rigid ideas. For example, if both of you are professionals, don't delegate responsibilities by saying "Well, you should…." Tell each other what you prefer doing, and then compromise on the jobs you don't like, such as throwing out the garbage, clearing the dishes, cooking, cleaning, vacuuming, laundry, etc., which are all of the things you'd have to do if you were alone anyway! Of course, you can always hire a maid!

John Bradshaw gives a great example on expectations in marriage and how they cause problems. He recalls expecting his wife to fill the sugar bowl and he'd get annoyed if she didn't. When he lived alone, he realized that he rarely filled the sugar bowl. It was no big deal to him. We have to wonder why the lifestyles we lead when we're alone are acceptable to us and then we contradict ourselves through the expectations we have in a relationship. Laziness doesn't work but you do need to give each other permission and space to be "lazy" occasionally. How do you define lazy?

Behavioral traits, whether learned or inherited, can change. In a George Benson song, he sings, "Learning to love yourself is the greatest love of all." I believe soulful love is about the inner work of getting to know who you are, what motivates you, what is important to you, and what is your reason for being, which in the final analysis, makes all the difference in the world. You will feel good about yourself and others really can't do that for you. If they leave or when they die, you still need to overcome the fears associated with predictable and unpredictable events, if you want to go on living.

There's a very useful technique which is crucial to good communication. It is known as a "reframe." You simply reflect back to the other person by stating – "What I hear you saying is…" (and restate the exact words you heard them say, not making any inferences). Then, ask them "Is this correct?" When they respond affirmatively, say "Tell me more." Doing this creates an environment of mutual support and caring which allows the other person to respond and repeat the above procedure without fear. This exercise requires practice until it feels natural because it's so different from the way you've spoken in the past. It's a useful technique to minimize conflict because you use a lot of "I" messages. Get accustomed to saying "I feel… I become… I get" versus using "You" statements. **Attack the problem, and <u>not the person</u>**. Typical responses usually make people defensive. Then, you stop listening for you're too busy trying to figure out what you'll say back to them.

It's crucial to acknowledge when you're angry by simply stating "I'm angry." If you find your anger escalating, it's better to remove yourself from the other person and find a way to cool down, either by walking aerobically, screaming in another room or hitting a pillow. You end up expressing your anger in a healthier way, where you don't take it out on the other person. At the same time, you still release the negative energy.

When and if your anger escalates to screaming, rage, breaking/throwing things or physical attack, it is strongly recommended that you remove yourself so you don't harm or hurt anyone, including yourself. Uncontrollable rage is not safe to be around. It's one thing when a professional works with an individual, however this is done in the safety of a therapeutic environment. There is no need to subject yourself or anyone else to irrational behavior unless you have severe personality disorders. This behavior is never justified.

Another helpful technique to use in minimizing destructive anger is to establish a policy that both you and your partner agree to. If you need to leave, then do so for no more than an hour. This establishes trust. It lets the other person know that you will return in an hour and they have the option of doing the same thing. When either of you return, agree to communicate within a twenty-four hour period so the anger is not prolonged and resentments don't turn into longstanding arguments.

Remember the rule **lets agree to disagree**. Avoid telling others they are wrong. Behavior is either mentally healthy or unhealthy. It is much better to think before you speak. Learn to give constructive criticism in a more positive way. For example, instead of saying "you always do that." Say, "I really feel hurt when you do this behavior." This statement reflects an "I" message, and it attacks the problem, and not the person. This exercise also reinforces respect. It's important to maintain respect for each other even when you don't agree. Do you need to have the same belief system in order for the relationship to work? I think if you have similar values, it's certainly easier.

Many are not aware of the impact that non-verbalized feelings create. You don't have to say anything to sense how someone feels because their body language and non-verbal vibration gives you the message quite clearly. When people don't know how to express disappointment, anger, etc., they tend to cover up their true feelings. Many are terrified to verbalize what they feel for fear of abandonment by the other party. Thus, the person who doesn't express feelings may throw or break things, scream, be physically violent, and verbally abuse the other. They may also become emotionally abusive via lying and deceiving.

In passive/aggressive behavior, it is clear that one party wishes to punish the other, and believes he/she can. However, this scenario can only take place if the other person allows it. You think to yourself, "Okay, I won't continue like this, and I'll make you miserable." If your partner has been to self-help workshops and learns about healthy behavior versus manipulative control, he/she simply says, "This is your choice, and I don't agree with it, so if you choose to not do this with me, then I'll do it anyway." This is not a healthy statement to use for bigger and more long standing problems. It can be as simple as wanting to see a movie and your partner saying, "No, I'm not going." You have the option of suggesting something else the two of you would enjoy doing or making other plans to either go alone or invite another person. It becomes problematic if you don't enjoy any activities together, and no changes are made. However, a familiar slogan says, "It's never too late to have a happy childhood!" It's your choice.

In closing, it would be dishonest for me to say that there's a way to get through pain easily. Self-exploration guides us through the labyrinth of new ideas, indecision and the great unknown. Most of us know about these times because we've lived through them. Trying to run from pain is a waste of time for it follows you or begs for your attention so you can get the message. By embracing our pain, we won't have to repeat it again. Pain and illusion often lead us to a new way of thinking; sometimes they jar us to see things differently, and we may choose a more spiritual approach to life. Learning to trust your innate wisdom and intuition is one way to live from a more enlightened perspective. How many times have you wished that you listened to your "gut feelings?" I hope you'll do so more often. I trust this chapter has opened your eyes if they were closed, and that you can use whatever information you find helpful to make your life easier. Here's a wonderful exercise you can practice.

Practical Exercise:

Allow yourself to take a deep breath, sigh, relax, and exhale all stress. Continue to breathe gently and rhythmically, as you release all thoughts you have. Bring the mind to rest by emptying it. Practice conscious, deep breathing several times a day. Keep your eyes closed or do an open eyed meditation as in gazing upon beautiful scenery.

In the next few days, become aware of any new insights or feelings that come up in you. Record them. Get in touch with the "aha" moments you experienced in reading this chapter. Feel free to explore what contributes to your peace of mind and pursue it. When you feel ready to share your wisdom with others, do so and may it be from a place of gratitude. You can now speak about what you've passed through. Know beyond a shadow of a doubt that you are more worthwhile and deserving to receive whatever you desire, as long as it is for your highest and best good.

Sometimes, we think we know what is best for us, but the "universe" has a way of working things out, that in the long run, is right for us. If you still don't believe this is true, you can always test the "waters" of your doubt again. Then, after you've experienced enough of what you don't want, try letting go and letting God. I guarantee it won't be a life of constant struggle. Keep a daily or weekly journal of the significant new changes you're making to create your future.

CHAPTER FOUR

Beyond Pain: Healing The Heart

To learn humility is to honor that your hurt and mine are one... That we share the gentle communion of being human.
Wayne Muller

"Become aware of your need for life without harm; with no tricks or betrayal; consistency."
Paul Wanio

"Whoever saves one life, saves the World entire"
Izaak Stern "Schindler's List"

~~~

This chapter became a necessity to help heal the emotional wounds many of us experience in our lives. Healing the heart is a dictum of our time. It is a choice because living in emotional pain is no longer an option. Acting as a "victim" doesn't serve anyone's higher purpose, including your own. We can't progress mentally and emotionally unless we first embrace and honor the painful passages in our life. If we don't do this, we end up wearing our "wounds" as a badge of courage in such a way that it continually reminds us of what we went through. However, our goal is to overcome the trauma and allow time to do its perfect part in assisting us to make the transition from victim to victor. Throughout this chapter, I have included excerpts from student comments made during a course I taught entitled, "Healing the Heart." In the words of songwriter Melissa Phillipe,

"To let go, you got to go through it. Can't go 'round it. What you're feelin', let it come through... In order to heal it, you got to feel it....You can work hard not to feel them. Try to conceal them and push them away. But that's the thing with emotion. It causes a commotion. Here's the magic potion: feel it."

I emphasize her song because so many of us have been taught to repress what we feel. In order to heal, we must allow our emotions to come out in ways that will restore us to peace of mind. Did you know that tears contain certain chemicals, which is why you usually feel better after you cry? Our physical systems are perfectly designed. Yet, we know only too well that any deficiency in our system can cause us to be off balance. When we are off center, the challenges we face many seem out of proportion to us. This imbalance effects us both physically and mentally. If we look at these challenges in a spiritual context, any desire to improve ourselves and our lives becomes an inspiration. Imagine that you are already the way you wish to be or that you have what you desire. To desire is to bring about. The Latin derivative of the word desire is from *"de sire"*, and translates in English to "of the Father." I interpret this to mean that our needs and desires are a part of our soul's longing and our personal search to accept that which is our natural right. When we honor these needs and desires, it is a way of giving expression to who and what we are. Why not try an experiment for a week? Allow your inner wisdom to guide your feelings. Feelings are the gateway to your emotional structure. In Greg Braden's video "Walking Between Two Worlds," he suggests that one of the greatest gifts we can give to ourselves is the ability to feel and emote. By expressing what is in your heart, the release of emotions creates new neural pathways in your brain. One result is that you feel better, simply because you expressed yourself. Secondly, you offer yourself a new way to see things. If you don't give yourself permission to grow, you will continually be haunted by a past that is no longer a part of your present.

One of our greatest fears is the issue of abandonment. When you realize that you are the only one who will never, ever abandon you, you start to experience life differently. It is almost like a wakeup call. From that moment on, you will never be afraid to be alone, because you'll realize that you are never really alone. Most people are amazed when they hear this for the first time. We have been so acculturated to feel accepted by others and look for validation from them because we were rarely taught how to validate and accept ourselves, which is where all growth begins.

Did you ever ask yourself what role you play in allowing certain situations to turn into personal dramas? Have you ever felt the need for revenge? This mindset is very toxic to your body and your thinking. A wonderful exercise which helps us get rid of this negativity is to write the following statement seventy times seven which equals 490 times. The sentence is, "I fully and freely forgive _____ for _____." You will find that the names will change with the circumstances. For example, you may start out writing, "I forgive myself for being so naive." Or, another example is a person who blamed someone for her unhappiness. She wrote, "I fully and freely forgive myself for putting up with that behavior for as long as I did." Mind you, it took her many sentences before she was able to accept the responsibility for her role in that scenario.

Try another alternative. "I fully and freely forgive "John" for "lying to me". When you start out using someone else's name, eventually you take ownership of the part you played in the problem. Perhaps then, eventually, you write, " I fully and freely forgive myself for accepting John's lies for so long." This process of nurturing and reflection takes you to a deeper level of awareness. It makes it easier to access the core issues of what you need to work on, what you need to forgive, and why. There is life after forgiveness!

A seminar participant once asked, "How long will it take me to forgive?" I responded, "As long as it takes for you to heal." One theory is that it takes up to one month for each year you were romantically involved with someone. Others know that it can take much longer. However, it is crucial that you honor your pain, sadness, anger, disappointment or any other emotion. If you don't, the negative energy will usually manifest itself in other destructive ways. Using drugs, drinking, gambling or practicing any other numbing addiction, only medicates your pain temporarily. If you bury your sadness, it will only haunt you. Instead, honor it. Your emotional healing includes crying when and if you need to.

Dr. Carl Jung asks us to explore one aspect of our personality, the "shadow." It represents those parts of us that we either don't like or are afraid of. It's worth your time to befriend your *"night- time shadow," (the dark side)*. This is nothing more than getting in touch with your greatest fears. Furthermore, while it is natural to have an aversion to your fears, I can tell you from personal experience, that unless you give yourself permission to honor what you fear, you will continue to fear it. I recall a powerful healing exercise given by the late, Danaan Parry, the founder of the Holy Earth Foundation. At midnight, a group of us at the seminar on <u>Warriors of the Heart</u>, stood together on a dock in the dark, each shouting out our worst fears. It was so freeing, not only to verbalize what we feared, but to hear the same responses from everyone else present.

For example, one common fear verbalized was being alone. Surprise? Perhaps one reason for this dreaded fear is due to never being taught how to be alone. Many have experienced being in a room full of people feeling lonely. What about being in a relationship and feeling lonely? What about learning to be alone in a relationship, so that both people have the space they need in order to grow and still stay together? If we allow our worst fears to take over, we'll experience the frightening psychological and physiological changes that accompany our sense of abandonment which is really a fear of dying. Surely you have heard the classic comment, "Who else could I meet out there?" This is in response to why people stay in unhappy situations. Initially, being on your own isn't about meeting someone else out there to take away your pain, it is about knowing yourself first. You might have heard the following expressions: "You can be with someone and be miserable; You can be alone and not be lonely, the choice is up to you." There are many different scenarios. Some choose to live alone and not get involved. Others choose to live alone, and have a significant other. Some marry, co-habit, or engage in a myriad of other arrangements these days. The truth of the matter is that you can create whatever you desire, even though the media tells you differently.

Can you imagine, if you wanted to marry, just having a spiritual ceremony so that you don't have to go through any legal entanglements? That gives you a lot to think about. Why do you think prenuptial agreements came about? Would you marry someone if you knew that if the relationship ended you would leave with what you came into it with? This question throws the whole issue of marriage into a completely different light, doesn't it? Yet, it is precisely these kinds of discussions which are so desperately needed today.

Other people fear not being able to change the qualities they dislike about themselves. It's interesting how we like to hold on to things, even aspects of our personalities, when they no longer work. It reminds me of the classic Peanuts comic strip where Linus won't let go of his age old "blankie." (blanket) It served him well and it was hard for him to let it go. I recall my own grief about the loss of my favorite blanket as a child, when my Mom got rid of it simply because she determined that the time was right. But right for whom – herself or me? I recall crying for days over my loss. While I obviously got over it, I wonder what would have happened had I been allowed to keep the blanket until I was ready to let it go?!

I wonder how and if that incident affected my inability to let go of destructive relationships as an adult. I recall the difficulty I had in letting go of a marriage with a man I knew for ten years in total and another eight year relationship where I wasn't married. In both cases, there was a lot of disharmony and all the wrong reasons for joining together. It took me over two years to completely heal from the former situation and approximately the same amount of time from the latter. I had to both forgive myself and take responsibility for choosing to stay as long as I did in both relationships. While many people face the same decisions, they may choose to stay in unhealthy relationships because of the fear of being alone, starting over, and last but not least, financial dependency. The people we allow in our lives usually serve as a mirror of what we don't like. They also have that "special" ability to bring out our worst emotions, some of which are highly unpleasant. Always ask yourself what the opposite might look like. I often ask people, "What would your life look like without this problem?" Oft times, they don't have an answer because they usually have blinkers on. It's important to do the best you can with the information you have at the time. When you are ready to change what doesn't serve you any longer, you will.

Healing is a process that has its own timing, and when you don't acknowledge your emotional pain as stated earlier, your spiritual and physical well-being suffer. It takes courage to face your life issues and do something about them. I recall my own torturous experience of when I was in so much emotional pain that it actually immobilized me to the point of creating a severe sinus infection. I wasn't convinced when my doctor told me I would have to be bedridden for about two weeks with nothing to do but sleep, take medication, drink fluids and have very little to eat. Have you ever experienced something similar? I long to pass on the wisdom of my own experiences to help you in your own process of self-discovery, if and when you find yourself in similar situations, or to prevent them from happening at all. Yet, no one can grow for anyone. Parents try to shield their offspring from pain and hurt and it doesn't always work. How else could we learn lessons unless we experienced what we need to?

Dr. Abraham Maslow, in his illustration of the growth and development pyramid, suggests that at the top of the pyramid is the goal of self-actualization. How do you interpret this? Self-actualization comes about when you are no longer concerned with your physiological needs, of shelter, food and water because you have secured them and feel safe from threat. In establishing safety, you create trust. After this stage, you seek out the security of loving friendships and relationships by belonging to a group. When those needs are met, your need for recognition and acceptance become crucial to your self-worth. At the top of the pyramid, you discover self-actualization. You realize that you can become anything you desire, and feel fulfilled in this life, having attained your purpose.

While many religions and spiritual traditions admonish us to know ourselves, does this self-knowledge improve our chances to live a life beyond pain? Zen Buddhists teach that all attachment brings suffering; therefore detachment brings joy. This is very much of an Eastern concept, and very foreign to most Westerners. However, if everything in life is transitory, might we not be better served to embrace a sense of detachment? As different as this idea may be from what we are accustomed to, it may assist us in accepting the transitory nature of this life. If we learn to find balance within ourselves, will we experience more harmony? Instead of adding negative energy to the outer, we will create more positive energy to surround ourselves by and thus invoke the same. We also have the opportunity to help others who may need our assistance.

How do we learn to "be in the world, but not of it?" I equate this to the formerly mentioned concept of Buddhist detachment.

Despite the seemingly unlimited nature of human desiring, Maslow says, human needs are typically experienced in the following hierarchy of predominance: 2

Figure 1
THE MASLOW HIERARCHY OF NEEDS

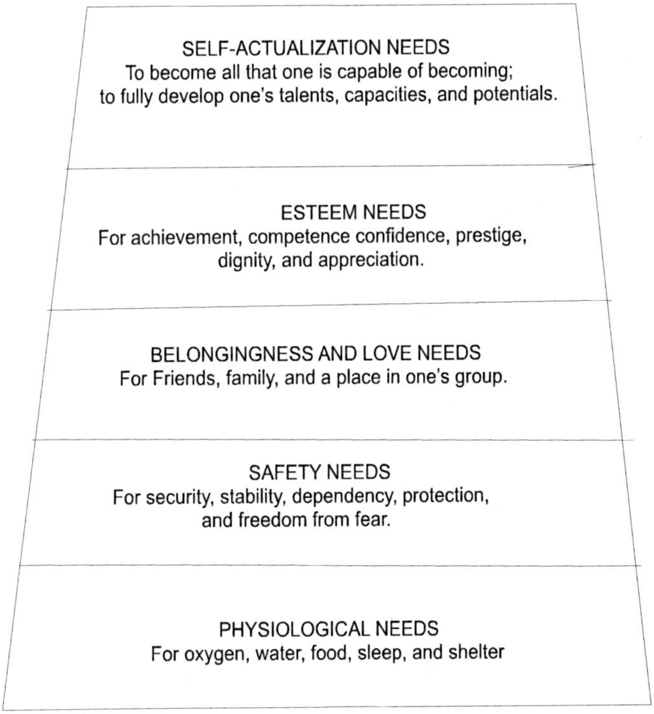

SELF-ACTUALIZATION NEEDS
To become all that one is capable of becoming; to fully develop one's talents, capacities, and potentials.

ESTEEM NEEDS
For achievement, competence confidence, prestige, dignity, and appreciation.

BELONGINGNESS AND LOVE NEEDS
For Friends, family, and a place in one's group.

SAFETY NEEDS
For security, stability, dependency, protection, and freedom from fear.

PHYSIOLOGICAL NEEDS
For oxygen, water, food, sleep, and shelter

2. Ibid., 35-47. The hierarchy illustrated in figure 1 is an adaptation of Maslow's list of the hierarchy of needs. By putting the lower-level needs at the bottom of the figure, where they properly belong, the adaptation adds clarity to Maslow's concept.

Yet, the words of a familiar song say, "No man is an island, and no man stands alone. Each man's grief is grief to me. Each man's joy is my own." This philosophy may exemplify one of the reasons we are born. Who amongst us has not felt the pain of another's tragedy and realized, except for the grace of God, there go I? In the final analysis, it is your personal and spiritual philosophy and practice that ultimately determines how you live your life. What is the impact you would have on others?

Do you care? There is a belief that as we evolve into the 21st Century, people will make more conscious choices to do less harm. What does this imply? How will it affect us personally?

One of the major causes of conflict amongst couples I have observed is their inability to meet each others' needs. Realistically speaking however, it is impractical to imagine that any one person can meet all of our needs. As a matter of fact, that expectation alone is guaranteed to create unnecessary stress. Many of the self help books over the last decade explore the value of self-esteem as a contributing factor in maintaining a loving, harmonious relationship of longevity. That is not to say there won't be bumps along the way. It infers that people in conflict will choose to do whatever they can to preserve the love, respect and integrity they require to sustain their relationship. It's not about "putting up" with behavior that you find unacceptable; it is about asking people to take responsibility for their own behavior. Then, you must have the courage to follow through with those actions that will contribute to your mental well being. The definition of insanity has been defined as doing the same thing over and over and expecting different results!

I believe it is time that we bring love to another level. I hear so much about the sadness and problems in relationships, but I very rarely hear about what is working. It is extremely rewarding when I have asked my clients to practice or "try-on" some new form of behavior, and they report working results, including more harmony and happiness. One woman complained that she didn't like the way her husband dressed because he looked shabby. He recalled that his Mother harassed him as a child and adolescent by constantly nagging him about his clothes. Consequently, his choice for a wife mirrored the same displeasure with his appearance and he used to argue with her and not do anything to change the situation. He became aware that he was re-enacting an old scene from his childhood, because now, he cares about his appearance, and himself. When they first dated and got engaged, he usually dressed well. However, a few years into the relationship, he reverted back to his childhood behavior in an attempt to heal the relationship with his family of origin member, in this case, his mother. He wasn't even aware of it at the time and so he responded as an adult to his wife as if he was still a child. You can often trace negative behavior back to a traumatic time in your life. It usually manifests when you become "comfortable" or "bored" in your relationship. You're not even conscious of why you're sabotaging your own happiness, but you know you're causing conflict from issues that occurred years ago. That is why "**knowing thyself**" is one of the greatest gifts you give to your partner as well as yourself.

We live in a time where we have access to many therapeutic tools for healing. When you can recognize your anger as a gift, you will see it as a message which lets you know something needs to change. Anger is energy. It needs to be released in transformative ways. We have seen the effects of repressed anger upon the body, as in backaches, neck pain, and other physiological symptoms that correlate to the pent-up feelings of holding on to anger and resentment. We hurt ourselves when we don't forgive, or release the condition that got us where we are. How can you move on when you stay stuck in the past? That it takes time is a given, but to hold on longer than necessary creates more problems. You need to research which techniques will help you to shift your blocked energy. What works for one may not work for you.

Earlier on, I described a time when I was unhappily married. I was only in my twenties and my body manifested a tumor the size of a grapefruit that had to be surgically removed. It is important for me to know that you, the reader, understand that I am not casting blame upon my ex-husband for this. In retrospect, had I known then what I know now, I never would have married him in the first place. My relationship with him, at that time, provided me a way to leave my home when I was 19. As in the case of many women, the only way they could leave their homes was to get married, especially if they couldn't afford to live alone or take care of themselves financially. This is why it is so important for us to become aware because if we don't truly know what we are entering into when we commit ourselves to another person, we'll have a lot of problems. Certain states now require couples who want to marry to attend pre-marital counseling or to enroll in continuing education courses that focus on how to have a healthy marriage.

When you are having problems it can be very helpful to work with a therapist you trust implicitly who can give you what you need. Your goal is to become mentally healthy and trust your intuition. Some of the therapeutic skills available to help you work through past traumas are psycho-drama; regression therapy, gestalt therapy, neuro-linguistic programming, role playing and rational emotive behavioral therapy. These are just a few in this burgeoning field. Finding a gifted therapist whose goal is to make you independent of them while allowing you to grow in the direction of your dreams is also one of your tasks.

When you make peace with your past, you get a larger perspective of your place in the world. You no longer have to limit your thinking. You will come to understand why you do what you do in your family and in the other roles you play in your life. Some of these roles are as a man, woman, brother, sister, friend, uncle, aunt, teacher, mother, father, etc. What is it that causes an individual to change? What inspires you to make changes? Do you notice a difference between the way you think and your grandparents or your parents thought? Much of our need to think differently stems from the fact that we no longer live in an isolated world. The fact that we can turn on our TV set and see what is going on around the world in a second contributes to our living in information overload. Consequently, it is really difficult to think the way we used to. We have a hard time disassociating from the stress of the world and that is why Dr. Carl Jung suggested that the collective unconscious affects each of us in a powerful way. For example, when you see a disaster, do you ask yourself "why is this happening, and why in this part of the world?" When I refer to healing the heart, you must recognize that it is difficult to separate ourselves from those things that affect us. Ask yourself, how do you react when you see an accident? Do you stop, say a prayer, or shudder and think, "That could be me." Or, do you not pay it any mind at all?

We don't live insulated lives anymore. We've become more connected to each other, and that's why these issues command so much of our attention It's time for us as a species to heal collectively and individually. Think of all the younger people you know who are dying of heart attacks and other illness now. How does knowing this affect *you*?

Life deals you unplanned circumstances much like random cards in a game. When you learn to play the hand you've been dealt, and decide to honor and work with it, instead of playing the victim and asking, "why me?", you'll finally be able to embrace your pain more easily by not fearing the move through uncharted territory. You can't just tell the pain to go away. It won't. It will return, or continue to remind you that your mental and emotional healing, through whatever trauma, is at hand.

You have all the tools available for healing, such as meditation, self-reflection, journalizing, psychodrama, psychotherapy, art and dance therapy, just to name a few. All of these healing modalities have come about over the years to lessen our pain. Far too many have sought relief in multiple addictions, which only numbs pain temporarily. When the effect subsides, you're left with the same feelings. Some questions to answer are the following:

- What do you need to acknowledge?
- How can you play your hand so that you will not be a victim any more?
- How can you redefine yourself and your life to maintain dignity and self worth?
- Ask yourself, "what will happen if I treat other people with respect, and dignity?"
- Will I accept anything less than the same?

As you're able to answer these questions, you will observe how your thinking changes. As you practice more self-disciplined behaviors, and bring your ego under control, your destiny changes. No one else outside of you can grow for you. Unless you give people permission to have control over you, they can't. It takes practice to allow the past to fade away, much the same way as a wound heals. It builds scar tissue and you are reminded of the experience every time you notice the scar. However, not all scars are visible from the outside. As you learn to honor the past, what you've learned will guide your future decisions and allow you to make choices that will create a new future. Relish in the possibilities of your life. Here's an example:

Usually, when I wake up in the morning I take time to meditate, center myself, and bless my day because I never know what the day contains. I always remind myself that "it's going to be a great day". No matter what happens, I always look for the good in it. This way of thinking is *not* automatic. I have spent many years teaching myself to think this way. This is not to deny that sad or bad things may occur, it merely emphasizes that behind every problem there is always a way to handle it.

I recall the day when I sat on my sunglasses and broke them. "Ha!, here we go again!" I thought to myself, "Deri, you always lose or break your sunglasses. Good thing they're not prescription." I began to wonder why I do this so often. The lesson is – a possible solution: simply wear them around my neck, or always put them into a case when not in use. That will require some discipline on my part and learning a new habit! Now this example is just with something simple, not catastrophic. You can well imagine the ramifications of more serious issues. For example, how do you react when you wake up and discover a flat tire on your car? I woke up to this reality one morning. I had to drive to Miami, and had little time for delays. However, I took a deep breath to calm my growing anxiety and realized how lucky I was this didn't happen on the freeway. I had the nail removed in the relative safety of my parking lot. Problem solved. And although the timing of a flat tire is never good, it could have been far worse.

When you get to the point when you can wake up in the morning and realize that life will present you with new and unexpected "stuff", you've arrived! What really matters is how you choose to deal with the stuff. It is only as individuals choose not to overplay their trials and tribulations that they will be liberated from thinking of themselves as victims of circumstance. In this way, a newly self-empowered generation is born. Self-respect is a key component in eradicating any and all kinds of abuse – including self-abuse. But, *you must begin with yourself.*

When and if a personal war in the form of people or circumstances presents itself in your life, assess whether or not you need to participate in it. Greater peace lies in understanding that your participation is entirely optional. I always remind people, you can excuse yourself, you don't have to hang around. If someone is screaming at you, you can say, "I do not choose to be around you when you're like this. When you calm down and act like an adult, I'll be happy to talk with you." Then move away and say, "I'll talk with you when you calm down."

Similarly, when your own anger approaches the irrational borderline, removing yourself from the scene is an excellent idea. Anger is an energy that can and must be channeled constructively. To prevent your uncontrolled anger from turning into rage, here are some helpful suggestions:

- go into another room,
- scream at the top of your lungs,
- beat the bed and pillows without hurting yourself.
- go for an aerobic walk
- take a shower
- call a friend and say you need to talk

And there's more, obviously. Find whatever works for you that isn't destructive. Although more drastic options are available, they're messier to clean up and can cause permanent damage to people and things – yourself included. Whatever you do, it is critically important that you learn to befriend your anger and make it work for you. Anger is a gift that lets you know that something needs to be changed. When you're calm you're better able to have a rational discussion. One of my favorite desk objects is a sign which read "An arguement is an exchange of ignorance and a discussion is an exchange of knowledge." Another helpful concept I encourage people to implement is "Lets Agree to Disagree". We don't necessarily have to agree with each other. Rather, we have to find what will work for us by discovering what will be of the greatest benefit to both parties.

We need to ask ourselves the right questions. Rather than wondering why you continue to subject yourself to negative situations assess how much longer you want to punish yourself? Do I really need to be verbally, emotionally and psychologically abused? The same considerations apply to business and professional settings For example: A manager with a fairly serious drinking problem would, on occasion, exhibit "dry drunk" or inappropriate behavior such as yelling and cursing. I declined to allow him to talk to me like that and told him so. Whenever I had to call to report a problem, this behavior would ensue. Consequently, I chose to deal directly with the owners. It was not until the bathroom ceiling literally caved in, that anything was done. Despite four weeks of advance notice and complaints because the roof had never been properly fixed the first time, it took an emergency to resolve the problem. His response was to scream at me. Mine was to remind him that he had no right speak to me that way. I explained that he was the designated person to go through to solve this problem. So I hung up the phone, and he called back, apologized and said, "I retract what I said and I'm doing the best that I can." I decided to write him a letter for the New Year and sent a copy of it to the owner. It said, "I choose not to enter into this New Year with the same communication we have been having for the last year and a half. I have always treated you with the utmost respect and I expect the same. Your response to "move out," every time I call you if there is a problem is neither an appropriate answer nor an intelligent one. This is tantamount to me calling the owner and saying "Your manager is incapable of dealing with the stress of his job." I received a beautiful Christmas card from the owners with best wishes for a pleasant holiday season with sincere thanks for my letter.

Another scenario depicting unhealthy behavior could have been to allow his behavior to intimidate me. Recognizing that his behavior is a likely result of unresolved anger issues and childhood wounds helped me understand why he behaved as he did. However, he wasn't coming to me for psychological help. The techniques for dealing with situations such as the one I described here are available not only to conflict resolution professionals, but to you as well. The approach is the same in either case.

It is sad to see how many people live in chronic turmoil. Sadder still is that many don't want to help themselves, don't recognize the need for help or, if they do, don't know where to go. Some people still believe there is a social stigma associated with counseling. Men, particularly, have been acculturated to believe that it is a sign of weakness to ask for help. The point is, however, that you can take control of your life. You needn't continue to be a victim to anyone or anything. It is up to you to do something or take some kind of action to change the situation. Unfortunately, this usually doesn't happen until you reach your breaking point, which can best be described as a dark night of the soul.

You need to face your worst fears. What is the source of your fears? If you never know what you are afraid of then you can't make peace with the ghosts. I often remind my clients to make as many phone calls as they can to get the information they need because someone out there can guide you to the next step. You'd be amazed how many people who work in the helping professions don't know where to refer people to go for help.

Dr. Brad Blanton, author of <u>Radical Honesty,</u> believes everyone in our society is extremely neurotic because of the lies they have had to live with. Even though it can be painful to tell the truth, it is better than living with deception. Did you ever get the feeling that you were "losing it" because people denied the truth to your face? Perhaps you've experienced going crazy when you didn't trust your intuition. For example, you know in your "gut" that something just doesn't feel right, and then when the truth surfaces, you say, "Yes, I knew it!" So, being able to speak the truth and accept it from others is a WAKE UP call for all of us. It is also very liberating despite whatever fears we may harbor regarding the consequences of the truth. How much can you hide behind?

I think there are ways to be diplomatic in telling the truth. However, traditionally, in unhappy love relationships, someone often goes out and has an affair thinking that will solve their problems. They've done this for over 5,000 years and it hasn't changed a thing. They went from one marriage to another then and they still do now. Although, back then, polygamy was acceptable! As a matter of fact, polygamy is still practiced in certain parts of the world. In their book, Sexual Arrangements, two psychologists explain that very few marriages actually stay together after there have been affairs. Some of them do repair, but in most cases it's very difficult because the trust has been violated. Now imagine what it would be like to actually talk with your partner and tell him/her how you really feel.

"We're having a problem here."
"We're not communicating well."
"We need to talk about this..."

Every relationship, no matter how committed, goes through challenges. When you enter into a marriage or other close relationships thinking it will be a bed of roses, you deceive yourself. The closeness of a relationship or the commitment of marriage is not a guarantee of anything. Rather, you grow together as you learn to navigate the inevitable conflicts you will have with each other. Rather than viewing conflict as a source of division, it can create a meaningful opportunity for improved unity. You must remain open. Consider that you just might find yourself in unexpected situations throughout your lifetime. Remember playing the random cards you've been dealt? Well, here's a couple of cards for you:

"I didn't know he was going to get sick when we married twenty years ago."
"I didn't know she would end up in a wheelchair."
" I didn't know he would gain so much weight."
"I didn't know he had a family history of alcoholism."
"You never told me your family members suffered from depression."
"How could I possibly have known that we would end up like this?"

Such is life. It's not always right or fair. We find out that our Princesses and Prince Charmings are human. As Rabbi Kushner explains in his book, "Don't ask why, ask what can I do about it now?"

Dr. Laura Schlesinger recommends that you find out as much about yourself as you can before you marry. She suggests that delaying marriage until such time as you know yourself better as the results of having traveled, lifestyle experimentation, and the development of an established set of preferences will ensure less divorce. How can you make a commitment to another if you haven't made a commitment to yourself? And how can you know who you are if you've never been given the chance to find out? For these reasons, most people aren't really ready for lifetime commitments until well into their thirties. It is critical to recognize that this idea is anathema to what previous generations believed and held true. The word 'commitment' meant something different to them.

When you've developed a healthy self identity, you won't require your partner to make you whole and complete, although popular music and movies suggest the opposite. In the past, the tradition was to bond so closely with another that your identity changed, which wasn't necessarily a bad thing. What brought about this change was a difference in the prioritization of needs. The focus shifted from I, me, and mine, to we, us, and ours. The result was that such a symbiotic fusion created ownership to some extent. However, what would often happen when a person died or left the relationship is that the other person would experience mental instability, emotional regression, spiritual detachment or physical illness. Although the loss of a loved one still creates these situations, it is the hope of today's generation that our survival won't be as difficult to sustain as it used to be. The message for this century is not to abandon your own sanity or remain very depressed for a long time. Help is available. Remember, *you are the only person who will never ever abandon you.*

You have to befriend yourself. You have to be able to look in the mirror and say "You know what, self, I love you." If you don't learn to love yourself - with all of your imperfections, you will spend your life looking for validation from other people and you won't always get it. As a matter of fact, we often get the opposite; that's our challenge. It's an exercise in the development of healthy self esteem to become aware of how divergent your thinking really is. You don't have to think like everyone else in order to be OK, loved or accepted. In fact, you will come to realize – that which others see in you may be what they have projected onto you based on their own low opinion of themselves. What can you do about this? Protect yourself from negative energy by freeing yourself from behavior that is less than conducive to positive interaction. Failure to do so borders on being self-abusive. Choosing not to accept or participate in the expression of another's devaluation of you is a new behavior. You didn't get an instruction manual, although following the golden rule of doing unto others as you would do to yourself might be helpful!

We can learn to free ourselves from the abuse or injury being inflicted upon us. When I use the word 'abuse', I'm talking about mental and emotional mistreatment. It is not always physical. To allow yourself to be someone's doormat or punching bag is, in effect, another act of self devaluation. It has been said the best way to defend against an attack is not to be there. You have to be aware of people's behavior. Perhaps you've experienced the sensation of having to walk around on eggshells because you never knew if or when someone was going to explode in the home or work environment. It's hard to be successful at treading lightly when people are out of control. However, you don't have to walk on thin ice anymore. You'll get to the stage where you say, "I don't choose to live like this anymore."

Look at animals. They respect their limits and needs, and naturally choose a path of safety. If the animals have to leave a burning forest, where do they go for shelter? More importantly, where do *you* go? How hot does your forest need to get before you'll evacuate? You need limits too. Your safety and well-being depend upon attending to your own needs. If you've forgotten how, remember that self-respect and self-love need daily renewal. It's helpful to get into the habit of setting aside quiet time for reflection, meditation and the use of affirmations. I have included some sample affirmations at the end of this chapter. After reviewing them, get into the positive habit of creating your very own to match your challenge of the moment.

Consider that our winged friends fly south when it's too cold, while brother bear grows a warm coat and hibernates. What about you? Do you sleep peacefully? If not, what prevents you from allowing your mind to rest? Knowing what is bothering you is half the battle. Doing something about it will relieve the stress. Because sleep is such an integral part of our lives, the negative side effects of sleep deprivation are quite serious. Among them are irritability, poor concentration, impaired decision-making ability, and not knowing how to handle stress. Sleep also involves more than just the mind. Remember that certain foods and caffeinated beverages also prevent you from getting the sleep you need. Good sleep contributes to your mental and physical well-being.

The point is that when you are troubled, you need to allow your subconscious mind a chance to rest, as in the saying, 'sleep on it'. You unconsciously create more chaos when you don't take care of yourself. So do other people. Have you ever noticed when people are angry with you, either out of resentment or fear, that it may have nothing to do with you? It can simply be misdirected energy. Such misdirected energy can be the result of a lack of sleep and/or some of the other problems we've addressed in this chapter.

We all need acceptance and emotional healing. Not everyone is open to this at the same time or even aware of the real issues. While we are all teachers of one another to some extent, we can't fix another person – not even someone we love. What we *can* do is be supportive and encourage them to get the help they need. This is not always as easy as it appears. The challenge lies in accepting that people must learn from their own mistakes. You can't force anything. Consider also that their willingness to seek help is part of the challenge. Finally, you must ask yourself if you could live with them if no changes were made. Such acceptance is one way we heal our hearts.

My years as a psychotherapist include a certain amount of experience in working with clients who have been completely devastated when their child or partner committed suicide. In each case, therapy was successfully concluded, and emotional healing was possible only after their realization that the outcome was never within their control and that they did the best they could. Knowing this provided a level of reassurance necessary for a calming of the spirit and a healing of the heart.

Sometimes we have to examine our own past to understand the present. We did this for several weeks in the course on "Healing the Heart". Among the exercises in the course were group discussions based on a list of questions that were developed from my research.

The comments that resulted from these discussions were sometimes overwhelming. In fact, it is part of why this chapter was written. It is my hope that you may be able to relate to the students' experiences and benefit from them.

Among the topics discussed were our relationships with our families of origin. One woman explained that she needed more from her mother. Many people in her family held a different impression of her mother that did not match her own recollections. As a matter of fact, even her father's side of the family recalled the mother in still another light. Her frustration is the result of not knowing who to believe. Her question was, "How do I find out what happened?" Believing that her recollection of her mother was unclear as the result of blocked, painful memories, my recommendation to her was to try Regression Therapy.

It's amazing how much the human brain can remember. Yet equally fascinating is it's capacity to block painful memories. People can be taught to recall events from their earliest childhood. Regression therapy is one way to unlock the mysteries of the past. Dr. Brian Weiss, a noted author in this field, has written many books on the subject. His premise is that many of our current problems are actually a carryover from unresolved issues, not only in this lifetime, but previous ones as well. In order to benefit from regression therapy, you must allow yourself to be guided into an altered state of deep relaxation, almost like self-hypnosis. In this state, it is easier to gain access to suppressed memories. For some people whose past has been extremely painful, this method of therapy brings certain segments of their past to the surface, allowing them to be resolved. Another student recalls his father this way:

My father was the prince of the whole family; so he is generally a lazy person. He depends on a lot of other people and women to help him to do menial things, things he could do himself very well, but chooses not to. "One of the things I learned about women from my father was that he feels that women are there to take care of men even though he never remarried and he's there all by himself and he loves it or he says he does. The other part is that any other relationship I have seen my father in is with any woman that could stand to be with him because of the way he treated them, he was so annoying and verbally abusive. He said he was really mad at his mother."

If you never work through your issues, your unresolved anger will influence all your other relationships. When you remain angry with your parents or significant others and you don't work through it, you might find yourself marrying someone who reminds you of one of your earliest care-givers. While this may at first seem like a strange thing to do, it is nevertheless a common occurrence because it creates a new opportunity to work through those issues with your partner – provided they're willing to help you through it. Many people play these roles unaware of what they're doing, and then wonder why they're so angry with their partner when it goes awry. For example, if you had a controlling Father, as a man, you may unconsciously seek out a controlling woman. Conversely, if you had a controlling Mother, as a woman, you'd seek out a controlling man. Sound familiar? The point being that behavior in one sex doesn't necessarily represent an opposite sex parent.

Another participant shares:

"One of the views that I got about love was due to my parents divorce when I was very young. I thought love was literally impossible. From a visual standpoint, that partnership would never be a true reality of harmony, but inside my own mind I knew that was different and then for so many years I always struggled with a fantasy, is this truth or is this real? Or is this the way it's supposed to be through aggression and fighting, and then how do I make the transition to healthy relationships? So I have never really been in what I would call a healthy relationship in my life and I'm 40 years old. I know that I will be. I don't have any doubt that I will be, but up to this date it has been a lot of preparation. A lot."

Many of us were never taught that we have to become the right person for ourselves before we can be "right" for someone else. After all, such relationships are not as much about *finding* the right person as they are about **being** the right person. As Glenn Close said in the movie Reversal of Fortune, "It is much easier to love someone than it is to live with them. Living requires work and most people are lazy and don't want to work. If you don't do the work, the love goes out of the window." When you become less needy and have a desire to truly experience and share life with another, then you won't operate from what is known as an "infant-hunger emotional attachment, a behavior that is developed throughout your early years. We display this hunger attachment when we feel addicted to another and it doesn't work. The term 'infant' applies to this behavior because infants can't express their needs in words. Rather, they use sounds such as crying, wailing or screaming to gain attention. Whereas adults *are* capable of expressing feelings or needs in words, they often resort to similar infantile behaviors.

When you think you can't survive without someone portends that you have an unhealthy addiction to that person. Couples who live miserable lives of quiet desperation illustrate this. Currently four out of ten marriages are intact. Of these, only nineteen percent are considered to be happy and workable. The other twenty-one percent who remain together aren't very happy about it because they're too afraid to make a change. The current divorce rate stands at an alarming sixty percent. The fact that six out of ten marriages fail clearly indicates that our society as we know it is unraveling. As you read the other chapters in this book, you will discover those answers that provide a solid foundation for the future. The nineteen percent who are supportive and work at their relationship do so because what they have created is so sacred that they wouldn't want to do anything to jeopardize it.

I recall the story of a man who was praying to be happily married. He was asking for two things: one was to be married, and the other, was to be happy at the same time. A lot to ask perhaps, but even more so for anyone who is unaware that happiness is a choice which is independent of external circumstances such as marriage. More simply stated, happiness is an inside job. Although we are taught from birth to look for happiness outside of ourselves, there is a Hindu saying which reminds us that at the beginning of creation, the gods placed man's answers within himself, the last place he would look.

You can add to another's happiness, but it isn't your responsibility to *make* them happy. Whether or not you are with someone, it is up to you to decide how you want to live your life and go about doing those things which add joy to your existence. There are those who can detract from your happiness, and others who can add to it, but not without your consent in either case. For example, a woman who has been married for a while and has children loves her husband dearly, but she is frustrated by his lack of interest. She says, "I just want to light a fire under his butt!" Perhaps, what she really wants is a partner to do things with. If he chooses not to participate, her needs will have to be met in some other way. It is also possible that they'll have to renegotiate the relationship.

There are ways in which we can light our own fires to sustain a relationship that has grown stagnant. However, each person must recognize and accept what they need in their intimate relationships and if they can't have those needs met, recognize that the relationship will be affected. Even the best of relationships have their challenges. Learning, growing and maintaining interest in life is an ongoing process. We may inspire each other, but the action is up to the individual. Learn to let *your* life be a living laboratory. Living, at its best, involves the proverbial search. We search the world for a perfect mate, a perfect career, etc. Very few things in life stay in a perfect, static, condition. We've all had our illusions shattered!

One person described her search in this way:

"No one seems to understand me. No one understood I was really crying for help. Now I know I can just ask for it. I'm available for people to help me. I want people to help me. I want people to be in my life and I want to help other people. It's not what it was; I don't have the isolation I used to have."

When I asked her what she had learned, her response was,

"I think if anything, it's more about my parents and how I really love them, I really understood that they did the best that they could and I love them dearly for who they are and whatever the upset I have with them, I want to be close."

If people you still have issues with are alive, I recommend that you get to a place of acceptance. We never know how long we are going to live. Take the first step. Write that letter, or make that phone call. Arrange a meeting and have that heartfelt conversation you've been putting off. You'll never know when or if you'll have another opportunity to do so. It's a rare opportunity for you to risk your neatly defined world and learn about those you've professed to love or hate. Many of us go through life *thinking* we really know our family members as people. When was the last time you asked your parents how their childhood was and what growing up was like for them? In the book and movie, The Bridges of Madison County, it wasn't until the Mother died that her children found out who she really was and the hopes and dreams she gave up as a woman to be their mother.

Another person in my course recalls her relationship with her mother in this way:

"The question about something that I didn't get from my mother was the one that affected me the most. I started making an emotional list in my head and it was a list *so* long that when I came to the group, I just said what I didn't get from my mother, was that I needed everything. And it was heavy for me to realize that I can't say a positive thing that I got from her which is awful, but true."

In order for her to see the experience in a more positive light, I suggested that she view the experience with her mother as a gift because it taught her that she doesn't want to live her life the same way. Her response was,

"Well, that's really true, because I am totally the opposite of who she is. That is a good learning experience, but from the article that you read about letting go of the past, I still feel like I have a lot of work to do because I want to let go of that and my Mom isn't capable of communicating any longer. So I tried to discuss it with her before she got Alzheimer's, deep into it, but she had no recollection of the events and things that I brought up, so I couldn't really come to peace with it, with her."

This is why we have ceremonial rites of passage. Dr. Florence Kaslow, author of The Dynamics of Divorce: A Life Cycle Perspective pointed out over a decade ago, when the divorce rate was 53%, that we had devised ceremonies for everything – weddings, birthdays, funerals, confirmations, bar mitzvahs…and all of it. What we really need is some kind of ceremony for our separations, a sacredness of respect to honor ourselves, the pain and the growth, and whatever else we've been through leading up to, and through divorce. Alan Cohen in his book, Happily Even After: Can You Be Friends After Lovers?" suggests that,

"A divorce or breakup is not the worst thing that can happen to you; but living in fear, pain, or frustration *is* the worst thing that can happen. Be careful not to write your breakup off as a tragedy. Seen from a higher perspective, it could be the best thing that ever happened to you. You may have lost a partner but regained your soul. With your soul intact, you are empowered to recreate your relationship from a point of strength, not weakness. "

More people are starting to think about what they can do to participate in their own healing process. Often, this begins with what is known as 'healing the inner child'. In Transactional Analysis (TA), and John Bradshaw's groundbreaking work in this field, he provides a framework to guide individuals through an experiential process designed to facilitate mental well-being as an adult. Even though we're all adults, we still carry within us the child we once were. Take out a childhood picture of yourself and observe the look upon your face. Do you still express and experience this state of being? Your child still lives within you whether or not you know it. Until you heal the hurts from that time of your life, you'll continue to carry them around and your adult behavior will be influenced.

Relief from these hurts begins with the desire for reconciliation. *Reconciliation* begins when negative memories and experiences with childhood caregivers become less painful, and influence you less negatively. Ideally, it would be best if your parents were present and involved, however, it's not necessary for them to be alive, mentally competent, or willing to participate. You can have resolution on your own. A trained, integrity-oriented therapist/ counselor can guide you through this experience.

TA teaches that we have three ego states operative in us at any given time; that of the parent, the child, and/or the adult. Although we are not aware of it, our behavior is the result of any of these three ego identities. Of these, the 'adult' is the healthiest ego state because adults ask questions and get information to make decisions and choices in their best interests. When we speak from a child or parental ego state, a critical or controlling behavior often results. Because few of us have received enough of the nurturing we needed, the result was a negative lesson about the issues of control. We learned to do whatever was necessary to get that nurturing. This manifested itself as controlling behavior. Consequently, our modus operandi in dealing with others is the unconscious use of controlling behaviors to get what we want. Perhaps, your caregivers gave only occasional nurturing. As a result of this inconsistency, you received mixed messages. Understand that your parents/caregivers passed on what *they* learned from their childhood to you. Chances are they weren't aware of the fact that they were reenacting learned behavior. If they did, even if they knew it was wrong or harmful, they may not have had the skills required to do anything differently. They did the best they could.

The approach to our present challenges is different because the excuses of yesteryear no longer suffice. Today, we have many more resources available for both parents *and* children. Unless we make use of them they are of no benefit. Often, the problem is not knowing where to turn. Equally difficult is what happens when children become recipients of mixed messages given by their caregivers. **Making children feel safe and comfortable is our priority.** Unfortunately, many parents instill fear, terror, and anxiety. How a child learns to adapt is a result of their conditioning. For example, they may have learned to put others before themselves, which isn't necessarily a bad thing, unless it results in behaviors that are destructive to themselves and others – unaware of the harm being done. Consider the alcoholic parent who demands that their child go to the liquor store under the threat or actual physical enactment of harm if they refuse to comply. Or, worse still is the parental abuser who asks a child to keep their 'special secret,' about anything from sexual abuse to lies. Consider the impact this has on a child! As a matter of fact, do you notice any of these negative characteristics or behaviors in yourself or others you know? And if so, be prepared to heal them. You no longer have to hide.

How do you experience anger? When you're angry, do you behave in a way that reminds you of either of your parents? When you were a child, did you ever hide under a bed, in a room, or a closet? Did you scream and make a scene? These questions are raised to help you become aware of whether your current anger reflects your former behavior. Oft times you may find yourself emulating the negative behaviors you learned from your father or mother. Do you ever catch yourself doing this and wonder why? At such times, when you find yourself caught up in the exact behavior you wish to refrain from, **stop**, and say, "I don't like the person I become when I am with you and I need to leave for now." Doing this will prevent further abuse. You have to be vigilant over your own behavior. No one else can do it for you. Although someone familiar with you may feel safe to challenge you on your behavior by reminding you that you mother or father did these exact same things, is this what you really want? How does this make you feel?

Assess what you need to change. One gift you have for getting to know yourself better is the ability to visualize how your thinking will affect a situation at any moment. You'll know whether or not your responses come from the parent, adult, or child ego states inside of you. For example, no matter how old or young you are, you don't always 'act your age'. Your parental ego state may be scared or out of control. The reason it's so helpful to be aware of how you respond is because it will enhance your interactions with others. Communication will become easier and more clear. Just imagine what the world would be like if everyone acted mentally healthy. The use of psychodrama and psychotherapy help us become whole, integrated people. Socrates said, "Know thyself, the unexamined life is not worth living". Dr. Maslow believed our ultimate goal is to achieve self-actualization.

Back to the classroom... someone asks, "Where is the spirit or the soul in all of this?" The answer is that every single aspect of who you are is never separated from the spiritual side of your nature, although it may appear that way. Our very essence is inherently spiritual. In terms of self-actualization, your spirit never separates from who you are. All stages of human development contribute to our spiritual nature. In your quest to be spiritual, observe your behavior. The spiritual, realized part of you, known in India as the "Atman" (the soul realized), is the true nature of your being. Arrival at this point of understanding is an 'ah-ha' moment. It is an epiphany. You know that you know.

It's very life affirming to understand something so completely that you no longer have doubts about yourself. We learn and we teach each other when we stop hiding. We'll never get real if we can't be ourselves. Being who you are demands a healthy self-respect. If you're family never taught you to respect yourself, you can still learn to do so. You can't replace your parents but you can re-create different role models based on those people whose positive qualities you admire and incorporate the best ones into your own approach to living. When doing this becomes as natural as breathing, you'll truly be honoring the gift you are and never abandon yourself again. You'll know beyond a shadow of a doubt that no matter what the challenges are, you'll survive.

As one participant in the course states:

"Deri covered this with me in a therapy session. At first it was very conceptual to me. I thought it sounded very good and you know, this is a great concept but I don't see how it's gonna' happen or how it's gonna' work. But, I just wanted to say, I now find myself, when I'm having those child moments and I get those thoughts racing in my head like 'what if this?', and 'what if that?' It's the fearful child in me. It comes from when I was a child that was afraid of disappointing people afraid of not getting approval, and being abandoned. When I get those ideas coming to me, I also hear someone else coming and saying, 'Now, why are you thinking that way, and why don't you stop and think about what you are saying here?' I have this other person coming in, and I know *that* is the adult. It's not even the parent I recognize; the parent thought comes in and says, 'now stop that!' So, when she was first covering this with me it was only a concept, and it sounded like a great theory. I was really not even thinking of it as a possibility, but I'm actually having the experience of it kicking in now. So I just wanted to share that it is for real. It does happen if you do condition yourself to it."

Another class member says:

"I just wanted to say that amongst the three of us there weren't really any positive comments. It was all negative, and it was really sad to me that we have all experienced deprivation, mis-understanding, not getting enough of what we needed, and not knowing how to ask for it and I think that's a common theme for a lot of people who do get involved in soul-searching. We are looking backwards so we can go forward."

In the same group, another states:

"For me, it was really the opposite. I always thought love was unconditional because that's the way I was treated, I'm not saying all behavior is acceptable, but it was alright to get angry. It was alright to express your anger and you were not going to be abandoned; you were going to be loved. When I got married, it was the opposite, because my spouse didn't come from a family situation like that. So when I would get angry, I was just venting and getting it off my chest and maybe I was getting louder as I did this. But, in my background, it was okay to do. Because he came from a more abusive household, you didn't do those kinds of things. It pushed him away and it frightened him. So, I can remember having arguments with him and saying, 'just listen to what I'm saying – not how loud I'm saying it.' And I learned with marriage that not all love is unconditional and there are responsibilities of how you behave with other people. This is a learning process for me, to recognize that it's not all just about me, it's also about others too. I can say with my children, I don't think I have been as good at giving them all unconditional love. I've tried, but I don't think I've been as successful at it. Maybe I still have to find out why."

Harville Hendrix's work in Imago Therapy is helpful for couples, parents, or children in conflict. You sit with each other and listen. If, for example, the parents are really angry at their child, and the child says, "Tell me more, Mom, tell me more, Dad," this is an exercise to remove defensiveness – a major stumbling block to effective communication. In the marital setting, imagine how helpful it would be if a husband were to say to his wife, "I'm listening; tell me more" – versus the traditional silent treatment or scolding response. The above scenarios portray a new way of behaving and responding. You can choose to live without verbal abuse. But, it requires the courage to change old habits passed down over the centuries and to be able to listen to what others are saying, even when you don't agree with them.

There is a big difference between conditional and unconditional acceptance of someone's behavior. You can unconditionally love your child or spouse, but that doesn't mean you accept or approve of their behavior. To say the least, there seems to be some confusion about what unconditional love is. We've all known people whose behavior we have found to be less than acceptable. However, love is not simply withdrawn even if you don't approve of what someone is doing or how they are living their life. You may threaten to leave or withhold your love from someone. However, in reality, if you don't get overly enmeshed with them, it is easier to practice unconditional love. What *you* think is best for someone else may not be a part of their path. We must all learn for ourselves. Love never really dies, rather it is transformed over time.

Perhaps, the purest example of unconditional love is seen in the love a parent has for a child. Practicing unconditional love is difficult at times. You can only hope that those you love will choose to work on their problems and rectify them, but that's not always the case. Have you ever met anyone who felt guilty when a family member committed suicide? One woman blamed herself when her son chose this route. He hadn't been able to stop using drugs over the years. Due to his chemical dependency, he would steal from his parents. Among the many attempts to help was to get him into a halfway house, and a job. Nothing worked for very long. Despite thousands of dollars, and years spent in chemical treatment, they could not prevent his soul's decision. The inevitable result is that he ended his own life. Why?

Each of us comes into this world with a purpose. We don't always understand what that purpose is. Both the survivor and the deceased have a lesson. No one can tell you what it is. You alone are left to discover it. Attending one of the many support groups available, listening to tapes, viewing videos, or reading books on this subject will help you to deal with this trauma. Eventually, your life will resume, and perhaps one day you'll be of assistance to others similarly bereaved. One of the guest speakers I invited to my psychology class was a woman who formed an organization for helping others to overcome the suicide of family members. She had lost a son over a decade ago and decided to help others by sharing her experience. Today she travels around the country giving lectures to university students who benefit greatly from her testimony.

The Prophet, Kahlil Gibran, points out in his treatise on children, that your children aren't yours to keep; they come through you, but one day they must go forth into the world to live their lives. Only when you see your child as an individual soul with a free will can you even begin to understand and accept suicide. Historically, many spiritual traditions have a viewpoint on death and the after life. Some validate the concept of reincarnation. If reincarnation is possible, as many authors suggest, such as Dr. Brian Weiss and Dr. Raymond Moody, then perhaps you may draw comfort from knowing that we learn from our mistakes throughout our lifetime. Your goal is to find what will give you comfort in this difficult juncture. One theory is that we keep coming back to Earth until we get it right. Learning to love one another unconditionally requires a worthwhile effort because you can't love another that way if you don't have unconditional love for yourself.

~~~

Unconditional love is a state of being that comes from within us, not the other way around. The paradox is when we stop searching for it, we are often surprised to find that we are already loved in this way. When we feel safe, we're better able to experience unconditional love and it becomes easier to invite others to share their love in the same way. However, if someone purposely intends to hurt you, would you subject yourself to being around them? It's easier to love someone unconditionally from a distance, or when you're not intimately involved with them. Perhaps you can relate to the comments made by former students on this subject.

- "We can be vulnerable. We don't always have the control, and people sometimes don't understand that. They see us maybe as intelligent, capable and able to handle things, but sometimes, inside, we are more vulnerable than we let people know."
- "One of the things I learned about women from my father was… well he was a real care giver, caretaker. Maybe I learned dependence from him."
- One of the things I needed more from my mother was; I still have a hard time answering that. I just would have to give that more thought I really can't answer this because I feel she's always been there for me in very healthy ways. My daughter said the other day something to the effect that the way she can handle stuff with my mother is different from the way she can

handle stuff with me because of the way my mother handles situations."

As a parent, you really have to set a good example for your kids. Hopefully, you do the best you can. When you become really conscious, there are certain things you won't tell your kids – the kinds of things they wouldn't be comfortable knowing anyway. For your children to know certain things about you before it's time, can cause them to lose respect. However, when they become adults, it's easier and more appropriate to reveal things unsuitable for younger children.

We are more than the roles we play. In my class, I once met a woman who remarked that her children viewed her as being more than just Mommy. They also saw her as a woman; a real human being. They got to know the real her. It's so important that your children get to know you as people, but don't expect them to be your caretakers while you're in emotional turmoil. I've seen mothers and fathers do this. They unconsciously use their children as scapegoats, or as a go-between to get back at the other parent. Another client, the eldest of 5 children, was told by her father before he passed away, "Now *you* have to take care of the kids." She was terrified of being put in this position. Her mother was still in the process of recovering from alcoholism at the time of her Father's death and the future was uncertain. She never knew what would happen next because she had no prior experience at shouldering family responsibilities. One day, after many years of anguish, she finally realized that she didn't have to be responsible for her entire family after all. Although she remains concerned about all of them, and continues to assist them from time to time, she no longer allows such overwhelming caretaker responsibilities to immobilize her. She now pursues her own goals.

I'm really grateful that my parents gave me the opportunity to know them really well while they were alive. I used to initiate dialogs with them and they were open enough to talk about themselves. I thank both of them for allowing me to know them as individuals; not just as "Mom and Dad." This didn't come about easily. It was when I was an adult and had spent enough time working on my own issues to the point where I wanted to know more about their lives before they met. Your ability to do the same, should you choose, will depend on your openness as an adult. You'll benefit by knowing that your parents see you not only as a daughter or son, but as a woman, a man, and as a separate person with your own ideas and beliefs.

We say "I'm your father, mother, daughter or son, but do you know what I'm like as a human being?" Do you know what my likes and dislikes are? Do you know some of the pain I've been through in my life? If you really want to have a valuable, different perspective, it begins when you can see yourself and others as individuals. I recall a client who told me that she didn't feel like a mother. How exactly are a mother or a father *supposed* to feel? How do you see yourself? One individual states:

"I draw from my own personal experiences. That children, of course, are great, no matter what age they are, are greatly affected when their parents divorce. But, my experience was, they were more cut up over how it affected them, not what I was going through. Due to current circumstances and additional pain in my life now, they don't want to be a parent. They really don't; you are always mommy and they don't want to hear it. It's largely about how it affects their lives. It doesn't mean they don't love you or don't care, but the point is driven home to me and I had to lighten up. I couldn't burden them. I was better off calling a close friend and finding other avenues and other places I could go to unload my burden and get healthy solace for what I was going through, and leaving my children alone because they really were only concerned about how this was affecting their lives."

Loving yourself *is* important. Never is this more true than when you're faced with a traumatic experience. While friends are helpful and often act as lifesavers, eventually they get tired of listening. Therefore, if you don't want to over burden your friends, find someone to work through your most difficult issues with. I refer to this as, "putting yourself back in the classroom." When issues arise that are difficult for you to deal with, having a good therapist who helps you move forward without taking advantage of you – is what good therapy is all about. I emphasize this because I've been in both roles. In my opinion, I cannot overemphasize the importance of working with a counselor who has been through therapy. I've been fortunate to have helpful mentors along my path when I needed them.

Some people think it's a sign of weakness to have mentors, or to seek the assistance of a counselor. I *know* it's very healthy to have teachers, sages, or people you respect in your life. They're critical to your emotional maturity and well-being. I have encountered them through word of mouth, at conferences, through recommendations, or simply by being in the right place at the right time! However, therapists are human and have problems too. Don't be afraid to disagree with them and let them know when you feel you're not being helped. You have to be your own advocate.

Children are too young to be *their own* advocates. It is not OK for you to dump your emotions on your children. To do so is really inappropriate. They can't handle it, and it's not fair to expect them to meet your needs. They can't do it. It's not their job to fill your "empty holes." While life is sometimes painful, and filled with stress, it is part of the human experience. Most people score over 150 points out of a possible 300 on a stress test. Why? Because, as people, many of the experiences are predictable. You may lose a job, change jobs, buy houses, sell houses, get married, or get divorced. Someone will die in your family, someone may get sick, and someone may have to be hospitalized. Life entails all possible dichotomies and the experiences that we have shape our lives. Moreover, our thinking and our response to what happens influence our destiny and the choices we make.

When you allow life to get the best of you, you're forgetting that we're all moving through this time and space together and that none of this is permanent. When you recognize these things, you'll look at life differently. Understand that tragedy and sorrow are woven from the same fabric as are joy and blessing. How do *you* cope? Is it a choice? Do you experience a void? You might find your answers in the stress test at the end of this chapter. When evaluating your results, bear in mind that your score will change at different times based upon what you are experiencing when you take the test. After completing the stress survey, you'll probably discover that you've already experienced many of the factors on the list.

Another seminar participant told the class, "When I was going through a rough time, I kept saying to my son, who's a professional person, 'this isn't about *you*.' I had to keep telling him, 'this isn't about *you*.'"

Your children can't be objective about you. In many states, including Florida, when parents with young children divorce, they are mandated to take a course on healthy parenting. More states are becoming concerned about the welfare of the children, and legislators want adults to handle their problems as adults and refrain from using children as pawns for emotional blackmail – or worse. In the event of a divorce, let children know it's not their fault, no matter what. Remember too, that regardless of age, they are not immune from being traumatized by divorce. Imagine if your own parents went through a divorce, and came to you and said, "I need you to help me." You ask, "How? What do you want *me* to do? I don't know what to do." It's one thing to go out to a movie and dinner, but to expect them to meet your emotional needs is unreasonable, if not overwhelming. If there's no honest expression of your discomfort, resentment will build and intensify.

When you're having this experience, the child must learn to say, "I need *you* to handle this. Please get the help you need." A parent's response often is, "But, *why?* Aren't you my child?" No matter how old they are, your children will have enough difficulty handling your breakup without having to counsel you. They can read books, get therapy, join groups and more – the same way you can! You see, what happens is, we unexpectedly put all this pressure on our family members or our children, and we end up alienating them. Then they don't want to talk to us at all. Is it not better to have a relationship with them where you can say, "I'm getting the help I need. Thanks for just being there." One woman explains,

"I don't have any children, and I'm not divorced or from a divorced family. If you expect a lot of solace from your children as a Mother, or Father, does it stop there? Do you expect them to take sides? Don't you think they'll wonder 'if I spend a lot of time with one parent, the other may feel that I must be blaming them.' One of them is getting the pity and the other is feeling neglected.

"…You know, from being a child that didn't experience a divorce, ultimately, what happened was that my mother wanted me to parent her. She was very needy throughout adulthood and I really didn't know how. I figured out that I didn't want to be the mother – I wanted to be the kid. Even though she really couldn't be the mother that I wanted her to be, I could still be the kid. And I could still be there for her in my own way even if it was hard for me. She had her own way of nurturing and I had to allow her to find her own answers."

Children and parents have to be careful not to take sides. Your children want to love both of you no matter what happened between the two of you. How can we know about things we never read about or discuss? This is the same concept as when you learn to tie your shoe, ride a bike, or add and subtract. We can't be adept at anything until we practice it. John Bradshaw tells a joke about gender. He said that when he was married, one day the toilet started overflowing. His kids and his wife came running, saying, "Daddy! Fix the toilet bowl!" He said, "What do I look like – a plumber?" The implication is that just because he's a man, he'd know how to fix an overflowing toilet. Similarly, does a child know how to take care of a Mommy or Daddy? I don't think so. When parents try to get their children to take care of them emotionally, the kids may end up resenting them. It can be very harmful if you never separate emotionally from your parents because what will happen when they die if you're not prepared for it? I have seen some people become overly traumatized in this way. For example, you may not know how to go about living your life when they're gone. Think about your current relationship with your parents. Think about the unfinished business you have with them. Most of all, think about the relationship you have with yourself. Are you in touch with your needs or do you sacrifice for everyone else? When you need help, don't be afraid to ask for it. Know where to get it. If you open up any Yellow Pages or newspaper, you'll see many support groups listed from Alzheimer's to Arthritis, and Lupus to AIDS, Divorce, Co-dependency and Incest. We're fortunate to have so much support available today unlike the past. Life would be like it was a half-century ago with all these problems shrouded in secrecy. We need to avail ourselves of the help that is out there. **Don't be afraid to ask for what you need.** Another participant in class shares the following:

"I could say something about my mother. When we were growing up, she would say "okay if you don't do that, I'm not going to love you." Is that conditional love? Yet, we knew she was there for us all of the time. She never hugged us, never kissed us, but she would cook plenty. That was her way of showing love, so we knew she loved us. I couldn't say that she didn't. Now I hug her."

Did you tell her you loved her?

"Then, when I was growing up? No."

Do you tell her now?

"Yes, oh yes."

Did you ever ask her why she wasn't able to do that when you were young?

"I'm going to ask her before something happens."

Another person states:

"I always saw my parents fighting, but I saw a lot of action with my mother's family. I saw it helping others, they would take the shirt off their back and give it to somebody in need. It was so real it was unbelievable. That's love to me."

Someone else says:

"I learned so much just by listening to others' experiences and views. To me this is the bread of life, what life is about. It's why I'm here, on this Earth, to experience this kind of life. Sometimes we get challenges that make us angry, fearful or whatever. We are still supposed to go through those things... and I feel like I'm growing just by listening. I realize now that the difficult things I experienced as a child were part of being in this life. I would have loved to have had loving parents and had a wonderful heavenly childhood. Because I didn't, doesn't make life any better or worse, it's just life. I'm learning that more...

When we get to the point that we can accept that this is life, with or without us, it's okay. We're here on this earth just as if we were visiting another city...We choose certain things about that city that we want to see, experience or do... We kind of have control of what we are going to be going through and so this whole life is just a microcosm of that...Tomorrow will take care of itself...I really learned by sharing experiences with people like yourselves and I thank all those who have shared. It has helped me a lot just to listen."

All of these comments cause us to reflect on our own experiences. How have you chosen to heal your own pain or are you still hanging on to it? Ask yourself what you gain by holding on to negative experiences. By shifting the way you see things, you can move forward and create the kind of life you want to have. It's all a lesson. It's up to you. My hope is that after reading this chapter it might aid in the healing of your heart.

Will stress in your life make you sick?

Score yourself on the Life Change Test

If any of these life events have happened to you in the last 12 months, please check Happened column and enter Value in Score column.

Item	Value	Happened (✔)	Your Score	Life Event
1	100			Death of spouse
2	73			Divorce
3	65			Marital seperation
4	63			Jail Term
5	63			Death of close family member
6	53			Personal injury or illness
7	50			Marriage
8	47			Fired at work
9	45			Marital reconciliation
10	45			Retirement
11	44			Change in health of family member
12	40			Pregnancy
13	39			Sex difficulties
14	39			Gain of new family members
15	39			Business readjustment
16	38			Change in financial state
17	37			Death of close friend

18	36			Change to a different line of work
19	35			Change in number of arguments with spouse
20	31			Mortgage over $10, 000
21	30			Foreclosure of mortgage or loan
22	29			Change in responsibilities at work
23	29			Son or daughter leaving home
24	29			Trouble with in-laws
25	28			Outstanding personal achievement
26	26			Spouse begin or stop work
27	26			Begin or end school
28	25			Change in living conditions
29	24			Revision of personal habits
30	23			Trouble with boss
31	20			Change in work hours or conditions
32	20			Change in residence
33	20			Change in schools
34	19			Change in recreation
35	19			Change in church activities
36	18			Change in social activities
37	17			Mortgage or loan less than $10, 000
38	15			Change in sleeping habits
39	15			Change in number of family get-togethers
40	15			Change in eating habits
41	13			Vacation
42	12			Christmas
43	11			Minor violations of the law
				Total score for 12 months

Note: The more change you have, the more likely you are to get sick. Of those people with over 300 Life Change Units for the past year, almost 90 percent get sick in the near future; with 150 to 299 Life Change Units, about 60 percent get sick in the near future; and with less than 150 Life Change Units, only about 30 percent get sick in the near future.

Reprinted with permission from Journal of Psychosomatic Research

CHAPTER FIVE

A Discourse on Love

"It doesn't interest me what you do for a living. I want to know what you ache for, and if you dare to dream of meeting your heart's longing.

It doesn't interest me how old you are I want to know if you will risk looking like a fool for love, for your dream, for the adventure of being alive...

I want to know if you can sit with pain, mine or your own, without moving to hide it or fade or fix it...

I want to know if you can disappoint another to be true to yourself; if you can bear the accusation of betrayal and not betray your own soul; if you can be faithless and therefore trustworthy.

I want to know if you can see beauty, even if it's not pretty everyday...

I want to know if you will stand in the center of the fire with me and not shrink back...

I want to know what sustains you, from the inside, when all else falls away.

I want to know if you can be alone with yourself and if you truly like the company you keep in the empty moments.

Oriah Mountain Dreamer

~~~

<u>Soulful Love: The Search for the Self</u> came about through my own transformation over the years. In the last three decades, I have been on a quest to find what we all want in this life – peace of mind and unconditional love we can experience and personalize. This work has also been inspired by the many stories of the people that I have counseled in the last two decades and specifically from a course I taught

entitled, The Path To Love, based on Deepak Chopra's book and other authors. The first line in the book is "All of us need to believe that we are loved and lovable." As you read this chapter, reacquaint yourself with the experience of love, and redefine exactly what it is for you.

We are consistently bombarded with ideas about love today via the media, songs on the radio, multitudes of books written on the subject, along with the overwhelming problems which have come about for this generation. A century ago, many of these problems weren't talked about. They were shrouded in secrecy. Many of the problems were not even identified. We didn't have names for them.

We each come from a background. We each have a family history and part of our search for love necessitates making peace with our past. Some of the ways we accomplish this are by attending classes, reading helpful books, going through various processes, which may include psychotherapy, different forms of counseling, regression work, or even body work, such as massage.

We all desire to experience wholeness and fulfillment. Yet, we are reminded that if we don't heal ourselves, we are bound to bring our neediness into our relationships and expect our partner(s) to fix those parts of ourselves which they can't. Ask yourself what has happened in the past when your partner didn't fulfill your needs. Did you get angry or mad? The Celestine Prophecy articulates the idea of control dramas. Control dramas arise because we are unconscious about our behavior. The more unaware we are, the more drama we create. Socrates' advice to "know thyself," and Abraham Maslow's theory of self-actualization are one and the same. Their focus is on relationships that have a spiritual significance. Most of us were not taught to look at relationships in this context.

We wanted to have our basic needs met – food, air, water, shelter and, for many, it has always been a matter of economics. However, the shift we've been forced to make requires that we view things differently. The previous ways we engaged in relationships left much to be desired, especially noted in the increased divorce rate and quiet lives of desperation lived by many. Consider that domestic violence was actually legal in England during the 1600's. A man could take a switch no bigger than the width of his thumb and beat his wife because his wife was his property – chattel. Approximately, four hundred years later, it is a crime punishable by law in the United States. Legislation and laws now prevent families from abusing each other. The reason for this is simply because too many people were being killed due to someone's uncontrollable rage.

Part of the path to soulful love is learning how to befriend your anger, and knowing how to work with it to produce those situations which are conducive to positive mental health. There are many effective avenues to pursue. Some include primal scream therapy, or release by physical action, as in aerobics, where no one is hurt and no property is destroyed. Some prefer to go into their garage and break bottles; you're not hurting anyone, but you'll have a mess to clean up! Some therapists recommend kicking your legs up and down while lying in bed to release the energy from your anger. You can also punch inanimate objects, like pillows, if that will help.

Many of us want to know how to communicate from a center of love versus a center of fear. It is the kind of love that really is unconditional – you want to do what is best for the other person, even if it means forsaking your own need. When or if you think of spiritual people, saints, masters, or others whom you consider inspiring, maybe you've wondered, "What is it that these people have in their lives that I don't?" The answer is it is not a matter of having "something." Your answers come about through developing an *awareness* that there's a different way to do things. You really don't have to travel down rocky roads anymore, unless you choose to. If you believe you must suffer, then you will create choices based on that need.

My goal in this chapter is to provide you with lots of information so that you can make informed decisions as to what is in your best interests and promotes mental well being. Along with this, you'll be able to incorporate your own wisdom based on personal experience to redefine just what love is. Let's examine romantic and platonic love, actually being friends with the opposite sex, as if it's not possible! What will remind you to tolerate nothing less than respect, whether it is in the workplace or at home? The Greek language offers a unique description of love because of its ability to express what the English language can't. They use three words to our one word to define love. Love is eros, agape and philia. Eros is the expression of love in a physical, sexual context. Agape represents a family-like love, whereas philia is the more universal aspect of love, which we know as brotherly love. These three definitions comprise the different aspects of the ways we love.

Phil Donahue's video, *Nature Versus Nurture,* explains how the human child, or the human animal, if you will – after all, we are the highest primates of the animal species, cannot survive as an infant without being cared for. Animals take care of their young, but then they are left to go out on their own. However, a little baby who doesn't receive daily nurturing, love and touch will die because it cannot feed or take care of itself. Consider, for example, how we take care of ourselves when we transition into adulthood. A man once asked, "Isn't it important for a woman to know how to nurture herself and take care of herself?" My response was "Yes, and isn't it important for a man to know how to do the same?" His response was "Well, how many people do you know who can do that?" I answered, "Most people can't if they haven't been taught how to." This is one reason why so many people fail in their relationships, especially if they are desperate. How can you expect someone else to take care of you if they can't take care of themselves? As we heal what is incomplete within ourselves, we won't have to suffer any longer because we will no longer tolerate unacceptable behavior.

Ken Keyes book, <u>A Conscious Person's Guide to Loving,</u> describes the importance of becoming aware of what you say, why you say it, how you say it, and when you say it. Now, you may be thinking to yourself "I can't walk around conscious like that one hundred percent of the time." You don't have to. You have a choice. Consider what would have happened if you never learned to tie your shoelaces, not because you couldn't, but because you were lazy. Similarly, you can choose to learn healthy, respectful verbal communication skills. We speak in foreign languages, yet we can't even understand each other when we speak the same language.

Don't be afraid to ask questions whenever you disagree with something you've read or heard because there's a lot of information available today. We have many articles, videos, cassettes and books that offer help relative to any situation. Our lives are a learning laboratory. Understanding love requires that we don't limit our definition of it. For example, Dr. Paul Wanio's article, entitled "There Are No Condoms For The Heart," suggests that there is no such thing as casual sex. While many people agree, according to the media and our personal experiences, casual sex does exist and is an option. Condoms may prevent disease and pregnancy, but they don't prevent emotional, mental devastation. Wanio explains:

"Sex is inherently an intimate act, whether we think so or not, and can only be separated from love through denial of the intimate aspects of sex, or rationalization that sex is merely a physically pleasurable act, or dissociation – a splitting off or numbing ourselves and making sex impersonal... If we have sex without love, we will never be truly satisfied. We will sense something missing in our lives, yet never quite know what it is, We will have pleasure, but that is all. True fulfillment in a relationship will forever remain a mystery."

His thoughts may reflect your own experiences or disappointments. Maybe you know of others who've suffered similar experiences. If sex is inherently a deeply spiritual act, performing it casually might leave one feeling empty. There are those who say "it doesn't make a difference." Wanio suggests it does make a difference. Many people I've worked with in my years of practice validate this concept because of their own experiences.

Although they may say, "We're two consenting adults," I've never met anyone who at some point wasn't disappointed or hurt by the person they were having sex with if they expected an eventual commitment. Why? Because, the idea of being really conscious before you get into this thing called "sexuality" is what will avoid a lot of pain down the road; unless you are both really clear on what your agenda is. Wanio states in his book, I Love You, I Think – When Sex Disguises Itself as Love":

"Do human beings have a natural need for sex? Yes and no. We have a need, actually a drive, a desire for sex, but only as human beings. It is simply bad science or psychology to ignore, limit or deny the complete aspect of our natures. That is, we must recognize all aspects of ourselves, biology as well as psychology, sexual feelings, rational thoughts and emotional needs – human, emotional needs. To the degree that we dissociate or split off any one essential part of who we are, is the degree that we have devalued, dehumanized and fragmented ourselves."

It is not unreasonable to have "healthy" expectations; however, if they aren't discussed with your significant other, both of you run the risk of not getting your needs met. I am often surprised by the amount of people I meet who expect their partners to know what their needs are. When you project your needs onto your loved one without communicating them, this is a setup for failure.

Tom Costa, a Science of Mind minister, stated in a video, "You know, after my marriage ended, I said 'Ouch! That hurt.' And then, after my next marriage ended, I said 'Ouch! That hurt.' And then, after my next...." He attempted several marriages. Perhaps like me, you're wondering, "Why get married at all?" The "OUCH" gets bigger and bigger. Consider your own family history; your genealogy. All my grandparents, including my parents, were married for over fifty years. As a matter of fact, everyone in my family stayed married but me.

Were they happy all the time? I don't think so. However, they were certainly committed to each other. Is that better than all the divorces today? In cases where there's abuse, be it mental, domestic or physical violence, certainly not. Don't stay. If it was more difficult for people to get married, perhaps there would be less divorces.

Take a look at an average life span. Now our life expectancy is longer than before. We don't have to deal with the challenges our ancestors did, but we have new stressors. The question to ask yourself is - if you are going to be with someone for a very long time, can you make the commitment? From the first throes of passion, to your loved one possibly becoming "sick or challenged," will you stay with that person? It's a difficult question to answer, but if you are looking for only good times, a commitment is unrealistic.

An article I wrote for the Canadian Peace Research Journal, entitled "Overcoming Family Violence" answers some of these questions. It has been said that we live in the Prozac-happy generation. Dr. Norton's book, Beyond Prozac, was written to help us deal with all of the challenges we face today in love, romance and self-actualization, which is the search for our self. In the 1600's, Wilfred Trotter wrote, "We are driven by primitive, selfish desires to satisfy animal instincts." Compare this to Dr. Norton's recent theory: "Twenty thousand years ago, we evolved to meet the conditions of life on the African Savannah. Our bodies and brains remained virtually unchanged from those of our Stone-Age ancestors. Yet, in the last few hundred years, a bewildering rush of cultural evolution has thoroughly transformed our world – a global village of nearly six billion. It has become a draining task just to empathize with the televised plight of our global villagers. Cumulative stresses of modern life have set off an avalanche of depression, anxiety and insomnia. Most people self-medicate, using anything from caffeine to cocaine. The way we sleep, the way we eat, the air we breathe, draw on the same account, weakening the specific neurochemical stress shield that Prozac is designed to bolster. In a certain sense, our lifestyles have made us Prozac-deficient."

Our biochemical makeup includes fourteen neurotransmitters in the brain. You may recognize these chemicals, such as acetylcholine, norepinephrine, serotonin, etc. What Prozac is designed to do is to increase the serotonin reuptake in your brain synapse. It helps you stay calm and not overreact. For example, have you ever noticed after you eat rice, pasta or turkey that you feel more relaxed? That's because these foods convert to tryptophane, which makes you more peaceful and sleepy. The point is to learn as much as you can about your body, the food you eat and its effect on your behavior. Have you ever noticed that when people are hungry, they can become easily annoyed and very moody? It is important to notice all environmental factors that influence behavior.

To help you understand more of what influences you, it is necessary to know how your brain functions and how this influences your perceptions. The more information you have about who you are, the way you operate and why you do what you do, the more you will know about human psychology. Interestingly enough, Metaphysics now refers to psychology as a "Science of Spiritual Psychology." The more information you have, the more educated choices you will hopefully make about who you choose to get involved with. You'll then have a barometer to measure your mental health as you learn to navigate the waters of healthy love. Wanio continues:

"You allow someone to get extremely close to you physically, without being logically prepared for the experience. In fact, it is not possible to be prepared. The psychological closeness requires trust. Trust requires a knowledge of the person that you are with. And knowledge and intimate knowledge takes time. It is naïve to trust mere words, first appearances and infatuation. To really know someone is a highly developed skill that does not occur in a night, a week or a month. Nor is it merely dependent upon time. It requires in-depth awareness, emotional sharing, honest communication and non-defensiveness. Some people never master it."

It is sometimes overwhelming how we affect each other. Imagine for a moment that you could learn how to love much the same way you learned to ride a bike. Many of us grew up in families that are today known as dysfunctional. Years ago we didn't have names to identify these problems. Dysfunction implies an abnormal or impaired functioning. When you look back at your grandparents and your great grandparents, do you think they knew then what we know now? How has the information overload affected us? No one knew what serotonin was. Research is a powerful tool, but, like anything else, we can abuse it if we allow our intellect and ego to take over, we'll never reveal ourselves. Wanio explains:

"Though sex can express intimacy, it can also substitute for it. We can learn to perform sex without ever sharing or knowing ourselves. Without an intimate and deeply personal knowledge of one another, love cannot exist."

Hormone elevation affects infatuation. Dr. Bruno Bettleheim says it takes at least five months to get to know another human being. The first three months are the honeymoon phase of any relationship. You look good. You feel good. You smile. They like you. You're great. Two months later, you hear – "I don't want to know you." His idea is to go slow. What's that?! I've heard people of all ages say, "It's really much easier to be alone and feel lonely than it is to be with someone and feel lonely." One of the ways we really learn more about ourselves is by being in relationship. Dr. Wanio suggests:

"You cannot love that which you do not know. You cannot love a stranger, only be intrigued by one. Sex is not a game. It's not a sport. If you're playing a game of tennis, it is not necessary to bring all of you into that relationship. It is not essentially personal."

Sex has been referred to as one of the most intimate acts because it reveals who you are to someone else. How do you feel if you never see or hear from the other person again? Maybe, at one point or another it was not important. The sexual morays of the '60's certainly proved that to be true. However, what has become really scary is the aftermath we have had to live with since AIDS. While there are cures for most STD's, (Sexually Transmitted Diseases), there are no quick cures for broken hearts. You know when you've been degraded, but are you aware of why you allowed someone to mistreat you?

I was once asked to explain that comment in a class. People need to be honest with each other in their relationships, no matter how painful it is. A male asked, "Do you mean if the woman I'm dating is going out with another man, she should tell me? And if I'm seeing someone else, I should tell her?" DUH! Why not? Wouldn't it avoid a lot of complications down the road if you both knew where you stood? Do you realize that just a half a century ago lying was an acceptable way of life? Why? How many people who were in unhappy marriages or unhappy relationships had the courage and integrity to say "I'm not happy. We have to do something to try to make this work, give it our best shot, and if it doesn't, then at least we can say we made a mistake." Most people, however, end up getting involved in affairs or relationships with similar people, only to repeat the same patterns again. By the time they get to marriage number three or four, it gets ridiculous. They experience the same behavior with a different partner, even if they aren't married because the lessons weren't learned.

Some believe that our life on earth is a school and we come here to learn. If we don't learn what we need to, then we keep coming back until we master the lesson. I can't tell you what is true for you. We all have to discover that for ourselves. When something speaks to you, it may not speak to someone else. What is relevant to you may not be universal. The key is to find what works best for you. I will tell you, though, that the more honest you are and the more integrity you demonstrate, the more at peace you will be, because you won't be hiding anything. Wanio continues:

"How would you feel if your mate said to you after an affair, 'Oh, it was only sex – don't worry.' Would you be relieved? Hardly. And why not? Because you'd know that even if the sex was able to be twisted into something impersonal, the intimate aspect of this loving act could potentially arise to further threaten your relationship. If sex were so casual, what reason would there be to prevent the affair from occurring again? If sex were casual, it would be as silly to object to an affair as it would be to shaking hands….Human sexual relationships are complex, basically due to the fact that we are human."

My hope is that you'll become really clear about what is important to you regarding your values and your needs. Communicate them; otherwise, people won't know who you are.

"Johari's Window," a psychological tool, suggests that the unknown self is also unknown to another person. If I don't know something and you don't know it either, then we can't share that information. But, if I know something and I hide it from you, I prevent you from knowing me better. If you prevent me from knowing you more, then the information is hidden. The way we can have healthier relationships is through revealing ourselves. It takes time to feel safe to do this. In our over-addictive, super-driven, consumption-oriented society, it is hard to slow down. Yet, what is the alternative?

Chopra reminds us that, "What you call flaws are really just the scars of….wounds accumulated over a lifetime." A common theme runs through much of this material. People say it with different words. We go through the various stages of growth. First, we leave our mother's womb, then our childhood, and eventually, we develop into adults. Chopra indicates that our circle of love widens more by our experiences which usually includes our family and friends first. Then, we add intimate partners, along with learning and truth which we can hopefully turn into skills that build healthy relationships. Unfortunately, many of us don't find out about healthy love until we've gone through severe crises.

Love is also about passion – a passion for life, not just passion explored through sexuality. What makes you want to get up in the morning? What makes you feel excited? Do you have a project you're working on? What's important to you in your life? Answering these questions will provide you with new insight. Insight may lead you to understand that your search is not so much to be loved or accepted, but rather, to make peace with yourself, as well as love and accept who you are. It is natural to desire companionship, closeness, nurturing, love and acceptance. However, no matter how much you love someone, what happens? Life. The other side of life we call death. We leave our physical bodies through death and enter another domain. In reality, no matter how much you love another human being, one of you is going to go first, unless you go together. This truth, which many people don't talk about, is one you're going to have to make peace with. What happens very often is that many people who have been together for a long time die soon after they lose their mates.

I observed that experience with my Mom. My Dad made his transition five years ago, on August 24th, and my Mom's health got progressively worse. She passed on March 12th, 1999. It was very difficult for her to go on without him. They had been married fifty-four years. That's a long time to be with another human being. A lot of the men and women I met in my support and bereavement groups keep their loved ones memory and spirit close to them by viewing photographs and talking to them every day. Many feel comforted by their loved ones' presence.

When I was fourteen, a very dear friend of mine died instantly in a car accident. Her parents moved to Florida years ago. I was close to them when I was younger. I recall when I "accidentally" bumped into them in a supermarket. We cried and they invited me to their home. When I walked inside the living room, my mouth fell open. There were pictures of my friend everywhere. Her mother didn't believe in life after death, but her dad did. I never imagined that he would share a similar spiritual view of death as I did at the time. He led me to believe that he had made peace with his daughter's death because he believed that she knew exactly what she was doing. They had always reminded her not to get into cars and take rides. She accepted a ride with a school teacher who was driving and was the only one out of five people to die instantly.

When a parent outlives a child, it is a very difficult trauma to overcome. Imagine, if you can, the same devastation suffered when you're older and have shared many years together with your partner. Love continues. When you love someone and they leave you or your leave them, the relationship may end. The love you shared changes. You don't really stop loving people you've loved. Hatred and love are opposite ends of the spectrum. When and if love becomes abusive in any way, the relationship can't exist at the same level you first discovered it. You can't sustain a relationship in which there is no giving or receiving. If you do, however, you'll be very unhappy.

There are as many paths to love as there are different kinds of love. One of love's goals is to teach us more about ourselves. You can learn more about yourself both in the time you spend with others and alone. It is important to not fear being alone because you can enhance your creativity and reveal other aspects of your personality. Simultaneously, we also learn some of our most difficult lessons through other people. We have those "ah-hah" moments where we get a revelation that finally makes sense.

Chopra suggests that, "Everything love is meant to do is possible. Knowing this, however, has only made the gap between love and non-love more painful." Why? He states:

"Most people have experienced love as pleasure, sex, security, having someone else fulfill their daily needs, without seeing that a special path has been opened to them. Socially, the normal cycle of love is simply to find a suitable partner, marry and raise a family. But this social path is not a path, because the experience of marrying and raising a family isn't automatically spiritual." *[There's that word again!]*

"Sad to say, many people enter lifelong relationships in which love fades over time, or provides lasting companionship without growing in its inner dimension. The spiritual path has only one reason to exist. It shows the way for the soul to grow."

What exactly is "Soul" growth? If you think of yourself as a mere human being living in a physical body, then what is this thing called the soul? And what of all your soulful revelations that came about through emotional pain and the dark nights of the soul? They are the wakeup calls – the clarion - indicating that there's more to life than pain and suffering. Life is a dichotomy. It is filled with opposites. Chopra believes that when you find your path, you will also find your love story.

How many have been through an experience in a relationship based solely on sexuality without a spiritual connection? I'm not referring to your particular faith, but rather, to a spiritual affinity. There has to be something more that you can rely upon to keep the relationship intact. If you choose to enter a relationship without an inner awareness of what sustains your life, you may be looking for trouble. You can't expect people to be who they're not. You can't ask someone to be spiritual if they don't know what that is, and you can't grow for another. Give them a book to read. Be helpful in that way. We've all known people who had to pretend. They were dishonest. Their lives were motivated by fear. What motivates one to lie? Self-interest and fear of the truth. Yet, all experiences provide some form of growth. It is up to each person to determine the level they want to grow to. If you don't know something, ask. Why go on deluding yourself or allowing others to do the same? Our path to love is inherently an act of self-actualization and self-knowledge.

It's up to you to begin to live from this frame of reference. When you truly find yourself, you'll also find love and you'll discover what it is like to live in a loving consciousness. There is a difference between universal love and romantic love because, as Chopra reminds us, "Falling in love is over and being in love begins when romance turns into committed relationships and the path changes."

We live in commitment-phobic times. One reason for this phenomena is due to the terror and fear people have experienced in their "love" relationships. Their wounds still haunt them and they have not healed. If you grew up in a family which was very toxic or abusive and you don't take steps to heal the pain, you may unconsciously sabotage yourself and keep creating the same. Emotional abuse includes lying, deception, and not being available.

We have become an addiction-oriented society because coping is painful and people want to medicate their pain. However, when you realize that you don't have to stay in painful situations, you will no longer hurt yourself. You will want to be fully aware and join others of like mind on a similar path. This is what our journey is all about – becoming conscious. Becoming conscious means that you realize you live in a spiritual state of awareness. It is in this state that a couple learns to nurture through surrender. They surrender the ego.

In a John Bradshaw video, he described his own dysfunctional relationship when he was married. Due to his alcoholism and before he went into recovery, he wondered why people thought he had the answers to everything! He recounted a story about his family. One night the toilet bowl started overflowing and his children said, "Daddy, Daddy, the toilet bowl's overflowing. Fix it! Fix it!" "No," he said. "What do I look like – a plumber?" He was reminding us that just because he is a man, he isn't necessarily a plumber! Similarly, because you're a woman, are you automatically expected to be a nurturer? Our roles have changed and we are relearning what the new roles are, and if they work.

Men now play the role of being caretakers in relationships and they are also fully-participating fathers. Other relationships find more women working outside the home and more men becoming involved in home making. There's no set rules anymore. Everything's been torn apart. Why? Because many of the old ways didn't work. Change happened, and we are the recipients of the growing pains. Like it or not, if we don't grow, we'll be unhappy. The way we once thought can no longer sustain us. We grow individually and as a society. Each one of us makes up that society. Every piece of information you gather can be shared with someone else and it might change their lives too. They might be led to think differently and find out more information.

So, one by one, each one teaches one. The "Hundredth Monkey Theory" was created by the late Ken Keyes. Monkeys in the South Pacific islands had washed their yams in the sand for years. One day, on another island, other monkeys started to wash their yams in water. Eventually, the monkeys discovered that yams taste better without sand, and they adopted the habit of washing their yams in water.

We are like the monkeys, too. We want to know why we should do something different. We say, "Show me why this is going to work for me." Perhaps we ask, "what will happen after I do all the work or "what am I going to get from this?" Then, there are the followers who adapt to the changes. It's not business as usual. One of my favorite statements is "I'm not going there!" This basically means I've been there, I've done that, and I don't want to do that again. Of course, you'll get tested over and over again if you want to do that "dance" again. In Dr. Harriet Goldhor-Lerner's books, <u>The Dance of Anger</u>, <u>The Dance of Deception</u>, and <u>The Dance of Intimacy</u>, she uses dance movement as a metaphor for anger, deception and intimacy. There are healthier ways to respond to destructive emotions.

Whether you're in a relationship or out of a relationship, you're still in a relationship – with yourself. A wise mentor once stated, "you are the only person who will never leave you or abandon you." Imagine what would happen if you ever "left" yourself? You'd be in big trouble! This doesn't imply that you can't learn to love others or be in relationship with them. What it suggests is that until we learn to love all the parts of ourselves, including the bad, good, indifferent and ugly roles we play, no one else will accept us. We must first accept ourselves. Drs. Connie Zweig and Steve Wolf, suggest in their book, <u>Romancing the Shadow</u> that,

"Hidden from our awareness, the shadow is not a part of our conscious self-image…the individual's persona, the mask shown to the world, is split off from the shadow, the face hidden from the world…Therefore we cannot face it in ourselves or tolerate it in others.

Denial is entrenched because the shadow does not want to come out of its hiding place…Eventually, we can learn to create an ongoing conscious relationship to it, thereby reducing its power to unconsciously sabotage us…We need to cultivate an attitude of respect toward the shadow, to see it honestly without dismissing it or becoming overwhelmed by it."

Shadow work asks us to stop blaming others, to take responsibility, to move slowly, to deepen awareness, to hold paradox, to open our hearts, to sacrifice our ideals of perfection and to live the mystery.

I once had a client who told me the following story about her relationship. She used to live with a man who would occasionally tell her before he left for work in the morning, "You know, you don't look so good to me today." Excuse me! Let's wake up and smell the flowers. What is the meaning of a statement like that and what happened to this relationship? It didn't work out because it couldn't. You could say, there was an unexplored issue in that man which he himself was clueless about. Due to his own emotional insecurities and immaturity, he projected his fears onto his partner, who was really a mirror of himself. What is pitiful is that this man went on in search of the "perfect woman," never finding her, because he could not accept his own imperfections. His behavior is indicative of an emotionally abusive relationship. Telling someone you don't like the way they look in the morning serves no purpose. Even professional models have bad hair days!

Regarding sacred marriages, Chopra believes they are created and based on a divine essence. He says, "As you grow, you exchange shallow, false feelings for deep, true emotions and, thus, compassion, trust, devotion and service become realities." He believes these elements will prevent the marriage from faltering. How many people today think this way? It seems that the divorce rate would suggest that most people enter into marriage "unconsciously" certainly not in devotion or service. Chopra believes that surrender is the door one must pass through to find a passion. In spiritual terms, he equates passion with letting yourself be swept away on a "river of life," which is eternal and never-ending.

I believe that our search for love is the search for ourselves. When you meet another human being and become involved with them, your life is transformed. You no longer are accountable to just yourself. We have to be able to express to each other what we like and don't like about ourselves. Healthy relationships promote positive change. Very often in couples therapy, I ask my clients to write down everything they like about themselves, and everything they dislike about themselves. Then, they write down everything they like about their partner, and everything they dislike about them. After that, they write down everything they want to change about themselves. Then they have to write down what behaviors they want their partner to change.

You may be very surprised to find that some of the things that you don't like about yourself are reflected in another. Or, those traits can cause you to work on yourself. When we change, the things that used to bother us no longer do because we've shifted our thinking, and when that happens, the dynamics of the relationship change. *All it takes is one person to change, and that alters the relationship.* Whether the relationship can sustain itself is based on the willingness of both people to work on their issues and get beyond them.

Life gives us stuff to deal with. When you get lemons, you can make lemonade! You have choices, don't you? You can let the lemons rot, or you can choose to do something with them. If you never know that you can do something different, you won't. Many people are "locked" into one way of thinking. One client limited herself to the locations and groups where she thought she could socialize and meet new people. When I asked her why she limited herself to that crowd, she was quite surprised, not having realized that she could open other doors to contact different groups. The more we free our thinking, the more we learn to love ourselves.

Being able to feel love in a spiritual context, you can also experience the same from others and thereby not limit yourself to the amount of love you're able to receive. Previously I have alluded to the concept that we are spiritual beings having a human experience and human beings having a spiritual experience. It is the human part of us that finds it more difficult to live in a continuous state of love. It's easier to love spiritually because we don't have any expectations then.

I've had some incredible transformative experiences. One I recall was with Rev. Barbara Lunde and her mother, also a Science of Mind minister. They prayed with me for a physical healing regarding a health challenge. The experience that I had in that room with Barbara and her mother was, indeed, out of this world. The three of us were moved to tears, and the environment was filled with so much light and love. I was healthy. This experience was living in a state of being, knowing that we move and walk in love. The movie *Cocoon* depicts how people's bodies house their spirits, demonstrating this phenomena by showing a beautiful, ethereal light emanating from their bodies when they removed their skin. After all, our physical form houses our eternal spirit.

Living in this physical, material world, we are daily bombarded by it. Our experiences can easily cause us to get off the path of love. Think of your reaction to traffic, long lines, and the stress you allow those situations to produce. What has worked for me in these areas are the following:

- Patience
- Not waiting in lines when I don't have the time
- Striking up a conversation while on-line
- Always having some reading material with me
- Getting acupuncture treatment and using Chinese herbs
- Ion-pumping chords which are two chords that balance the electrical system in your body. The negative and positive polarities are placed on four magnets which you place at different meridians or acupuncture points on your body. One position for the magnets is in the middle of your wrists and on your foot, between your fourth and last toe. This treatment is called "Relaxing Yang Way." According to Chinese medicine, it relaxes dominant energy.
- Walk aerobically, bike ride and take classes at a gym three to five times per week.
- Yoga, stretching and meditation.
- Reading and relaxing.

In order to maintain a loving state, you must take care of your body and you must do those things that make you feel good. Your endorphins, the body's natural opiates, relax you.

The body is the temple of the Spirit, yet, many abuse their bodies because they need to medicate their pain, not knowing how to heal it. There are many avenues for healing. Deepak says that a path implies a beginning and an end. In talking about a path to love, "the beginning is a reality in which Love is longed for but uncertain." Fear and anger can overwhelm us, and forces of hatred produce anything but love. Yet, what is required – the deepest healing of all – is the healing force of universal love applied to every situation.

RITES OF PASSAGE

We need rites of passage to help us heal. We have very few of these. The ones we really need have yet to be developed. What exactly is a rite of passage? In Judaism, when a boy enters manhood or a girl enters womanhood, they go through a bar or bas mitzvah. In Christianity, teenagers go through confirmation. In African and Native American cultures, groups are sent out into the wilderness and taught how to survive and overcome fear. Rites of passage also include births, baptisms, weddings and death. We still lack rites of passage for divorce, illness and other challenges, however we are developing more rites of self-acceptance. Answering the following questions may provide more peace of mind and suggest a modern day transition into healthy adulthood.

How can you tell the difference between love and infatuation?
What do you need to feel safe to become emotionally intimate?
How do you make peace with your past?
How do you learn to express constructive anger?
How do you build self-esteem?

You can go through life without answering these questions, however, contemplating them might ensure more happiness. Write your answers in a journal and be aware of how they change as you grow in spiritual understanding and maturity. This growth requires the practice of self control. That is not to say you shouldn't allow yourself emotional outlets or verbalizing your feelings. However, when you are in charge of yourself, you will feel more comfortable with yourself and your decisions. Being aware of your codependent traits also helps transform them into healthier behaviors.

We all need tools to know how to relate to others in all kinds of relationships, be they familial, romantic, or business. We need to understand each others' psychology; for example, why men prefer to be silent about their issues and why women need to process verbally. We need to learn from each other and this requires time, patience, practice and willingness. Self-knowledge leads to a greater understanding between yourself and your partner. Better communication results in not being afraid to speak your truth all the time. Trust your intuition. Allow yourself to grow and watch your goals change. Recognize that giving and receiving are opposite sides of the same coin. Be aware of the difference between what you need and what you want. Be willing to learn what love really entails. Understand what went wrong in past relationships, so as not to repeat the same lesson.

In Brenda Schaeffer's book, <u>Is It Love Or Is It Addiction?</u>, she provides characteristics of healthy belonging. See if you recognize some of them. People in healthy relationships have the following characteristics:

(1) they allow for individuality. They experience both oneness and separateness from a partner. Part of being in relationship is coming together and coming apart. For example, it is going out and exploring your day and then coming back and sharing it. When you first meet someone, you're interested to find out about their past, who they are, their lifestyle, etc. Then, when you think you know everything about the other person – boredom sets in. Boredom in a relationship happens when you are bored with yourself and expect your partner to motivate you. This places a tremendous strain on the relationship. We are each individuals, even in a relationship, and you have to discover what your interests are. I often hear the complaint from couples – "He/She doesn't do anything." You may need to accept that that is your partner's choice, but don't expect them to change. We do learn from each other.

(2) Bring out the best qualities in a partner. Remember, this is healthy love.

(3) They accept endings.

(4) They experience openness to change and exploration.

Schaeffer writes in depth about what being open really entails. Regarding the ability to accept endings, she writes:

"The death of a relationship is painful, but mature people have enough respect for themselves and their partners to cope when love is over. Mature people know how to let go of an unsalvageable relationship, just as they are able to survive crises in a healthy one. Even in their grief, they do not doubt they will love again someday. We can survive pain, though there's no denying its power over us. I've witnessed strong people crumble into tears when they are sexually betrayed by a lover, even when they may have themselves cheated on their partners…

In order not to lose such vital openness, a wounded lover must transcend the natural tendency to react with anger, fear and panic. 'I'll get him; I'll get her.' We have the power to surmount pain and grief, and to once again forgive and love. It sounds difficult, and it is. It takes one's spiritual side to overcome the strong, self-destructive rule of pain and anger. In time, mature people are able to accept reality, even when it hurts, and to move on to the next chapter in their lives. They face up to the problems and sorrows in the most rational, healthy way, even though it isn't easy."

Have you ever had a similar experience? I did. I knew someone over twenty years ago who wanted to marry me. We were very good friends at one time, but we could never sustain a long term romantic relationship because our lives were headed in different directions. We expressed that we would always love one another and try to stay friends, acknowledging what we were grateful for. What more can you ask for when you're open and you're honest? We both cried at different times and the healing we experienced was different for each of us. I believe this interaction is what Schaeffer implied – that we can accept the change that comes about, even if we don't want it or like it. That's the part in us that owns up to being honest about our feelings, rather than being in denial or lying to ourselves or others. That only makes it worse. More qualities of those in healthy relationships include:

Experiencing more openness to change and explore.
Inviting growth in the other partner.
Experiencing true emotional intimacy vs. sexual intimacy.
Feeling the freedom to honestly ask for what you want.
Experience giving and receiving in the same way.
Not attempting to change or control the other person.
Encouraging self-sufficiency in their partner.
Accepting your own limitations and those of your partners.
Accepting commitment.
Having high self-esteem.
Trusting the memory of the beloved; not being afraid to be alone.
Expressing feelings spontaneously.
Welcoming closeness and risking vulnerability. (How can you be in a relationship without being vulnerable? It's not possible.)

Caring with detachment.
Affirming quality and personal power of self and partner.
Not seeking unconditional love.

I have come to really accept the statement "THEY DO NOT SEEK UNCONDITIONAL LOVE:"

"In a good love relationship, we no longer crave unconditional love from our partners...because you give it. The only time we needed that kind of care was in the first eighteen months of our lives. We no longer need it from others because we can grant it to ourselves."

This is a powerful concept; unconditionally loving yourself. How can you expect someone else to give to you what you can't give to yourself?

"Unconditional love is a state of being that comes from within us. It's not the other way around."

Growing up, though, you may have believed it was the other way around. Do this for me and I'll love you. Be a good girl. Be a good boy, or you won't be loved. You'll be punished.

"The paradox is that when we stop looking for unconditional love, we are often surprised to find someone loving us just that way. Perhaps it is because experiencing ourselves as unconditional love, we now give the safety that invites another to share their love."

Isn't that what it's all about – creating safety? Do you create safety in your life? How do you know when to trust yourself and ask for what you need, whether it's with your employer, friend, romantic partner or anyone? One easy clue is recognizing when you're feeling uncomfortable and sharing what that is about. Know the difference between being in love and living in love. Most people would like to live in love, although it's difficult to remain in this state all the time. The following comments were given in a course on Love:

"It's easy for women to discuss and share their pain with a man. It is in our relationship with our men, and our main man in life is our father. We found out that if we don't have that relationship with our father, that carries on with our marriages and our whole life."

"In my case, personally, my first marriage was not a very good one, and I did not have a very good relationship – with no communication at all, but I did have it with my father...My father was a doctor, so we always communicated very well. I don't know how I attracted that person. I grew tremendously in that relationship. I did find out that I didn't have to depend on him for me to be happy; or that I didn't have to be his support, which I did for many years. I was the overfunctioning person in the family. I really grew spiritually."

"I found that we didn't have a spiritual relationship in any way, and that's what I wanted in my life. I had to break out of that relationship, and I did. I walked away myself. Then I went into healing. I found Unity, Science of Mind, all the books and all the therapy. I put myself through it."

"In growing with the energy nourishing me, learning who I was...and what I really like in life. I was lost completely. I got married very young to this individual. I was seventeen when I got married...thinking I'm in love. That's what it is exactly; falling in love. Leaving that place – I think that was the most wonderful experience of my life. Yes, I think that is my lesson and I'm very grateful to him for all that I've learned."

"We have a beautiful daughter, and I've always thanked God for her. So, today, I'm happily married, and I think the reason that we discussed this was that maybe the key of finding the right relationship, the relationship that I had with my father, when I had respect and honor and wonderful values, was because I made the choice of growing and healing myself. Finding love for me – taking care of myself – and respecting myself – I found that relationship."

"The one question we grappled with was – why do men stop making love to their wives? My husband ran around on me for years. I felt that he did that because he could not get close to me. So, then, sex, for him, became a way for getting close to women. But it was not close, it was just sex; yes – after twenty-five years. We never discussed it. He told me about the affairs, and how many there were, and, you know, my father also had affairs. So my mother allowed it and so did I. It was familiar, and I convinced myself it didn't matter that much – that I had children. Then I put my emotional life in my children. But I still made it on my own with other things. When he would go out of town – he was very discreet, so I never knew, but I knew. So the kids and I would party when he went out of town.

We'd go buy steaks and strawberry shortcake and ice cream and he was very conservative. So I made the best of a bad situation."

In an article I wrote about John Gray's book, <u>What Your Mother Couldn't Tell You And Your Father Didn't Know</u>, I suggest the secret that many families lived with for centuries is that of women being emotionally abused by their husbands. Originally sanctioned in early European lifestyles, it was more or less accepted, if not tolerated, that men have mistresses. Is it any wonder that modern day couples lack the ability to share their feelings and communicate about issues that weren't dealt with for centuries? Many sense the complex undercurrent present in our experiences with ourselves, the opposite sex, and with each other. We are the ones who are in the process of creating and redefining just what our relationships might look like in the future.

As one man stated in a former domestic violence group,

"I believe our relationships in the future won't contain the violence we've lived with for hundreds of years because of the new information we are learning about with regards to nonviolent relationships and communication."

If you can understand what you're unhappy about in your marital relationship, you won't have to go outside of it to resolve the problems. You may need professional help, but having affairs won't make things better. It may appear to improve your self-esteem, but you're still going to have to face your partner and come to some decisions. Very often, the person that you end up having the affair with is only a catalyst in your process of self growth. Equally important is knowing the cultural traditions we come out of. As stated earlier, while men in Europe had mistresses, men in China had concubines.

The sexual revolution caused women to go out and repeat male behavior. They thought – I can do the same thing. Then we had irresponsible sex, causing sexually-transmitted diseases. Tit-for-tat didn't work; it never does. Ultimately, we are all accountable for our own behavior. Yes, we're changing as a species, as a culture, and in the final analysis, as human beings. It's exciting and scary to be part of this change. Our stories create our lives. If you don't like the picture, you can change it, and the cost is usually a great emotional upheaval. Learning to live without pain and emotional distress would create a wonderful life.

The next question in the course asks, "To what extent do you perceive qualities in your partner that strongly remind you of those in your parents?" One answer was:

"I have Harville Hendrix to thank for that. Getting the Love You Want is the book I was referring to. It was actually after my divorce that I realized (after reading the book), how many qualities my ex-wife was manifesting that I related to about my mother. It was also very interesting, on reflection, that probably the qualities were more on the negative side than they were on the positive, which relates exactly to what Harville Hendrix talks about – when you actually attach yourself to somebody in a difficult relationship. It reminds you of your mother or father, whose qualities, both negative and positive, you are, in a sense, trying to regain or re-establish, particularly if you've had a long break from being close to your parents.

...I found initially I was turning a blind eye to the negative qualities, and also turning a blind eye to her development as a human being, or lack of development as a human being...In fact, ...I'm remembering the qualities that she manifested in her family life, either seeking or rejecting in the marriage with me. It's very much the case that you do go back to your parents as a starting point. It's the only reference point that you have from day one, and if they are ineffective, then, until you understand them and learn to go beyond them, you remain ineffective in relationships.

And that was what was happening, because I could see that we reached – the great gift that she has given me is to realize that, number one, you can't change a person unless they want to change; and, number two, don't try to."

Another participant states:

"We spoke of how you define love. The three of us came to an agreement that it's really self-love and getting to that is an understanding of your own soul...Finding that place, finding that within, is important...whether it's God, Prana, Brahma, Great Spirit, or whatever...When you love yourself, you give out love or energy that others become attracted to, and then you can be loved by others.

In the other question – what is the difference between being in love and living in love – once again, we come to an assessment of feeling that being in love is learning to love yourself…It is okay to be in love with yourself. Sometimes, I have to tell people I'm number one. I have to be number one. Many times, I wasn't, but if I can't be number one, if I can't love number one, I can't love number two. It's not possible, one and one in that instance doesn't work.

The other thing that popped out for me (only due to some experiences many years ago), is the question – do men experience shame for their desires to be nurtured by a woman? And I'll leave out mommy. I'm not into that. It's only been within the last couple of years that I have come to terms with being at war, not only with myself, but at war. I'm an ex-Navy Seal. Going into the military at the young age of eighteen, with a year of college behind me, you don't ask the sergeant when you're in a fox hole and he says – "duck" – you don't say why. I was the corpsman, so doc got protected at all costs. It was a live-in world that I lived in for a while. You had to shut things out. You had to build up a wall, and it's the old prophecy of forgetting to drain the swamp and up to your butt in alligators, I think it was – or something to that effect.

Another gentleman told me one day that when we build walls, it's like a castle tower and you're up to your eyes and armpits in defecation, when the easiest thing is just to pull a block from out of the bottom row and let it drain. Well, we all forgot that. In some of my days, that shell was the only thing that kept me alive. They teach you how to do things on instinct in the military. Sometimes, our fathers teach us to do that as well. We forget our feminine side, which we do have, and it takes a hammer and a chisel for a number of years to get through that and find the Goddess within.

"Over the past couple of years, I've been very fortunate to be a part of a Native American group out in Arizona. I have found that being out there in nature has taught me many things, not only to accept myself as being alone in this world and do for yourself, but to find that Goddess within because…finding that balance of emotional, physical, mental, spiritual, south, west, north and east…if you can't do that…you can't find your center."

Nature teaches us about ourselves. If you've ever gone into a park and observed nature, including animals and the movement of trees, this very much reflects a part of who we are; our connection to the earth. Our human side is incomplete without recognizing our spiritual nature and its connection to the earth. That which is unspoken can be heard within every sound.

Another participant chose the question – do men's experiences make it difficult for them to share pain with a woman? She states:

"Speaking from a woman's point of view, we're trying to suppose and assume how that works for a man. From my own personal experience, very recently being involved with a man who was unable to share a lot of himself because of his previous experiences, I say that yes, that is a true statement about men. And I only base it on my own personal experience.

Then, the man in our group said that society as a whole prepares men to be less willing to share their pain, that they must be more stoic and conservative about their feelings and emotions in letting them out. He expressed that....being unwilling to share his emotions as far as being able to cry or being able to express joy at times, having been conditioned that that's not okay for a man. I suppose that I probably felt that, myself, personally, in relating to men that, yes, its a conditioned way of behaviour, but to hear it from a man is a confirmation actually, and it makes it more understandable, as a woman - hearing it from a man."

This subject is always of interest. At every conference I've attended, the issue of gender and relationship always comes up. The majority of the people who attend are female. Today, however, more men are willing to open up, share, learn, grow, and receive. Women are also learning to embrace that which might be called masculine, such as the traits of willfulness, courage, and strength. We need to accept that all traits represent a combination of both the masculine and feminine.

Clearly defining these qualities helps us discover more about our lives and our journey. This chapter explores different literature as a way of understanding ourselves better. In exploring this subject of love, it is important that we process, experience, and work on our issues. The other half is knowing the theory behind behavior. Thus, the intellect interprets the meaning of what people say about love while you seek to interpret it through your own intuition and thereby make sense of your dreams. The greater your awareness, the greater is your ability to understand yourself and others.

To experience the universal level of love in your life that Deepak Chopra spoke about is to awaken to the spiritual essence found in the intent of love itself. We all seek to be loved on a personal level, which is natural. Yet, it is the one area that we have the most challenges with. As previously stated, it is much easier to love someone than it is to live with them. Living requires work and most people are lazy and don't want to work…then the love goes out the window (Reversal of Fortune)

The three areas identified as love in the Greek language are found in the family, brotherly love, and in the expression of physical love, (Eros). Deepak advises: "When you feel love, act on it. Speak your heart. Be truthful. Remain open." What does he mean? Very often, we go through life wishing we had said something when we didn't; or we may regret not having taken action – doing nothing. When you are conscious of what your intent is in your communication with another person, it fosters openness. This doesn't imply that the other person will give you the answer you want. Rather, being open to what that person has to say will give you necessary information to help you make decisions along the way.

This helps us to grow in relationship. When we look at emotional pain, we can view it as a great teacher. We have even been admonished with the idea of "No pain/No gain." What is interesting, however, is that most people don't seem to learn a lesson without pain. Many spiritual teachings suggest that we can overcome pain. The dichotomy is, that if we don't learn the lesson, we are doomed to repeat it over and over. So the next time you experience hurt or wonder why you're in a situation you don't like, ask yourself if you've ever gone through this before, and decide to stop hurting yourself as soon as possible.

Perhaps the various spiritual teachings remind us that we don't have to go through repetitive experiences because we only need to get the lesson once. Life is a wonderful teacher, even if we don't like the message. It has a great way of presenting lessons until we get it.

Does this make sense to you? We all know the risks involved in loving another person. You open up your whole being and expose yourself. You choose to take the risk to practice love as a conscious effort - it's not mindless. This kind of love is applicable to all relationships – familial, romantic, and platonic.

It amazes me that so many families are estranged from each other. The amount of pain that people go through is often overwhelming when they cut themselves off from their brothers, sisters, fathers and mothers. The reasons for their behavior are many. One of the major causes is due to abuse; mental, verbal, emotional, and physical. It is said that while you can choose your friends, some believe that you also choose the family you're born into. Most people don't think they choose their families. However, if we look at the experience as a lesson, then we can see what our mother, father, sister or brother is teaching us. You decide what you can accept. You may get to the place where you say to yourself, "I don't need this behavior anymore," and because you can only change yourself, not another, you know what you have to do even if it isn't easy.

Relationships are more difficult if you and your partner don't share a similar spiritual outlook. You can learn a lot by observing other relationships. Judging doesn't work. The goal is to assess what you can accept and what you can't, so you can do what you need to in order to free yourself from unhappiness. Dr. Brad Blanton states,

"Lying kills people. The kind of lying that is most deadly is withholding, or keeping back information from someone we think would be affected by it. Psychological illness of the severest kind is the result of this kind of lying. Psychological healing is possible only with the freedom that comes from not hiding anymore."

The great Persian poet, Rumi, offers the idea that the blessing of "falling in love" comes from Spirit, but it can be blocked by the ego. It's also interesting that Eric Butterworth, in his book, <u>Spiritual Economics</u>, wrote about not letting yourself "fall in love," but to "rise in love." Butterworth suggests the following about the traditional institution of marriage:

"Rather than commit your lives until death do you part, commit your lives one day at a time and see what tomorrow will produce as you live in the present moment."

Another article written by Leslie Camp, entitled "Sharing Life's Journey – Creating and Keeping Healthy Relationships," suggests:

"Conscious relationships today are very different from the relationships we experienced and our parents experienced. Instead of mating, we're partnering. Instead of child-rearing, we're co-parenting. Instead of fighting and flighting, we're using our conflicts in relationships to heal childhood wounds. The biggest problem in relationships is that people give their power away to maintain the relationship. They walk on eggshells so that the relationship survives. It's a myth that this works at all. And we've seen that over the years, with the current awareness of the disease of addiction."

ADDICTIONS — OUT OF CONTROL

I'm not just speaking about the traditional addictions of alcohol or drugs. I'm speaking about gambling, sex, eating, etc. – all the multitudes of addictions to cover up our pain. Our challenges ask us to rise above the limited identification of our egos and move into a new way of life. Camp says, "Indeed, the development of one's magnificence is what makes a person attractive." Yet, most of us were brought up with messages contrary to this idea. Fairy tales in childhood told us that men were encouraged to rescue women, or, "the princess" would come along and kiss the frog to turn him into a prince, or perhaps we believed the woman would be swept away by the prince, or the knight in shining armor would come along on a white steed and off we'd go into the sunset, happily ever after. What have we found out? Is it all a myth? Does it really work?

I know it gets tiring to hear that you have to become a whole person, but what's the choice in not progressing? The answer is found in math, a perfect science. One times one equals one. ($1 \times 1 = 1$) A whole person times a whole person equals a whole relationship. When you have less than that, you have a half times a half, diminishing it into a quarter. ($1/2 \times 1/2 = 1/4$) Is it okay? Sure. The question you need to ask yourself is – are you happy? Camp asks,

"Would I want this person to be the father or mother of my children?" She indicates that the answer is a good barometer to check out when you're getting to know someone, if you're in that stage. She continues, "I think the purpose of relationships is to heal, and it's important to be aware that's what the other person is doing in your life."

Imagine what wounds the people in your life are helping you to heal. Let them know what it is that you want them to know. Again, ask for what you need, validate yourself. You may find that when you ask another for what you need, you may not get it. This response lets you know that the person is either not capable of giving you what you need, or you need to give it to yourself. Perhaps you need to look elsewhere. Don't limit yourself. Camp cautions, "It's different than being with someone to fill the hole." Most of us were taught to fill the emptiness with anything so we wouldn't have to feel our pain or loneliness. Progress will be made in this century through communication which will ease the struggle.

Most of us go through life terrified of "abandonment." Yet, as Phil Donahue pointed out in his video on *Nature Versus Nurture*, throughout our lives we want to ensure that someone will always be there for us. From the time we're first crawling around on all fours, we keep turning around to make sure someone's back there. Another challenge is knowing that we can take care of ourselves even if no one else is there. However, the ultimate test is knowing that one day we will leave these bodies, and return to that which we came from. No matter how much we love another, we are always being taught or asked to let go at some level, because none of us will stay like this forever. I believe that making peace with this truth and honoring it will help us live from a more sacred place.

RELATIONSHIPS

Intimate relationships show us more clearly and deeply who we are. Relationships may be confronting in the sense that you have to face yourself, not only the other. On a deep level, most of us need some contact, a sense of sharing our life's journey with someone. I take issue with the concept in <u>The Course in Miracles</u> which suggests that there are no "special relationships." If this was true, ask yourself if you'd have the energy to maintain the kind of intensity it takes to have a "special relationship" with all the people in your life. The reality is, with only twenty four hours in a day, stop and consider your own personal chores, tasks, work and any other activities that are scheduled into that time period. To have more than one intimate relationship simply burns you out. How many people can you be intimately connected with? I don't mean sexually. When I say "intimately," I'm referring to "emotional intimacy." There are special "sacred relationships." You may love everyone universally, but you don't necessarily like everyone's personality, and that's okay, too. Chopra said,

"You never receive more love than you are prepared to receive. You cannot give more love than you have to give. The love reflected from another person has a source in your own heart. Out of our loneliness, all of us seek a source of love that will fill up the lack that we have inside."

This is exactly what happens, folks – no more and no less. The path to love begins when you realize that separation – that loneliness and the pain of isolation – are "real." Yes, they are real – why? Because you are human. Chopra says, "Not many people want to face this fact; therefore, they resign themselves to a sadly constricted amount of love." Many people have told me that their partners are not emotionally supportive of them, and what they do is they go outside of the relationship for their emotional support, which is not to say that this is wrong. What I've heard from "happily connected people" is that they trust their partners as their friends, and they can share any truth with them without the fear of being judged. The idea of having friends outside of that system is not negative at all; it's a matter of how much you share and what you share with whom.

Chopra states:

"Duality has always been an illusion. There is no one out there waiting there for you. There is only you and the love you bring to yourself. In Spirit, you are united with all other souls, and the only purpose of separation is for you to rejoin that unity."

Imagine that for a moment. I know it's hard to understand. When he says there's no one out there waiting for you, it suggests to me that we bring ourselves into any situation. We are the ones who add meaning to our lives. Thus, as we become more aware of who we are and what we want, we won't settle for less. Thus, the byproduct is we learn from one another. It's the same thing as knowing where to go when your tooth is bothering you. You go to a dentist. It's really not that difficult, and yet we make it so hard. I often wonder how my grandparents and parents generation chose to stay together over many years with many sacrifices. You have to wonder what has happened.

The concept of <u>Soulful Love: The Search For The Self</u> contains the idea that there may be more than one partner or one mate for everyone in this lifetime. I've also known men and women who, upon losing a long-term spouse to death, never remarry. Some say they never met anyone they wanted to be with. They are content and have a full life. Others look to fill the void.

Chopra says, "The path to love always opens unexpectedly." (When you least expect it, it happens.) "Actually, there is nothing but love once we are ready to accept it." If you're already in a relationship and your partner is not loving that day, what do you give your partner? Love and space. Kahlil Gibran said "Let there be spaces in your togetherness." If you need to have fifteen minutes, a half hour, or a half day for down time, take it. When you walk in the door at night, tell your partner "I need some alone time." Everyone needs time to themselves. Don't see your "alone" time as a separation. See it as a healthy space in your togetherness, be intrigued by your partner but recognize that a certain level of maturity and trust are necessary.

Have you ever noticed in a restaurant if couples talk to each other? Silence can be golden. Yet, it also can be deafening. What do you bring to the table? In Chopra's chapter on "The Path," he writes:

"In the west, what we generally call love is a feeling, not a power. When love and Spirit are brought together, their power can accomplish anything. Then love, power and Spirit are one. We do not accept the power love can create inside us and, therefore, turn our backs on our Divine status."

Right! Mere mortals going through suffering and pain. He continues, "In India and in the east, every person is Divine, but not everyone recognizes it. What is the path?" You may not agree with him. I really do. Remember, that's okay, because we agree to disagree. He says, "The most valuable thing you can bring into any relationship is your spiritual potential." Many people went into relationships based on lust and physical attraction. Eventually, the endorphins wear off and you get bored, want to switch partners, and you say, "This isn't exciting anymore." Staying in a purposeful relationship is much more than sexual attraction, although our sexuality is a gift and plays an important role in the relationship.

Chopra continues,

"When you begin to live your love story – that's being who you are at the deepest level – your spiritual potential is the seed for your growth in love. The unfolding of spiritual potential has been the chief principle of all the great seers, prophets and masters. Theirs was a carefully charted quest for the Self, a far cry from our notion of love as a messy, emotional love affair."

Yet, we are bombarded with messy, emotional love affairs in the media, our own lives, and the lives of our best friends and family members. Chopra believes, "The goal of the path is to transform your awareness from separation to unity. In unity, we perceive only love, express only love and we are only love. "We all know this is not an easy task. Try living in a state of love twenty-four hours a day – well, sixteen if you're sleeping eight hours! Remember, though, that you do have a choice to honor all the experiences that come into your life – even the most challenging ones.

Jungian psychology has defined for us the anima and the animus – the masculine and the feminine. Part of Anais Nin's philosophy over half a century ago allowed us to develop our so-called masculine qualities in a female form, and similarly our female qualities in a male form. Why? Because the idea of being compassionate, willful, strong, gentle, and nurturing are attributes that are part of both sexes. It becomes a sexless quality, or androgynous as she called it. For thousands of years, our culture, based on patriarchy, has taught us differently.

That's why we are now struggling with the ability to co-parent and co-partner versus the traditional model of power, domination and control. (PDC)

Chopra sees the path of love as a way in which two people can escape the trap of separation and suffering. Yet, in our most intimate relationships, many people do suffer. In fact, many espouse they'd rather be alone and be lonely than to be with someone and be lonely. Perhaps you have known the immense suffering of being with someone you love who's not there for you. The question has been asked, why go through the suffering? There are many answers, some of which are codependency, addiction, habit and fear. Yet Chopra insists that,

"The freshness of life is love and nothing else. When two people can grow into that knowledge, the promise of lasting happiness becomes real. The question arises. Well, why should I choose a path at all? Relationship, with or without romantic love, has existed for a long time. Being in love with another hasn't required making any conscious spiritual choice other than, perhaps, go to the same church, or what faith to raise your children in. Therefore, it's worth asking how this is actually achieved. And whether we can ever attain security without embarking upon a spiritual journey."

So, ask yourself, do you think it's possible to be in a relationship with someone (even with yourself) without having a sense of spiritual awareness or being on a spiritual journey together? Of course it's possible. It does happen. As a matter of fact, perhaps you've experienced it or maybe you know someone else who has had this kind of relationship. It is certainly purposeful when two minds are on a similar path. Have you experienced more frustration without having a common purpose? This idea does not imply that there's no meaning between two people who aren't conscious of why they've come together. However, it does suggest that there's a deeper meaning if you can share your feelings with someone on a very soulful level. Chopra believes that level goes beyond pleasure. He states:

"It is all important to found our happiness upon a basis that doesn't change. The solution is to find a source of happiness beyond pleasure. If you took away the pleasant feelings associated with it, most people would be hard pressed to define the experience of love. But love has the power to heal, to reveal Divine essence, to restore faith in your own being, to bring harmony to all levels of existence.

And all these effects lie far beyond feelings. They are tangible results based on Spirit. Fortunately, for all that love is abstract, scientific research reveals that it is as dramatic and potent as medicine, both when it is present and both when it is withdrawn. Do you feel loved? You are more likely to recover than those who do not.

In patients who have been diagnosed terminally ill, the correlation between recovery and this response is higher than for any category, including any previous physical status."

When you feel emotionally hurt, it is usually because you have trusted and given your power over to another, even if that trust wasn't warranted in the first place. Being hurt is usually a matter of power. This doesn't mean that I have given my power over to another to hurt me. Rather, I have come to understand what the lesson is behind the hurt and the pain. Chopra says, "the powerless are in no position to offend or antagonize the powerful." This reality was brought home to us on the playground a long time ago. It is a old holdover habit; trying to be nice. Being nice, we expect niceness in return. By placating someone who threatens us, we hope to ward off their aggression. In the name of being hurt, we stay in a defensive posture. You can't come from love when you're defensive. I've always encouraged clients to speak their truth without needing to be defensive. There is no need to walk on eggshells. Walking on eggshells keeps you in a state of fear and trepidation. It prevents you from really actualizing who you are as a person.

In the last decade, having worked in the field of domestic violence, I can say that it's a pretty sad state of affairs out there. The amount of people who abuse power is frightening. It's not only physical power and threats, but the emotional power of verbal threats and psychological blackmail which drains our spirit. Let's not forget to mention that property damage is also a violation. We had to create laws which mandate that you do not have the right to hurt another human being. I believe there was a similar law over 5000 years ago "Thou shalt not kill, steal, etc." Sound familiar?

The recurring theme is to be aware of what happens to you and any other people you are involved with any time there is a power imbalance. There will never be a win-win situation when people vie for power. All relationships, be they between men and women, parents and children, employer and employee or those who would be considered advantageous over the disadvantaged, or the economic disparity between rich over poor, all portray power plays.

It's up to each one of us to choose a more respectful environment where we learn to speak from the heart. No matter how much or how little money you have, no matter what your background, we can all learn the native American practice of "walking our talk and talking our walk." No one else has power over you except you, yourself and your Creator. You might be thinking to yourself, "Why did I ever give my power away in the first place?" One theory is that we were never taught to esteem ourselves. If you're never taught to love yourself unconditionally, what ends up happening is that you look for other people to validate who you are. Then you get disappointed when they can't or won't do it. But guess what? Very often they don't know how to validate others, especially if they never received any validation themselves.

The whole idea in having healthier relationships is learning to love on a more conscious level. When couples come to me for counseling, I ask them, "have you done everything possible to try to heal the wounds in your relationship?" Some of them say "yes." Some of them say "no." The opportunity, is for them to choose to work through their conflicts. It is wise to do all you can before you determine that it would be best for both of you to separate. Your thinking changes throughout the course of a lifetime. No matter how many years you are together, if you don't keep abreast of the individual changes you make, you won't know each other anymore.

That's why Marriage Encounter and other nationally offered workshops are so helpful. Everyone needs healing in their relationships. In an article I wrote entitled "Beyond Oppression – Transforming Destructive Conflict," my friend, Larry Kaiden, a psychologist, states:

"The responsibility for change lies in each of us taking responsibility for our prejudices and our points of view and getting away from the idea that...we are right and the others are wrong. Awareness and acknowledgment are the roads to resolution. What blocks us from resolution is fear. The answers to change and for change lie in our own willingness to change."

Pain often causes us to change at the deepest core. Pain teaches us what we don't want. Dr. Debra DuNann Winter also speaks about power imbalances in relationships, availability, abandonment, and alienation. Her article, "<u>Boys Will Be Boys.</u>" speaks to this problem. In Webster's New Collegiate Dictionary, the word 'patriarchy' is defined as 'a social organization marked by the supremacy of the father and the clan of the family.' The task of recreating relationship amongst the sexes requires that we each rethink what role equality plays.

Much has been said and is probably overstated by now about the patriarchal system. However, the reason there is so much discussion about this subject is because of the massive confusion we are experiencing today. A model that was based on control and power can no longer function in our society. The inter-generational patterns of dysfunctional behavior have been passed on throughout the ages. Many men abandoned relationships and women were forced to work to fend for themselves and provide for their children. To explain what happened is to understand why and how women really suffered. Having no husband to support her, not being able to survive without skills to take care of herself or her children, the welfare system was born. Any class in sociology today covers this history.

The ideas in <u>Soulful Love – The Search for Self</u> explore these themes in depth. No matter how much we love another human being, we still have to love and care for ourselves. We're always being reminded of this. Whether or not we are being forced to change in this new century, we must learn how to do relationships, don't we? Is it any wonder that the struggle for self-esteem is a constant challenge? Being in a personal relationship can be very threatening because many women and men are no longer willing to put up with the mediocrity and dishonesty that our forebears lived with. The belief that they had no other choice but to suffer is being replaced by another model which says you don't have to suffer. What a revelation!

We are the building blocks for creating healthy relationships in our own lives and for leaving a new legacy for our children and grandchildren. In an article by Judith Sherman and James Sinowski, they wrote,

"Women and men are the only building blocks we have to form and transform society, yet our schools do little or nothing to prepare boys and girls to have the skills to communicate with one another with respect and understanding for their differences. We need to rethink what is required before a couple is granted permission to receive a marriage license and procreate. Mandatory classes dealing with how to negotiate mutually satisfying conflict resolution should be a part of every curriculum."

Wouldn't you agree? We learn how to read and write, but we are not taught how to communicate. It's sad to say that even though there are many wonderful programs being implemented in schools and mental health facilities, many of them fall by the wayside due to lack of funding or priorities being in the wrong place. For example, it would be much easier to train people already on-the-job in conflict resolution and mediation skills versus hiring a consultant that could only visit a location once a month.

What does this suggest? History repeats itself. These programs need to be consistent and continuous. Curriculum of all kinds, now in elementary, middle schools and universities, doesn't imply that everyone adapts to the changes recommended. It will take at least another two decades before we observe change at a deeper level. You may start to notice that your children will make more conscious, different choices than before. Your grandchildren will also be taught to rethink things and do them differently. Why? Because many of these rules that previous generations practiced no longer work.

If we think about the people who created the Declaration of Independence and their thoughts on freedom, we are still a far cry from that vision. Yet, part of the dichotomy in the path to love is learning to live in freedom and what this implies is your ability to make healthy choices. Additionally, you cannot deny responsibility for those choices. True freedom is really a double-edged sword. You have to know how to use it wisely or you will get hurt.

We often want immediate answers to questions. Your answers may not come when you want them to. We learn to live in the moment; one day at a time. Yogananda suggested that we should live each moment completely and the future would take care of itself. A motto that works for me frequently is "When in doubt, do without."

It means if you can't make a decision, don't. Not making a decision is a decision and when it's time for you to know something, you will. Everything falls into place in its own timing. That's the next step you take. What good would it do to know about something if you're not ready to act on it? Think about that the next time you are really impatient, and ask, "What is it that I need to know that will help me now?" If you can practice this thinking one day at a time, you may notice that your steps will be guided in the best way possible. It all works out one way or the other. Metaphysical laws suggest "If not this, something better!"

Realize that you don't always need all the answers. Your ego may not know what's best, but your spirit usually does. It doesn't lie to you. The same is true for the book <u>The Path to Love</u>. It's about living in a spiritual framework. Many wonder what it means to be spiritual. My definition is that we are in a conscious state of awareness about what we say, why we say it and how we say it. Do I do this all the time? No. I'm still learning! We all get opportunities to experience this because we have to learn to think differently if we are to survive. However, we're all in this together and the goal is not just to survive, but to enjoy the gift of life.

One of the ways we learn is by incorporating knowledge into a practical application of it. Chopra suggests that "Being hurt is usually a matter of power." Define the word "hurt?" Do we hurt because we don't understand why people do what they do? It is critical to know that you're not responsible for other people's behavior. The only person's behavior we are responsible for is our own. It is a true adage that you can't change anyone. Yet, you owe it to yourself to be honest.

The co-dependent's Serenity prayer states: "God help me to accept that the only person I can change is myself and to know the difference." Chopra says,

"The absence of love is as devastating as it is beneficial. The word love applies to many situations, from intimate affection to abuse, to dependency to control, from lust to ecstasy. Asking if someone feels loved is unreliable. We feel love. We feel numb and traumatized by our love stories. Once it has grown to fullness, a love that is based on Spirit has no fear of being wounded. Imperfect forms of love are much more vulnerable. Almost everyone has asked for love and received rejection instead.

We have taken our frail self-images into situations where they got battered, where hope died and our worst imaginings came true. The effect of rejection, failure, humiliation and other traumas is to numb one's feelings. However, love requires sensitivity. It must have openness. Whatever has numbed you makes it much harder for you to feel love. Therefore, people who are numb at the emotional level can't recreate love stories. And part of that is meant to take time to heal."

Processes of growth take us through the pain so we can become open to love again. You can't run away from your feelings, however, you must learn to embrace them and verbalize them to move through difficult emotional terrains. "To value yourself is to love yourself. It is really from here that your love from others comes." What is known as a mid-life crisis, for both men and women is really a re-evaluation of what's important for them at this stage of growth. Although we have traditional ideas where men feel their sexuality is ebbing away and they use that to explore other options, women may feel the same or suffer the empty nest syndrome. Judith Viorst, the author of <u>Necessary Losses</u> points out that through all the phases in our lives, we must grow through our losses.

A woman who had been married for over 30 years was divorced by her husband who ended up dating a woman six years older than their daughter. This woman who always portrayed an image of "total self-esteem," gained 50 pounds in eighteen months, required knee surgery, walked with a limp and had to get bifocals. She aged so rapidly in that short time and giving over all of her power to her husband over the years, rendered her helpless in the end. When someone you love leaves you, it's true that you will most likely be devastated. However, if you give your power over to that person to determine your happiness for the rest of your life, you will be miserable. I don't think that's our love story or how our lives are meant to be.

Chopra states,

"When you are faced with a losing enterprise, it's only natural to give up naturally. When you're young, all of us can pursue a certain amount of hope and optimism backed up by energy. It takes energy to carry out any passion. For some people, the energy has run out. They say they have no time for love. They feel that they do not need it in their lives. What we are actually experiencing then is the lack of energy, the loss of enthusiasm that follows repeated failure. But energy is a self-renewing commodity, like water from a spring it is not diminished by what you take away. People who cannot live their love stories have not found a way to renew their energy to tap into their source of passion."

How would your perspective change if you knew the source of your passion?

Robert Muller, the former chancellor of the United Nations, wrote many books, amongst them was <u>Most of All They Taught Me Happiness</u>. He also wrote a universal <u>World Core Curriculum</u> adaptable for all schools. Its basic premise is founded on three questions: What is my purpose; why am I here and where am I going? Imagine if your relationships were based on that! Each of you knows your purpose, where you're headed; and why you are living. The answers to these questions can only lead to clarity and help you to understand the larger picture; that your individual life has meaning and there is some worthwhile contribution you can make.

The late Ken Keyes, wrote <u>A Conscious Person's Guide to Loving Relationships</u>. One of his major contributions taught us to "uplevel" our "addictions" to preferences. This means to state what you need, what you prefer, and what you choose. People who are addicted to other people, substances or circumstances can't take control over their own lives. Consequently, it is much healthier to be interdependent versus codependent. The choice is up to you. There are many qualified therapists and programs you can choose from to change your life and your behavior.

BIOLOGICAL INSTINCTS

The human body is wired to produce certain chemicals. One chemical produced by the human brain, known as phenylethylamine, is also called the "cuddle chemical." You feel so good when you are loved and loving. You enjoy being held and caressed. In a <u>Time</u>

Magazine article entitled The Right Chemistry, the author, Anastasia Toufexis suggests that

"Love is a natural high... but phenylethylamine highs don't last forever, a fact that lends support to arguments that passionate romantic love is short lived. As with any amphetamine, the body builds up a tolerance to PEA; thus it takes more and more of the substance to produce love's special kick. After two to three years, the body simply can't crank up the needed amount of PEA....

Fizzling chemicals spell the end of delirious passion; for many people that marks the end of the liaison as well. ...Still, many romances clearly endure beyond the first years. What accounts for that? Another set of chemicals, of course. The continued presence of a partner gradually steps up production in the brain of endorphins. Unlike the fizzy amphetamines, these are soothing substances. Natural pain killers, they give lovers a sense of security, peace and calm. That is one reason why it feels so horrible when we are abandoned or a lover dies.

As the article indicates, it is natural to regenerate loving feelings over a period of time. However, when life becomes overwhelmingly stressful, passion fades. With time and understanding, however, diminished feelings of love can grow to even greater depths of passion and love. ISD, Inhibited Sexual Desire, is a common disorder today. Many couples who are overly stressed because of jobs, children, extended families, illness, etc. lose interest in sex when they are overwhelmed by life's demands. I recommend that couples try and take at least one weekend every so often to get away without their children. Everyone needs to create spaces of togetherness in order to re-ignite the initial feelings they once had. Of course, even if you don't have children, it may be difficult to get away. In that case, take at least one day and evening a week to create some alone time for yourselves as a couple. If you don't devote enough time to appreciate each other, it is not hard to imagine why the relationship could falter and might disintegrate.

NEW IDEAS

Many peace conferences now focus on creating outer peaceful conditions by cultivating inner peace techniques. A group known as Individual and World Peace present their ideas on relationship issues. Some of these topics focus on withholding information, which is a form of seeking to control others, avoiding communication, denying when there is a problem and showing disrespect. In addition, when we judge each other we create mistrust, resistance, and confusion. As you learn to change needs into preferences, your relationships will start to mirror healthy interactions where you participate instead of withhold, and you communicate instead of avoid. Rather than become frustrated by your partner's evasiveness, imagine that they may not have an answer and might feel ashamed. Acceptance plays a critical role as well. By accepting each other's limitations, you automatically become supportive. You realize that you're not in charge of another's learning.

One of the great gifts my Mom gave to me during her ailment was when we were able to have a heart-to-heart dialogue. It was so healing for both of us to be able to cry together, comfort, hug, and support each other. It was wonderful to hear her say, "I think I finally have to learn to accept your limitations as well as accept my own." By acknowledging our humanity, we agree to learn from one another and in honoring our differences we can create a gentler world.

In John Bradshaw's books Healing the Shame That Binds You and The Family: A Revolutionary Way of Self-Discovery, he describes his theory on healing the "inner child." The theme is to return to the original times when your emotional wounds were first inflicted. The first five years of your life are the ages where you initially learn your behavior. If you can't remember that far back, and most people don't, then you may repeat negative patterns on into adolescence and adulthood. Hopefully, as you mature and grow emotionally, the people you attract into your life will be healthier. (Oh that it were so!) I know that you're wondering if this is true. However, I can guarantee that you'll no longer seek to repair the "old wounds" of your former relationships with your Mom, Dad, or other caregivers because of your new awareness. Your partner will no longer remind you of old behaviors. I fully support individuals to make peace with their past and I see it work out over and over again. As you improve your own mental health, you'll be able to emotionally support the people you care about to work through whatever issues they have to deal with. Supporting an individual is different than becoming overwhelmed by their problems.

In Ken Adams book, <u>Covert Incest</u>, he describes the problems that come from emotional incest which has nothing to do with sexuality. The theme relates to those parents who make their children their companions. They do this quite innocently because they don't know how to ask their partner for what they need or they fear rejection. They expect their children to be there for them emotionally and rescue them. This not only causes a lot of confusion; the child loses out on his or her childhood by being expected to fulfill the parents wishes. Consider what Kahlil Gibran wrote about children:

"Your children are not your children,
They are the sons and daughters of Life's longing for itself.
They come through you but not from you,
And though they are with you yet they belong not to you…
You may house their bodies but not their souls…"

Thus, we're inclined to ask ourselves questions. Especially when we read something like the above, it triggers us to ask even more questions. The reason is because as Rainier Maria Rilke reminds us, sometimes we have to learn to live with the questions. This allows us to feel our emotions and honor the questions that emerge from the soulful journey. Questions elicit responses so that we can try them on for size, in other words, see what feels right. One of our goals is to seek personal happiness and live a more peaceful, purposeful life.

What happens when the honeymoon dies? Well, how do you define the "honeymoon?" Does this mean that reality sets in? If passion is a phase of the honeymoon stage and you haven't developed communication skills, including openness and honesty with one another; then when the passion diminishes, you have nothing else to sustain the two of you. You can create an endless cycle of searching for passion over and over again, however, unless you find someone that is committed to resolving problems, then passion alone won't provide the needed skills for a harmonious relationship either in or out of the "honeymoon phase."

Some suggest that it's not necessary for passion to die. While there is a primary passion, if given the right circumstances and the right nurturing, that passion is there forever. One person states, "In fact, not only is it there forever, but I think it can be enhanced as time moves on." This being true, it is also helpful to understand the biological components of what makes you feel "in love or lust!"

You might want to look up various definitions of passion, write down your own definition of passion and then define what inspires you. Share your lists with each other and verbalize your thoughts, feelings and ideas without judgement. While this may be hard to do, if you can remove your ego from the exercise, the benefits will far exceed your egotism. The objective of the exercise is to bring you closer together in understanding what is important to each of you. Consider some of the following dialogues which were initiated in the class about relationships. See what you think.

"…About the question of what do you value about your role as a man or a woman… four women in our group…discussed that it changes all during our lives. Three of us are moms, and that for a while, for myself, it was being a mom. I kind of lost my role as me because I was always taking care of the kids, and now I'm looking for myself again in certain areas. I have to have my time for me and time for the children. And another thing was about being healthy first in your role to attract any other or anything else."

A man asked, "How controversial do you want me to be?" He states:

"I don't think men know where they're going, because a lot of the direction they used to take has actually been taken now by women. Particularly, the previous role of hunter/gatherer which then became the role of provider through the workplace, is now changing dramatically. Unfortunately, the male role – he cannot take on the female role, which is reproducer of offspring. So, if the male claims that his hunting and gathering has been taken from him by the female, he can't then jump in unless he becomes a house-husband, into taking over the role that women have had, which is producing a great deal of confusion for men."

His comments allude to the adjustments we are being forced to make due to step-parenting, re-marriage and learning to integrate step-families into our lives. Alan Cohen remarks,

"The notion of the nuclear family is a relatively new and unusual one on the planet, and it may not be the healthiest. For most of humanity's history, people lived in extended families, via tribal collective or polygamy. While most of us are not ready for polygamy, we have unintentionally created extended families through multiple marriages and step-relatives. I have a thirteen-year-old goddaughter who has three fathers - her biological father, her stepfather and her godfather."

Consider how more men are choosing to be the "nurturers" of their family. Some men want custody of their children and to share in the upbringing of their kids. Women, who were seen as the nurturers for many years, are now wanting the option to have a different role. Although men can't physically give birth to children, they are certainly invited to be a bigger part of the birthing process now-a-days. It takes two to create offspring; although that has changed due to test tube and genetic engineering. Men and women are being forced to learn new roles, both from each other and the world we live in.

In the last two decades, more people than ever before have been involved in empowering each other. This means that both sexes are able to take care of themselves financially and emotionally, improve their self-esteem and understand the purpose for their lives. While this is certainly not a wide spread concept throughout the world yet, many of the universal problems we face today are being explored on a daily basis by those who seek to live a different life. Think about some of these comments. One man states:

"If men no longer have to be the principal wage earner, this means a great deal of work between the sexes; they need to nurture each other, help each other, talk to each other, far more than they've ever done before in order to achieve a sense of balance that they both want to have. Because otherwise, the upheaval is going to be monumental. And my fear is, as Susan Jeffers points out, is that there can be a huge male backlash with regards to what's going on. And men will have to "regain" their power that they feel they've lost through losing the "power" in the workplace. The workplace is where men do their hunting, and because it's genetically inbred, we are now having the genes altered by the structure of the planet. Unless we deal with it, and unless we deal with it very quickly, there's going to be a huge explosion of male anger and it will be directed wholly against women. That will be terrible."

We've already witnessed the tremendous backlash which reared its ugly head in the form of domestic violence. Rather than yield to fear, we have to realize that there are enough people on our planet who care deeply enough to change what isn't working. Just as we saw the shift occur when the Berlin Wall came down, and Russia's attempts at (Glasnost) democracy, we also see evidence of other progressive changes. We don't have to go the route of "Armageddon" unless we choose to. Consider another idea:

"Perhaps the death of Princess Diana has, in a sense, triggered this, as well. What I found extraordinary was the fact that basically the whole world saw in her a woman who cared about the underprivileged, the underdog. And her death prompted an outpouring of grief such as, I believe, we've never seen before, except, perhaps, in the U. S. with President Kennedy. And that maybe this is a paradoxical shift of major proportion that will encourage us – that we will be the ones who pick up the sword that she put down. We will be the ones who will, in turn, collectively help the underdog, male and female, children, babies, animals, and the planet."

Princess Diana really symbolized what was deferred for so long for many women. The truth came out of her life of struggle and oppression. What is really symbolic is that Mother Teresa died soon after. Think of the magnitude of their contributions to humanity – so different, yet so powerful. A man states:

"Women are recognizing that men do need certain guidance. In fact, most of the sacred pipe carriers that hold space for us in Native American ceremonies are women. It's not that the men haven't done it; it's just that very few men have gotten to that level as quickly as some of the women have…when we don't listen to them, that's when things go awry.

Even though men, in some way, after a certain period of time will learn what they've been telling us for a hundred years or more. We have brotherhood circles. We have sisterhood circles. And in each of those, things are passed between both of those circles that help us understand what those roles are. We make agreements, and depending on the type of work that we're doing or the things that we're after, it gets beyond our basic needs – air, water, clothing and shelter. It goes to the next level of wants.

A relationship is easier to hold if you understand where the other person is coming from, and they understand where you're coming from, and I don't really see it as a role reversal. I see it as a role-enhancer.

And in these agreements, in knowing what has been said daily, in your emotional, physical, mental, spiritual and sensual agreement, when anything goes awry and you look back upon the former questions and answers that you've given each other, they may have to be updated. And sometimes, agreements need to be updated every three or four months."

The overall purpose in this transition between the sexes is to work through every problem. We have to be willing to move on to the next level, whatever that is. Sometimes, you have to ask for clarity. When you learn not to give your power away to another, then they won't have control over your emotions. This behavior will change things. Consider that it's perfectly okay to disagree with what someone else says. Practice a new dictum, "agree to disagree."

More men in the global community are verbalizing that they would like to learn certain things from women in the same way that men help women to understand the things that they weren't expected to know. Since women were the caretakers of society and raised the children, the sons were acculturated and raised by females. Both men and women must be the parents of today's children. Here are some other reactions:

"We spent most our time on what's the difference between being in love and living in love? We needed more time for this. Being in love is something you start with, your mind, and your feelings. Living in love is something that's actively and continuously done. One example is an arranged marriage – they seem to work because people accept it from the beginning. It's expected of them to make it work, and they consciously and constantly work at it. So they're actively living in love. They don't lose it, whereas a lot of us start out being in love, and that's it. They lose it, they don't follow it; they don't deal with it."

"Do women need to feel and do they have a need to be maternal and nurturing to men? We think that's not really the case, not necessarily do we need to be maternal to them at all, but nurturing as in loving, as in a partner, as in caring; and the men do this for their partners, if there's real love. There's a nurturing of the male to the female. It's not a paternal or a fatherly kind of thing at all. It's strictly nurturing, caring, as one human being to another who happens to be a partner in your life."

We ask men what they wanted from women? "Do you want nurturing, mothering, or both?" Some answered that they'd like to see many of the characteristics of mothering or a mother in women, such as caring. Do the same qualities exist in men? Both sexes have to feel safe to express their needs. The difference lies in how we interpret responses because of generational differences. For example, what you might term as affectionate, can be nurturing. Some consider nurturing in a negative context and thus equate nurturing to mothering (or smothering) which equals meddling!

One man said, "Nurture me to the hilt, but mother me not." Much of the negative perception of women needing to be in control was due to the fact that for many years women felt they had little or no power over anything. Consequently, their behavior was seen as manipulative and meddlesome when they overly dominated their children or husbands. As women have gained more self-confidence and have greater control over their own lives, they are equally concerned with everyone's happiness, including their own. When we refer to society, there is a mindset about the roles that we've been programmed to play. We've been raised in "boxes," and it's becoming easier to step outside of them. Walking the path to love allows you to be in a child-like mode, aware, yet safe enough to express the innocence still in you.

MEDITATIVE PRACTICE

Close your outer eyes, and open your inner eyes. Take a deep breath, and slowly exhale, and again, a nice deep breath and slowly exhale. Thank yourself for your ability to express who you are, which makes your life whole and complete. Feel your connectedness through the energy that flows through you. Invite this energy to be a part of your day, your week. Allow it to restore you and replenish you. Feel the energy as it nurtures and heals you. With this inner knowing, celebrate your new level of awareness and your wisdom. Accept these gifts and share them with those people you encounter this week.

~ ~ ~

The path to love is found in the wisdom of the statement, "If I knew then what I know now, I would have done things differently." Guilt and blame don't serve a purpose because you could not have gotten from "there to here" without going through those experiences. Would you disagree? Ask yourself what the lesson was that you learned. Whenever I hear people say "Why me?" I always thing of Harold Kushner's book, <u>When Bad Things Happen to Good People.</u> He reminds us not to ask why; ask *what* you are going to do about it. What are you going to do about walking this path to love? Understanding is paramount to giving and receiving. How do you show understanding in your relationships? In order to be understanding, you have to be understood. A very simple technique that works is "reframing." When someone makes a statement and you feel attacked, you might automatically say, "You always make me mad." However, a healthier response is "What I hear you saying is that I always make you mad." Then ask, "Is that correct? Tell me more." This practice removes the need to be defensive. By not saying "It's all your fault," or "you do—", you take away the instinct to replay the old "tit-for-tat" scenario. You also remove the need for people to respond offensively. Mirror to others the same kind of behavior you wish to receive. You disarm others when you choose not to engage in old behavior.

If you want to change things for the better, you must learn the art of reframing. It's nothing more than repeating back to the person the exact words you heard them say. Avoid your tendency to add things that weren't said. When you do this you might notice the other person's bewilderment since they have become so accustomed to defensive responses. I guarantee that as you practice this behavior you will see different results in time because who will argue with you if there's no one around? The following examples are given to help you practice this exercise:

"Pat you make me sick." "Steve, what I hear you saying is I make you sick." "Tell me more."

"Maureen, you always make me feel that way!" "Bob, what I hear you saying is I always make you feel that way. Tell me more."

"Bonnie, I hate when you do that." "Carol, what you're saying is you hate when I do that. Tell me more."

"Lou, it's always your fault." "Diane, what I hear you saying is it's always my fault. Tell me more."

These responses may seem rote and elementary, but what occurs is a lessening of conflict by making it safe to communicate. You won't necessarily know the outcome, but it's a very safe way for everyone to discuss their feelings. If the other person should continue on in a heated fashion, when they raise their voice and you're becoming tense, simply say, "I can't talk to you when you're like this. When you calm down, I'll be happy to talk to you." Many folks aren't even aware of when they are being verbally and emotionally abusive. They get addicted to arguing; they love fighting. It's amazing when you stop and think about it. Remember people in intense states of anger can't be reasoned with.

When asked the question, "what is the opposite of giving and loving?" the response was "receiving and hate." Do we really want to hate? When we give love, we also allow ourselves to receive love though it may not come from the source we give it to. I recall an exercise I was involved in. The facilitator asked a group of people to form two circles – one in the center and a group on the outside. For those of us in the center, we were number one, and the outer circle people were number two. It was the job of the one's to receive all the unconditional love they could from the two's. I was overwhelmed by the amount of people on the inside who wept. When they changed places, they were no longer crying. It's much easier for many people to give love than to receive love. To receive love means that we are vulnerable – to just open ourselves up to that, which Deepak says "is baring your soul." There are no guarantees in life. We don't know if someone's feelings will stay the same. Make a commitment one day at a time. Imagine that you both choose to work on whatever issues arise. Imagine that you loved yourself enough every day to take care of yourself as you would take care of someone else you loved. Consider that you can bring something new to the relationship which is what drew you to that person in the beginning because you were always sharing something.

When did you stop learning about each other? Did boredom set in? Maybe the TV overtook your sharing and you stopped communicating with one another. We can't always learn from each other; you may want to take classes together or apart or do something different. Make time to listen. If you're listening to the TV or radio in the background, chances are your attention will be diverted. Listening has been described as an act of love. When you spend a full day at work, or have a stressful day, you need to schedule time to talk with the people that you really care about, the same way you schedule appointments with doctors, your hairdresser, or for your car. People want to feel valued; like they have something to give.

One common denominator that has emerged in conflict is known as PDC – Power/Domination/Control. People try to control other people. The greatest realization you can have is that no one has power over anyone. We can learn to exercise self-control. That's the lesson. It's the perception that someone can control you. We buy into this notion at a deep level without being aware of why. We may think if I say this, I may be left alone or this person won't like me. Guess what? If that is the case, they don't have integrity or respect in the first place. As you become more aware about the ways you give and receive love, then you'll verbalize exactly what you want to say. You won't mislead others or yourself. In order to be honest, you have to allow that much love to develop in yourself, let alone another person.

It's a different way of loving. What you say, the tone of your voice, and the intention from which you convey a message creates greater feelings of trust. If you practice looking into someone's eyes when you speak to them, and you speak from the heart, then you are really encouraging openness. I can't tell you the amount of times I've seen emotional healing occur amongst family members who hadn't been speaking for a very long time or they wouldn't talk about certain issues. Through their willingness to solve their problems they came in and opened up. They put all their cards on the table. There's no judgment, no blame. We use "I" statements. An hour and a half later, through tears and much growth, they feel lighter. They feel new. But it takes great courage to do this. You become a warrior of the heart. Deepak says,

"Love, however, has the power to unite. Metaphysics teaches that the world is both imminent and transcendent. Imminent means material, changing, subject to time. Transcendent means it's eternal, timeless and beyond the material. The lover sees a more real world because he or she looks at ordinary things and finds the spiritual life that is actually there. The rest of us miss the transcendent and therefore claim it doesn't exist. We are doing the best we can, yet we cannot claim truth for our side because we're not there. What is mysterious is that being engulfed in your beloved is also divine. But the visitation of spirit is a subtle phenomena, and a very empowering thing. Either spirit takes you with it, or it departs.

From a spiritual point of view, infatuation opens us up to these same insights." The beloved serves as a trigger like the mountain, the spacewalk or the near-death encounter. This is not to diminish the allure of the beloved, for the transcendent wonder of infatuation has no difficulty shining through the visible light. In love, the imminent and the transcendent are one."

What he's talking about is being in a very high state of awareness. It's hard to be in a high state of awareness all the time. One of the greatest admonitions is – "Be in the world but not out of it." No matter how great a relationship you have with someone, it is bound to go through challenges because we change. You have to tell the other person what you're feeling. We have to be willing to give ourselves the freedom to learn from our mistakes. The same is true for those you love whom you can't control.

Parents, very often, have a problem doing that with their children. Can you watch your children fall flat on their faces so they can pick themselves up again? I often hear parents say they have a teenager that they don't get along with. So I say, "you have a teenager." She says "yeah, it's driving me crazy. You know how teenagers are. I remember what I was like," So I say, "Well, learn from your experience and pass it on to your son. He'll grow for it. If he wants to dye his hair purple and pierce his nose, let him do it. He'll grow out of that phase. He'll want to get his nose unpierced and he'll want to look like everyone else down the road. Don't take it personally." That's a little quip on adolescence!

In a chapter in Deepak's book Seeing Beyond – Loving Practice, he suggests that we can become intimately acquainted with our intuition as we proceed along the path to love. Think about the following questions.

When you look at a sunset or a full moon or something of great natural beauty, have you ever felt yourself expand as if you were no longer enclosed within the physical limits of your body? Have you prayed and had your prayer answered? Sometimes it's not the answer you wanted and it's still an answer. Sometimes when you can't make a decision, that too is a decision. Your decision is to make no decision at all. That's being gentle with yourself. You can't force yourself to be where you are not. You can beat yourself up in the process, but you can't make yourself get there any faster.

Many times when I have taught a class on metaphysics I begin with an affirmation which is, "Let's close our outer eyes to the world, because very often that which is felt is unseen. Can you trust your intuition, feelings, and knowing your gut reactions? It's there and it's a gift." Deepak tells us to "go through our most vivid experiences we've had of spirit, of soul, of love, and look again at the messages that have been there for you. As you learn to attune yourself to spirit, you may hear the gentle whisper of intuition." Chopra explains,

"Spirit isn't a phenomena. It is the whispered truth within a phenomena. The phenomena is that which cannot be explained. As spirit is gentle, it persuades by the softest touch. The messages never get louder, but they do get clearer. If you have the slightest hint of communication from spirit, ask for clarification." Imagine feeling really loved, safe, watched over, at peace. Things are okay, really because you are making them that way.

When you look at a newborn baby, what do you usually see in the child's eyes, in their smile? You see a miracle, innocence, purity, no fear, and joy. Years ago, Crosby, Stills, Nash and Young sang "If you smile at me, I will understand, for that is something everyone, everywhere speaks in the same language." The smile. Ask yourself if you can operate on that level; knowing the lessons you've learned and still be willing to trust. Rather than thinking nothing will work out, stop seeing through the eyes of fear. It's all a learning experience. We get wake-up calls. Cultivate your ability to see differently. Native American traditions provide vision quests where you go off into nature for several days on your own with few possessions to distract you. In order to find your path, you must take time apart from the daily madness and allow your dreams, daydreams, and visions to guide you. Do one thing after the other and your process will unfold.

A friend of mine runs an international/cultural homestay program for high school students from abroad. She had a student from Finland. The host family didn't work out so she invited the girl to stay with her family. This girl ended up marrying her son two years later. My point is that when we follow what is in front of us to do, the vision unfolds. Having faith means that even though you don't know what your future will look like, it is still unfolding everyday by the choices you make and in the people you meet. This can be both exciting and exhausting.

Change can become detrimental if you need too much excitement. According to one addiction theory, the three E's, known as enticement, excitement, and exhaustion creates a roller-coaster-like effect in your life. This is what most co-dependents suffer from. They become exhausted by being preoccupied with what will happen in the future instead of doing what they can each day. I have heard a co-dependent joke that before you're about to die, you see someone else's life flash before you. Today well lived creates tomorrow. Rather than obsessing about what you can't control, do what is in front of you. There is a timing and synchronicity to everything, even when it looks like the opposite.

You must put an idea into action; make it real. If you don't, you may become overwhelmed when you discover that other people have taken the same idea you had and did something with it. The collective unconscious does not discriminate. All people have access to the realm of divine ideas and infinite possibilities. Eliminate what you don't want and thus you may create what you do want. It's all a process of elimination. You might say, "Well, this doesn't feel too comfortable. I don't want this experience. I'll let this one go, and I'll be open to another one." As you refine your intuitive skills and learn to listen to your inner wisdom, you'll be able to discern that which is for your highest good so you don't have to put up with garbage anymore. And there's a lot of garbage out there! If you allow it to come into your life, it will, and yet, most of us learn by experience. Hopefully, we can eliminate the experiences we don't want by making wiser choices. It's hard, but it's possible.

Eric Butterworth taught people to move their feet and do something. Don't just stand there! In other words don't just think about something or pray for it, take action. You will notice that when things don't go in the direction you want them to, the universe is giving you another message. Out of left field, another experience comes along. When the student is ready the teacher appears.

Some comments made on this subject are:

"I have no expectations, but when it happens, I'll know."

"Better communication, how to speak my truth at the time that I know is right, and how to trust and find my gut feeling."

Once again, these statements reflect an intuitive awareness. How do you develop intuition? You can hug trees, meditate, or get in touch with that which is unseen. It's really that simple. You may ask, "What do you mean by hug trees?" The idea is to develop an awareness about what you feel, so that you can almost touch it. Trees for example, are very grounded in the earth. When you hug a tree or stand with your spine erect to the trunk, you will feel a certain energy emanating from the tree. What it does is alter your sense of reality. Reality is defined on both subjective and objective levels. A good example is found in physics. No matter what you see, the truth is, the molecular structure of the object vibrates at such an incredible rate so as to make the object appear real. It's all electrons in motion. The

very same principle is at work in our bodies. Behind all form is energy. Chopra talks about separating truth from falsehood in relationships. He states,
"Only when you first begin to feel safe does your psyche permit you to look at the fears which were too intense to confront before." (You have to feel safe.) "It is common for either partner in a relationship to relive in contemporary form the traumas and survival threats of their childhood. It isn't surprising, then, that a man and a woman may not permit themselves to be in a healing relationship at first. They need the courage to see that the doubt and fear that surface at odd moments is coming up to be examined and released, not blindly acted on. The most destructive effect of feeling threatened is to cut yourself off from the feeling of love. If you were not taught about love in childhood, being able to be undefended is much more difficult. Loving parents must teach their children that reality isn't simply harsh. All of us were imprinted one of two ways. Either the world is dangerous with moments of safety, or the world is safe with moments of danger."

The above is similar to the question we address when we ask, do we see the glass half-empty or half-full? Chopra concludes that no matter how hostile the world appears, a loving family remains secure as a place of nurturing and protection. What ends up happening, (I've seen this over and over again) is that if we didn't grow up in families where we experienced unconditional love, where we were nurtured and supported, then we unconsciously pick out partners who will reinforce that message for us in adulthood. We try to create the opposite of what we experienced, but we usually won't get it until we work through the earlier issues from our family of origin, our mothers, fathers; the people who raised us.

Even if the people have passed on, there are many rituals available that can help you to heal old wounds. Process work includes letter writing and sacred acts. Some people choose to burn their letters, take them to the gravesite or an ocean and sprinkle the ashes. This is similar to what people do in cremation ceremonies. This process frees you from whatever blocked you. Regression therapy is anther helpful tool. There are many ways to heal your past and live in the present. You can release old traumas. It works.

When we look at the field of psychology itself, that too is changing. Consider that while Freud was a great contributor, he ended up hating his protégé, Carl Jung, because Jung disagreed with his ideas. Today we have many new forms of psychotherapy. Many people have advanced the cause of using a psycho-spiritual model, also known as transpersonal psychology.

I recall, when I was growing up, that I never understood what people meant when they said "you control your mind." I used to think that was impossible. My mind has to control me. However, as I became more aware through the practice of meditation, I began to see that our super conscious mind really can control what and how we think. You are the gate keeper when you control what goes in your mind and out of it. You've got to be aware of what you're thinking, because your thought creates your experiences. I'm not saying that we're responsible for other people's behavior. I am suggesting that we are responsible for our own reactions. All you can do is be honest; just speak your truth. Remember that you can't change anyone. "Have courage to change the person I can, and the wisdom to know that it's me."

Think back to some of your most difficult times. Did you notice while you were growing, the process you went through? Did you see yourself as a victim? If so, be grateful it's over. Once again, learning to love yourself is an important lesson. A relationship can last 45 years or 4 years. It's not easy. Who said it would be? Why do you think they wrote "breaking up is hard to do?" It's an emotional wrenching of your gut. It's someone you have bound yourself to for a long or short period of time. Even two weeks can seem like a lot for some people! Life does go on. And love is as perennial as the grass. The question you must ask yourself is what have I learned from this experience?

Einstein said that we can't solve a problem at the same level we discovered it. Sometimes, there are no direct answers, but there are feelings. Honor them, whatever they are. Certain unfathomable mysteries come about that we may never have the answer to. We conjecture on what causes people to do what they do. But very often, you ask someone, "Why did you do that." They say, "I don't know."

Well, how can you figure out why someone else did something if they themselves don't know.

There was a woman involved with a man she had known for about three years. He wanted to end the relationship, and he ended up telling her, "it's not you. This has nothing to do with you. It's all about me." Years later, the same behavior continued. He would go from relationship to relationship saying, "it's not you. It's about me." This man would have made life a lot easier for the people he chose to get involved with by telling them up front that he has a problem making commitments. That would have been acting out of integrity.

I, myself, befriended a man whose integrity I really admired. He said that he dated lots of women, and that he was never going to get married. He said he told all the women that he went out with that he wasn't interested in getting married. He advised them not to think they could ever get him to marry them. He told them he would date them for a while at the same time he was dating three or four other women. His honesty entitled women to know what they were getting involved in. That's integrity. That's honesty. Then you can evaluate if you want to date someone who's not available? Honesty removes a lot of the garbage that people deal with. What causes people to lie in the first place and be dishonest? Fear. They won't be accepted. They're going to get hurt. They might be thinking, "If you knew what I know about myself, you'd hate me and I'd end up being alone." We all have to get in touch with our shadow.

I recall and admire the late Danaan Parry, the founder of Warriors of the Heart and the Earth Stewards Network. He taught people to embrace their fears. He helped many to do just that by travelling to Belfast, the Gaza Strip, Brazil, and Vietnam. One of the exercises he engaged people in was to stand out on a pier at 11:00 p.m. in the darkness where they couldn't see each other. For a half-hour, you shouted out your greatest fears. What do you think were some of the things people said? I'm afraid I'm going to be alone forever. I'm afraid I'm going to get divorced. I'm afraid I won't get married. I'm afraid I'm going to die. Every possible thing that has ever come into your mind comes out on that dock at night. Why? It has been explained that we are human beings having a spiritual experience and likewise, we're spiritual beings having a human experience. Being able to embrace your fears is one of the greatest gifts you can give yourself. You no longer need to push your fears away. You embrace them so you can move through them. If you keep pushing them away they'll just resurface. Remember the statement, what you resist persists.

In Jewish mysticism, the Kabbalah teaches that a dream is an unopened letter to yourself. Understand that if you have a recurring dream, you need to get the message. You psyche is your intuition. It's your higher, guiding force. It's there to give you information, so honor it. In Jungian analysis, and also according to the Senoit Indian technique, Native American dream interpretation looks at the symbolism in a dream. For example, you can identify the things you're dreaming about. Write them down as if on the spokes of a wheel. After listing as many possible ideas related to the dream, choose the four that have the most meaning for you and see what the message is.

In John Bradshaw's book <u>Healing the Shame That Binds You</u> he illustrates this technique as a way of making your dreams relevant to your current life. Sometimes we dream of those things that are lost in our lives. For example,

Deepak says that passion must contain surrender in order to be authentic. He asks us what we surrender to? He says the frankness of declaring a strong passion is refreshing! It reminds us that the spiritual union of lovers isn't separate from the sweat and mingled breath of their sexuality. Sex allows you to blend the needs of the self with the freedom of your self. That's what he calls the new intimacy with yourself, the passion to surrender. But, surrender to what? Intimacy. True intimacy is shared self-expression. For some people, it's a release, an opening, or a contradiction. He talks about passion in a sexual context and says,

"If a man feels himself to be a hunter, conqueror, or ardent pursuer, that is his own choice. If a woman sees herself as prey, prize or an unattainable love-object, that is her decision. No single code operates anymore. And by making intimacy an agreement, both parties can approach sexuality openly as something they mutually want. But there is a price to pay. In many ways, sexual freedom is frightening because of the loss of boundaries. The old social code linked love and sex. Now that this has become a matter of agreement, there has been a lot of disagreement. Love and desire are essentially separate – a matter open for intelligent discussion. <u>It is surprising how many people enter sexual intimacy with no idea of what they are agreeing to.</u> To rob sex of its spontaneity makes it both false and ugly. (However, we all have different roles to play.) Suppression is not good; however, it is only expedient. Society requires we draw limits on the expression of desire, which makes it all the more necessary to love at least one area of your life that is completely free and uninhibited." Intimacy is meant to be just such an area. What is it that makes sex free or uninhibited, loving or merely pleasurable? Whatever blocks our pleasure also blocks our love because in sex, pleasure is the doorway to love. Intimacy starts not with a physical approach, but with a set of beliefs.

"Sex becomes a problem when it becomes mixed with hidden emotions like anger, shame and guilt. Values are personal. If you understand where you are in a sexual situation, meaning that your emotions and values are in awareness with your clarity, then your drive doesn't stand apart like a raging intruder. It is a part of you that is loving and acceptable."

The Indian author, Krishnamurti, says, "The pursuit of pleasure throws life out the window." By life, he means the sacred being at the heart of existence, the mystery that can be known only by not resisting, by being natural. The difference between sex, love and chastity doesn't exist. They are one. In a world where imitating other people's ideas and values is forced on us in thousands of ways, sex is left as a means of escaping ourselves. It is a form of self-forgetfulness that is many people's only real form of meditation. Such is the promise of intimacy, that it can deliver us into a place where experience of the spirit is genuine and undeniable."

Be aware that surrendering yourself on a sexual level, (unless you're really aware of what you're doing and why you're doing it,) can end up doing great injury to yourself emotionally, which is what Paul Wanio explains in his article, "There Are No condoms For the Heart."Passion isn't purely sexual. It is also emotional. It is creative. Beethoven had a passion for music. So did Mozart. Your passion is about your life. It's what propels you forward and gives you a reason for living. Consider the beautiful poem, Desiderata, found in a church in the 1600's. Think how these words written close to 400 years ago might affect you now.

Go placidly amidst the noise and haste,
And remember what peace there may be in the silence.
As far as possible, without surrender, be on good terms with all persons.
Speak your truth quietly and clearly.
And listen to others.
Even the dull and ignorant, they, too, have their stories.
Avoid loud and aggressive persons who are vexations to your spirit.
If you compare yourself with others, you may become vain and bitter.
For always there will be greater and lesser persons than yourself.
Enjoy your achievements as well as your plans.
Keep interested in your own career, however humble.
It is a real possession in the changing fortunes of time.
Exercise caution in business affairs.
For the world is full of trickery.
But let this not blind you to what virtue there is.
And everywhere life is full of heroism.
Be yourself
Especially, do not feign affection.
Neither be cynical about love, for in the face of all aridity and Disenchantment, it is perennial. It is as growing as the grass.
Take kindly the counsel of years.
Gracefully surrendering the things of youth.
Nurture strength of spirit and self-love to shield you in sudden misfortunes.
But do not distress yourself with imaginings.
Many fears are born of fatigue and loneliness.
Beyond the wholesome discipline,
Be gentle with yourself.
You are a child of the universe, no less than the trees and the stars.
You have a right to be here.

Whether or not it is clear to your, no doubt the universe is unfolding
As it should for you.
Therefor, be at peace with God, whatever you conceive God to be.
And whatever your labors and aspirations, in this noisy confusion of life, keep peace with your soul.
With all of its sham, drudgery and broken dreams, it is still a beautiful world.
Be careful, and strive to be happy.

CHAPTER SIX

Prescriptions for Living: Remedies For Well-Being

I thought it a useful idea to include a chapter on Prescriptions for Living in <u>Soulful Love: The Search for the Self</u>. The following text is based on many years of study in the fields of metaphysics, psychology, spirituality, and philosophy. As we have been reading about throughout this book, life presents us with circumstances, which can cause stress. I want to point out the discipline that is required in learning to think positively. It takes years of practice. This is not to imply that you have to think positively about everything that happens; sometimes that's just hard to do. What it does suggest however, is that you'll begin to see events unfolding as part of their own pattern and whether you call them good or bad matters not.

Our reaction to events is precisely that – a reaction. Our emotions cause us to feel the way we do. We have been learning to integrate the mental, physical, and spiritual aspects of our being. To do so is crucial for our total mental well-being. Over the last two decades, I have explored various spiritual psychological disciplines, which have assisted me in my own mental and physical well-being in addition to deciding to be happy.

It's easy to forget that we've been given extraordinary powers since the time of our birth. Einstein pointed out that we use a very small percentage of our brainpower. We see the world as we are period. Letting go of what you don't want to embrace anymore is a key to mental wellbeing. The energy it takes to picture something different will result in outer changes. Clarity of thought generates the energy, interest, and enthusiasm which creates a magnetic force field that draws into your life the very things you focus on.

Turn your attention away from that which is negative. You can direct energy however you choose to. Energy is your thought forms and only you limit yourself. Some dreams take longer to manifest and taking action in a loving way and seeing yourself as a perfect image of the creative life force also removes negative energy. You can bring out the positive side of life by choosing to be positive. It is you who allows others to change your thinking either for the good or its opposite. We have a choice to live fully or not. You're 'desert' experiences can bloom by what you do with them.

How do you see yourself? Do you believe the world can change because you're in it? What do you stand for/represent? What do you share with others? All of these questions are meant to spark or reinvent your identity. Seeing yourself as a precious messenger creates a space in the world that only you can fulfill. A spiritual life is reality. As we discussed earlier, the Buddhists regard this world as an illusion (Maya). Your mission is to bring love whereever you go and stop trying to control outcomes. Only good can come from bringing love from wherever you are.

Greet each person as if they have value. This is an outward expression of the Sanskrit word Namasté. It means I behold the best in you. Does life give you clues? What are you discovering? Do you pick up on them? Do you use your experiences for good? It has been said that a saint is none other than an ordinary person living the life that God intended! When you're facing a challenge, ask yourself, "what is it that I need to know about this situation?" Will I be present and learn from it? Are you living an authentic life? An authentic life happens when you learn to follow your intuition. It will guide you.

Imagine, if you can, that you can change your world for the better and live the quality of life you desire. As you become more adept in managing your thinking, you'll know that anything you need to know will be revealed. You invite the right people and experiences to teach you that we're all unique, special. Life makes a place for each of us what happens to you occurs through your consciousness when you know something is right you don't question it. Similarly when you feel something is wrong you'll release it.

When we take risks, we may have failure, but we know that we are supported by a gentle spirit which moves us forward through the inspiration we receive. You reinvent your ideas every time your focus is on receiving an answer. When and if you are confused, just by knowing that you are in the right place at the right time doing the right thing will open new doorways. Your confusion is a gift in letting you know that something needs to be cleared away so that you can open new doors and opportunities. Imagine how different your life would be if you knew about the Law of Attraction – the right people at the right time. Enjoy the beauty of each day even when it seems that none is present. Create it in your mind through visualization. Things happen to teach us we are each the inlet and outlet of the universal expression which finds its way in us. That which you are seeking is also seeking you. Your knowledge of the truth sets you free. How you interpret truth colors your experience. Do you believe that you are entitled to happiness? If not, why?

Change always involves a process of letting go. This principle never changes. Have faith that there is a special plan unfolding in your life and watch it happen. Don't sit idly back; but follow through on your intuition, and take the action that you feel led to do. In challenging times again, the reminder is to ask what is the lesson? If you want to change a negative situation, change the way you think. See the outcome the way you would like to envision it! God will guide you out of your own way, if only you'd learn to go with the flow by observing what is going on around you. What does it really mean to let go and let God? It means being willing to change. Don't vacillate in your thinking. Affirm the positive, declare it, accept it and allow the unfoldment to take place.

What begs to return to you does so by way of your consciousness. If this involves a painful situation, ask yourself, "have I suffered enough?" if the answer is yes don't continue to be mired down in non-supportive, negative environments. Father Leo Booth says that spiritual people shock us. They wake us up by inviting us to go beyond our comfort zone and **stretch!** You can only bring your awareness to a new level by being willing to transform your mind, spirit, and soul. The word 'angel', means messenger. Sometimes you become your own angel when you dare to be real. Other people may not like your honesty. However, when you are open enough to talk about the many things that people don't want to discuss, Father Booth says, "You make God smile."

Spirituality is God given and religion is man made. Spirituality includes insight, wisdom and harmony at work. Your presence is clearly felt. In becoming your own angel, you bring these qualities into your work and the world. It is the work of spiritual transformation. Your culture, your roots, and who you are contributes to the greater harmony we can all experience. It has been said that we are God in expression. Of course we don't feel this way when our emotions cause us distress which then may create physical illness. When you learn to trust that which created you, you know what you're not allowing, in working out your challenges. All healing requires the balance of your mind, body and emotions. Never give up on God and you. No one can save you but yourself. No matter what decision you make, you are always guided by your thinking.

Wipe the slate clean. That's the only way newness can come in. Be about your purpose, whether it is fulfilling a vision, creating a dream, or building a new project. You can change your life by answering three questions.

1. What is my purpose?
2. Am I involved in that purpose for living?
3. Do I make things more difficult for myself?

Stop creating obstacles, awaken to the pleasant scent of your favorite fragrance and infill your spirit with the same essence that created the fragrance. Make a decision to have integrity. In doing so you'll create more peaceful conditions for yourself and those you care about. You've got to give up pre-supposition. Nature allows itself to be. We may think we know what is best for others and ourselves, but that is not always the case. Your spirit knows, that is the wise person in you. Once again, your consciousness is critical to the way you live your life. Be available to the way life is, not the way it was!

Sometimes we are betrayed by our own concepts. This is challenging, for you have to be willing to let go of anything at any time and trust that everything is working out as it should. The question is, do you believe in randomness or a plan unfolding even if you can't see what it is. There are three things you can do to make things easier.

1. Show up. Bring your complete attention to the moment. Don't let your mind wander into the past or the future. Be here now.
2. Be honest. It takes tremendous courage to be honest..

3. Trust. Learn the art of surrender.

You can start by expressing your innate gifts, and not stifling them. What you have to share with others is valuable and important. Do you live your dreams out loud or do you restrict your life through fear? Your inner wisdom will always give you the truth. When you live out loud you enjoy your life more. Think compassionately and the impossible becomes possible. Your sub-conscious mind creates in the outer what you radiate from within you. For example, your environment will be influenced by the way you think. How do you prefer to think? Notice I use the word prefer, to imply that thinking is a preference.

You'll notice when you don't go on automatic pilot that different experiences will show up in your life because you have invited them. There is nothing drab living a spiritual lifestyle. Your life will be more peaceful as you align your actions with your words. Your entire thinking process is renewed by practicing great joy on a daily basis. When you learn to say, "If not this, then something better," you have to be ready to receive what you've been asking for. For example, I recall a time when I worked at a job I detested. Every day I would go in and say to myself "God, please open a new way for me." I was sending out resumes and opening my own consciousness for a change but I was scared. A few weeks after I began this treatment, one morning I walked into work and my employer said to me "I'm sorry to have to tell you this, but we can no longer afford your services." Inside I became elated although I was scared. What he did for me was a favor because that decision forced me to do something different, which I did. The moral of the story is to be prepared for change when you ask for it.

In the case of companionship, perhaps you've never heard it put this way, but there is a saying that all true marriages/relationships occur first in the mind of God. In an etheric sense new thought suggests that it is the attraction of the masculine and feminine energy within us first that brings forth the manifestation of being drawn irresistibility to another. Noted author, Joel Goldsmith, writes in his book <u>The Gift of Love,</u> "Marriage on the human plane is really the consummation of mystical marriage, conscious union with God." In Ernest Holmes' book <u>The Science of Mind</u> he states, "I shall make a home for you, O my wonderful love, and we shall journey through life, hand in hand." (pg. 513).

Marianne Williamson eloquently states that

"...what is natural is our desire for the beloved." I know this is true, for what I have personally experienced is a continuous turning of my face to the beloved in prayer. Prayer is a perfectly natural way to experience a deep union with divine love. So many people try to meet their perfect mate, but have never experienced the highest love of all. So many people long for a deep soul relationship with another, but haven't plumbed the depths of their own soul. Our love relationships on a human level may or may not lead us to seek a deeper relationship with Spirit. Our deeper relationship with Spirit will always outpicture as a human relationship.

There are many different theories on why relationships show up in our lives. Some say it's because we attract what we need to heal. Some say it's because there are unresolved issues in our lives and our partner is our guide. I say it is because our partner is our love for Spirit, humanly revealed. If we have been praying deeply and earnestly, for years, or perhaps for lifetimes, to see the face of Spirit and to know this Presence fully and freely, then why would we be surprised if this prayer revealed itself in such a magnificent form? Answered prayer is answered prayer; we don't get to judge what it looks like, but we are certainly privileged to celebrate its arrival."

DECIDE TO BE HAPPY

I came to believe that happiness is a choice. As a student of metaphysical thinking, I recall reading the first sentence in Scott Peck's book, <u>The Road Less Traveled</u>, "Life is Difficult." However, the second sentence states,

"It is a great truth because once we truly see this truth we transcend it. Once we truly understand – then life is no longer difficult."

Wow! The idea that we can transcend difficulty is powerful simply by knowing it. The way we think about experiences clearly demonstrates our ability in how we choose to overcome them. Many people unconsciously create struggles. Yet it has also been said that we learn the most through difficult passages. Consider what Raymond Charles Barker has to say on the subject, "Happiness is genuine satisfaction with your present experience." This reflects Ram Dass' idea in his book, <u>Be Here Now</u>.

Today well lived creates tomorrow and allows us to be in the present. Barker continues, "Happiness is not a constant, but satisfaction can be." He defines satisfaction as a deep, underlying sense of fulfillment, a sense of doing a good job with life. Having a sense of fulfillment comes about by allowing your creativity to express itself in your body, mind and emotions. We stagnate when we're not creating and boredom sets in. Dorothy Bryant in her book, <u>Ella Price's Journal</u> clearly depicts this in her novel about an American middle class woman caught in the throws of redefining her life.

Barker believed that people are unhappy because they don't see themselves correctly. They want to change events, conditions, and people. They don't want to change themselves. It's easier to judge others and tell them what we think they need to do instead of looking at our own lives. When we experience unhappiness, it is usually because we don't see the whole picture. Barker recommends, "A change of consciousness is the answer, and very few people want to change their consciousness."

We see mental and spiritual laws at work by the changed experiences an individual has. How many of you would accept responsibility for the idea that things, situations, and events don't just happen of their own volition, but rather they are caused by your thinking? In the film, <u>A Field of Dreams,</u> Kevin Costner's idea clearly produced the end result. Barker knew that the material world makes us comfortable, but it doesn't ensure happiness. Thus, your creative ideas govern your everyday experiences. When I hear people complain of boredom, or see the many ways they punish themselves, again, I am reminded that our state of mind creates the experience. This is not to be judgmental. Find something meaningful that speaks to you personally. Life is about having a forward moving consciousness. Problems serve as symbolic warnings.

The solution to any difficulty is as close as your next thought. However, you must control what you think. For what you think affects what is around you. In Jungian psychology we speak of the dream state and the waking state. In essence, what you see outpictured in your day to day life is a kind of dream state in that it represents your experience, which forces us to look at either what we don't like or want to change. The things we're satisfied with, we don't even notice.

Barker believed that thinking which is based on exciting, new ideas is the cause of happiness, however this doesn't happen randomly. You must build a consciousness and then apply it by transforming the beliefs you were taught which didn't work to what is now possible. It's all about reprogramming your subconscious mind. Begin by affirming ideas that reflect your belief that you have a right to be happy. Drifting into the past doesn't serve a purpose, unless we choose to learn from it. Barker says, "we always stand between the old that is familiar and the new that is unfamiliar."

It takes practice to accept the unknown new while releasing the well known past. Purposes are borne and new goals are achieved through growth. Those chronically unhappy remind us that we can't make them happy. To change the sub-conscious pattern of being unhappy requires new thinking. We can all change ourselves when we decide to. We've done it over and over again. While prolonged unhappiness is self-destructive, it is a misuse of your spiritually endowed creative mind. People who are spiritually unaware cannot change until they wake up to live their life differently. **When you do what you've always done, you'll always get what you've always gotten.**

What you give your attention to acts as a powerful force because emotions follow where mental attention goes. Giving your attention to those attitudes, situations, and people who will add to your well-being, is what is called affirmative prayer. Blessing those you perceive to be your enemies, as hard as this is to do, will set in motion a deliberate change. Negative patterns will yield to creative solutions that can produce what you say you really want. Very often we get fooled by appearances. Your fears prevent you from experiencing the good you desire. Self-discipline is motivated by desire.

I'm not suggesting that you have to be happy twenty-four hours a day. That's unrealistic. However too many people are happy too few

hours a day. The idea is to use what causes you sorrow as fuel for transformation. Building a consciousness of satisfaction can ensure that future problems won't demand as much of your mental attention as before. They'll be solved with more ease. The more you give yourself permission to experience happiness, the more you will come to accept that it is also your inherent right. Try the following experiment for one month. Keep a log/journal of your experiences. One day at a time,
1. Stop all complaining.
2. Stop telling others of your unhappiness.
3. Find things to praise.
4. Watch your conversations.
5. If you're negative, immediately offer a creative, interesting idea.
6. Know that your spoken word has power.
7. Use your words to produce what you want.
8. Do not discuss what you don't want.
9. Declare that you're finished with unhappiness.

Just imagine what our world would look like if we all practiced this kind of mental discipline. Doing different things, reading positive literature, and staying in circulation with others will get you started. God usually works by means of people. Finding the humor in situations often changes your experience. Be gentle with yourself and do what you can. Assert daily that you have a right to be happy. When and if you are challenged, see the situation differently and ask yourself what is the lesson.

Laws of Life

Raymond Holliwell, author of, <u>Working with the Law</u>, provides good ideas about various situations we encounter at different times in our life. Consider some of his ideas and see what your thinking is on the subject.

Money does not make a man. Finally magical results come not by change or accident, but by discipline.

When you discipline your thinking, you'll experience wisdom and understanding.

Something always has to be sacrificed for something else. We sacrifice every day of our lives whether we want to or not, whether we know it or not. No matter what we want of life, we have to give up something in order to get it.

Freedom is not living an obsessed, undisciplined life. Freedom is being able to control your life and make it what you want it to be. An undisciplined life is an insane life!

Think back to when you first decided to do something. For example, I recall when I decided to pursue a doctorate in peace studies. It was not something I consciously set out to do. Rather, through a series of what I call serendipitous circumstances, I was led to meet certain people whose suggestions sparked an idea within me. However, embarking on this path was a conscious choice and in so doing I was sacrificing my former way of life to embark on a very disciplined, focused one for a period of three years. That's why, when I finished my program and graduated, I didn't want to write anything ever again! But, that idea was short lived. I did take a break though. Following this spark was like following a dream because I was able to pursue understanding a subject that had always baffled and intrigued me. While I didn't completely know why I took that path then I realize today that it has become an integral part of my life's mission and work. This has brought forth great good into my life and the lives of many others I've been fortunate to come in contact with. Perhaps you can make a list of those paths you've chosen to walk down and see how they've changed your life. Remember, you can always change your experience by changing your thinking.

I've experienced much freedom in discipline. I realize this sounds like an oxymoron. Following what I've been drawn to has created more balance in my life. I schedule time for relaxation, work, play, exercise, meditation, socializing etc. We all have the ability to create a meaningful life. I can easily remember those times in my life when I wasn't disciplined, nor was my thinking through some very trying times. In retrospect I now see how each passage brought me closer to my desire to live a more conscious, peaceful life. In addition, the work that I do has taught me that most people want to experience peace of mind and happiness. Living a disciplined life, while maintaining a carefree attitude, will help you to create worthwhile, meaningful goals at the different crossroads of your life.

The Law of Success

In order to understand how this law operates, you need to define what success is for and to you. Consider that the dictionary offers, "the achievement of something desired, intended, or attempted." Imagine too, the hundreds of people who achieved success only after many failures. Sometimes our desires are tested.

I am often dismayed when I meet people who have suffered through terrible psychological traumas in their families or who have never taken the time or opportunity to heal from old wounds. Throughout the many classes I've given, I've heard numerous stories of people carrying grudges for years, sometimes for decades, without ever seeking resolution to their problems. I would consider it a great success if you have a good relationship with your family members. Most relationships require work and a willingness to accept other's ideas, even if you don't live by them or disagree with them. This is especially true in what has become known as the classical "dysfunctional family."

When I took a class in this same subject, I was asked to define what I considered to be my three greatest successes up to that point in my life. Although both of my parents are no longer living, I am very grateful for the close relationship we developed. Ask yourself in what ways it might be possible to improve relationships with living relatives. Recognizing that you can't change them, but you can have some kind of healthy, emotional boundaries and some form of communication. If not it is better to realize in the long run that you've done your best. So perhaps another way to define success is found in the original meaning of something attempted.

Another area that people define success is in their working career. Corporate research reports that very few people keep the same job for the length of time as our forebears did. Some people may know what they want to do from an early age. Others, like myself didn't have that luxury. I call it a luxury because it is difficult to navigate your ship when you feel lost. In Soulful Love, we explore the many paths that bring us to greater peace of mind. Such is the search to define our purpose.

I never knew or thought in my earlier years that I would pursue an advanced degree. It's almost as if the work that came out of the degree pursued me. See if any of my story sounds familiar to you or anyone you know. Through the people I had met, and the recommendations they made, I discovered a vehicle that would allow me to research what was really important to me at that time of my life. It was the Union Institute in Cincinnati, Ohio which offers a very progressive approach to higher education. I have recommended many others to explore their options in pursuing their studies with the Union because more traditional institutions may have been unavailable to them. The biggest difference being the way intelligence was measured; test scores versus adult learners who were working and making significant contributions in their field without a degree. As such, this whole area of education is now being assessed in a new light today with brain compatible assessments. This is certainly an accomplishment in moving our educational institutions toward a more enlightened approach when it comes to learning. Consider what Dr. Diane Ronis has written:

"Brain–compatible learning is about the growth and development of a human being with a wonderfully unique brain. The standardized tests that claim to measure student performance relative to other students in this country or in others only measure what students don't know, not what they do. Therefore, an attempt to apply standards based upon a flawed method of evaluation is a flawed concept itself…"

The problem here is that "demanding" does not necessarily mean "better." The current drive for **performance! achievement! success!** Comes at the expense of discovery, curiosity, and exploration, the very foundation of brain compatible learning…

It would be unrealistic to expect the same performance level from everyone because some students simply are more able to master challenging material than are others…Instead, standards must be set so that they are within reach but still require dedication and hard work, a challenge that would encourage learners to seek their maximum potential."

It might seem strange to include so much information on brain compatible learning and education under the Law of Success. However, this subject is very much a part of feeling and being a successful person, which is, after all, being the best you can be and finding out what that is. This by no means suggests that those who don't pursue higher education are failures. As a matter of fact, there are many who consider themselves to be successful without any degrees. Once again, it is up to the individual to define what success is. Think of your accomplishments. Most people don't rest when they finish a project. They may take some time away, but eventually, they feel the pull of creativity within which sparks them into action.

In much the same way I consider my earlier work as a pioneering minister in the Bahamas to be both a successful chapter of my life as well as an unbelievable odyssey. I originally wanted to meet with people who shared a similar way of thinking. The ad that was placed in the local newspaper attracted quite a few people which formed the nucleus of a very strong support group. I never knew that I would do this type of work back then. Yet, I am humbled when I think of the countless people who have been helped by this ministry which is alive and well today. This group changed faces and eventually became a financially viable center which to this day is known as Unity of the Bahamas.

One of the tenets I live by is "tikkun olam." In the translation from Hebrew to English, it signifies the repair of the world. Somehow, my belief in wanting to make a contribution to the advancement of civilization through humanity became important to me over time. Some people see the amassment of material wealth as success. Others see it in what they can do and yet, oddly enough, money helps many good works get accomplished.

Mental balance and peace of mind are very important to all success. Good health is also a contributing factor. Whenever we're out of balance, our body is too. It's a signal and sign for us to slow down and do what we have to in order to restore ourselves. If any of these stories or ideas ring true for you, then perhaps you'll look at success in a different light. I believe that another aspect of success is found in gratitude and forgiveness.

The Law of Attraction

All of the ideas I'm sharing here are based upon my own life, studies, and the wisdom and suggestions of others throughout the ages. While it has been said that there is nothing new under the sun, we learn to make it relevant to the times that we live in. Ernest Holmes suggested that when an individual earnestly desires something, he/she sets up a line of force that connects them with the invisible side of the good that is desired. In fact, when the good demands it, it is sooner or later realized in part or in entirety. Have you ever experienced this?

Whenever I felt something strongly I usually followed through on my intuition. Often that which I was meditating about would make an appearance. In Jungian terms, this is known as the waking dream; what shows up in your life on a daily basis. Be aware. You have to allow yourself to let go of the "stuff" which isn't in your best interest to prepare for what is. In the Science of Mind textbook, we are advised "Desire connects you with the thing desired and expectation draws it into your life." (64:209).

Furthermore, "Only desire that which will round out your life to make it fuller and happier, and also that which will enable you to help others into better and happier conditions." (66:218). This is particularly true, even when some desires are thwarted. Do you stay open to new experiences even when you know they are temporary? Personally, although I don't always understand why certain circumstances and people come and go from our lives, I am reminded, once again, as Rabbi Harold Kushner advised us, don't ask why it happened, ask what you will do about it now. This is one of the major dichotomies of life. Forgiveness requires a lot of mental work. However, the one you hurt both mentally and physically when you hold on to anger and non-forgiveness is yourself.

By thinking of what gives you joy, wisdom, and satisfaction, Holmes reminds us that, "we see in life that which interests us the most and pass blindly by that which is of little or no interest…We may be so interested in things that are not prosperous, joyful, and healthy, that we pass by the very things we desire most and overlook the means of our health and prosperity…With our interest so engrossed in seeing the lesser, either through habit or ignorance, we fail to attract the greater things that are all around us." (69:230). I am sure we've all gone through many turning points which have been challenging, to say the least. When you really want to be involved in some worthwhile project or with someone, the opportunity manifests, sometimes without any struggle or strain. However, you must take action, make plans, meet and communicate with people of like mind who can help bring your ideas to fruition. When we desire, we expect, and as we expect we can achieve. The law of forgiveness is as much a part as the law of attraction as air is to breathing. Observe what happens in your own experience when you permit yourself to suffer through the remnants of the past. The choice is up to you.

The Law of Forgiveness

Forgiveness means that I am the one who is releasing myself from all burdens, people, conditions and limitations of the past and present. It means that I also take responsibility for allowing myself to be in a "negative" position in the first place, which is also to forgive myself completely. Holliwell reminds us that we should "seek by every means at our command to overcome, abandon and forsake every emotional tug that has a debilitating and disturbing effect." ... "The law reads that certain ideas must be dissolved and cleared from the mind in order that other ideas of a different character may replace them." With new thinking, you can grow spiritually and mentally and thus your outer life will reflect the newness in the people and experiences you invite.

Denial, on the other hand, means that I am not consciously honoring some thing or some condition because of not wanting to deal with the effects of that conditioning; whereas forgiveness means that I am consciously choosing to work the "spiritual law" of letting go of past hurts and conditions from the people or situations that I believe caused my unhappiness.

Just "forgetting" about something means that it might resurface some time in the future unless I consciously forgive the person or situation as well. The truth is that you cannot truly forget what you can't forgive, and likewise what you don't forgive, you won't forget.

So herein lies the difference. It is not a complete process without bringing these two components together.

The Law of Observance

Originally, this was called the Law of Obedience. However, since I have such an aversion to that word, I looked up obedience in a thesaurus to find other words that express the inner core, one of which is observance. The dictionary defines observance as " a rite, practice, or custom." Furthermore, it is described as "the act or practice of complying with something prescribed, as a law or rule." Seen in this light, you'll notice how your practice of new customs works with these principles to guide your experience.

You'll be surprised how the future takes care of itself when you live in the present, doing your best everyday, and letting go of the past. If one of your goals is to have an easier life, become more observant of everything on a daily basis. You'll notice how your thoughts and actions influence your thinking and your experiences throughout the day. Usually, our difficulties result from not following our intuition and listening to the voices of many others. Very often we see the answer in nature.

First think things into existence from within before you see them in the outer. Most experience is the outgrowth of your own creation. Your purpose is to choose what is for your highest good. If you don't know what that is, following The Law of Observance, will allow your intuition to guide you. If you're preoccupied with outer conditions, then you can't become still enough to discern what is in your best interest. Listen to the inner promptings you receive. When you govern your thinking and living, you won't doubt the results to be gained: happiness, peace, and prosperity to name a few.

I realize that many of these tenets are difficult to accept, especially as a first run. However, in time, that which was once bizarre becomes commonplace. This is similar to the idea that a luxury used long enough becomes a necessity. Chances are if you're reading this book, you're no doubt looking for answers to some of the more perplexing anomalies in life. As my search led me in the same direction, hopefully you will find yourself too. Remember, **you're** the only person who will never ever abandon you. However, if ever you should, watch out, you'd better become really observant!

The Truth About Substance

What is substance? It is defined as:
1) a. Matter that occupies space and has mass.
   b. Matter of a particular constitution or kind.
2) a. Essential character: essence.
   b. The most basic or important quality or part.

Why even bother to discuss the relevance of substance in a chapter on Prescriptions for Living? One reason is found in the very definition 2b—the most basic or important quality or part of your life depends on you. I interpret one aspect of the truth about who we are as being the inlet and outlet of spirit moving through us. In essence, we are the "handiwork" of God and we know God through each other. However, if you have difficulty in believing in a "god", or a higher power or anything other than your self, chances are none of this will have any meaning to you. Yet, many of these basic ideas are found and seen in nature. You don't see the wind but you feel and see the effects of it all around you. You can see and feel the rain, but you don't know the process involved in the rain's production. You can feel an earthquake, but you don't know it's coming. All of these ideas suggest that there are only certain things we have control over. When you get to this realization, it's not hard to know that there's something else to this thing we call life. I've always believed that by centering our minds and hearts on relaxation and meditation, we learn to master the outer, and develop a peaceful feeling. No matter what the situation, we'll be okay. Knowing this, is living in a different mindset. Yogananda reminds us in his book, Inner peace: How to be Calmly Active and Actively Calm:

"It is a good idea to keep a mental diary. Before you go to bed each night, sit for a short time and review the day. See what you are becoming. Do you like the trend of your life? If not, change it."

I've lived my life this way for a very long time. It's what has gotten me where I am now. While there have been many scary times, by centering myself, I knew that whatever I was experiencing was guiding me over these temporary circumstances to something far greater. Eric Butterworth suggests that there must be a need before we attract an answer. What are your current needs? Are you taking charge of your thinking daily? Make an experiment one week at a time. Be aware of your needs, write them down and affirm that they are being met in the right time and in the right way. Thus will your answers respond.

    Powerful words guide us into powerful works if you allow them to. I recall my years as a young girl. While I liked myself, had lots of playmates, and felt loved and secure in my family, I remember that my adolescent years were fraught with much turmoil. I didn't quite know who I was and I questioned and rebelled against everything. My awareness then was very strongly influenced by the peers of my day, which included music groups that were then popular, like the Beatles, Jimmie Hendrix, and Janis Joplin, to name a few. Most people will recall the late '60's and early '70's as times of turbulent change. As Bob Dylan sang out, "For the times, they are a-changin." The clothes we wore, the places we went and the experiments we lived made us feel at that time as if we were part of our world. I realize that today many of our youth are confused and perplexed by different problems. Yet, they too are facing a similar challenge although in a different century, trying to understand who they are and what their place in this highly technological society is. If we go back to our basic definition of substance, to be a part of something, then perhaps it's easier to understand why it's so hard to define the "truth" today. What has happened to our values? It's quite clear that everyone all over the world is grappling with issues of soul searching, seeking to define their role and place in the world today.

    As we begin to mature emotionally and psychologically, our lives will change. This in turn will assist you to become more effective in your work, whatever that is. Don't be surprised to find that your work will change as you do. I believe the prevailing mindset of the era contributes to our feelings of high or low-self-esteem. Although we may not be aware of it, change is usually made for the better when we have done our inner work. I am so pleased that there is so much valuable information and education now being offered for both men and women alike who have an opportunity to be positively influenced more than at any other time in our history. If this is not change, I don't know what is. Perhaps you will start to look at the words **"substance"** and **"truth"** a little differently from now on. Maybe we can also look at the word **prescription** in a different light. Instead of needing medical remedies brought about by overwhelming stress, now seen more in the younger generation, it can't hurt to practice different remedies for a new way of living. Please write to me and let me know how and if these new habits are affecting your life.

CHAPTER SEVEN

The Art of Making Peace With Your Life

This book began with a sincere, soulful search that has been consistent throughout my life. It is not that the search was constant, but rather, an ongoing one, at various points in my journey. I've observed that each one of us searches for a life that makes sense. This journey is really an unfoldment into the new phases of our lives that present themselves. Experiences show up that we are ready for in one way or another. We all have something we are dealing with. It is unfair to compare your lot to someone else's, for everyone's lesson is different. Hopefully, you'll choose not to repeat the tough ones.

There are many self-help books out there written by people proclaiming to have the answer. I don't claim to have "The Answer." What I offer is a variety of ideas and philosophies that have developed through time. These hard-won realizations have been my road to travel. Talk to someone else, and you will get their understanding. The key in making peace with your life is to develop your own internal wisdom, guide, and mentor so that you really begin to trust yourself. You'll find new meaning to your existence and life will take on different dimensions. Your conscious intention is to take charge of your life. Let simplicity mark your every effort. There is a great rhythm which flows through everyone and everything. Become aware of it.

To make peace with your life, yourself and others, it becomes necessary to explore. I believe you've discovered this theme throughout the text. The search for the Self ultimately culminates in a feeling of having arrived. Where might you ask is this place? I call it the higher self, the God force, the life force, the spiritual force that animates our life. You become one with it, and it with you. You'll allow yourself to be guided in your daily actions. It's the kind of feeling you have when you're happy to be home. You know yourself and what is important to you. I've often regarded the wisdom in Eastern spiritual philosophies to be practical, helpful and very easy to

understand. I've drawn great comfort and sensibility from the words of Paramahansa Yogananda, the founder of the Self-Realization Fellowship over the years. Consider some of his following quotes:
"To become a peaceful being, it is necessary to not merely read about spiritual truths, but to apply them."
"Introspection is a mirror in which to see recesses of your mind that otherwise would remain hidden from you. Analyze what you are, what you wish to become, and what shortcomings are impeding you..."
"The best way to live is to take life as a cosmic game, with its inevitable contrasts of defeat and victory. Enjoy the challenges as you would in a sport, no matter whether at the moment you are victorious or vanquished."

What comes to mind when *you* read the above? Over the years, most people have told me that what they really want in their life, more than anything else, is to be happy and feel at peace. In this chapter, I offer psycho-spiritual approaches because so many people are perplexed by combining the two sciences – that of psychology and spirituality. Most problems begin in the mind. If not there, then where? Although we are physical beings who may think that physical ills start in the body, as I've mentioned earlier, many studies throughout the years suggest the strong correlation between physical illness and mental stress. Therefore, the solutions to our problems must be found in the mind.

Psycho-spirituality is also known as Transpersonal Psychology which has been around for several decades. Furthermore, Dr. Carl Jung alluded to this same concept in many of his books on dream interpretation and symbology. Many writings exist on this subject and more medical doctors and other professionals in the mental health field are gradually coming to accept these ideas. More clinics devoted to a body/mind/spirit approach are being seen in hospitals where alternative treatment methods such as acupuncture, energy work, and hands on healing are common.

When a person suffers from a personality disorder, such as ongoing depression or anxiety that prevents them from living a normal life, all they want is to relieve their suffering. They normally expect to find and experience peace of mind and happiness. Life is

Soulful Love : The Search for the Self

not so much about sacrifice as it was decades ago. More people are starting to believe that suffering is optional. However, when you experience a stressful situation such as the loss of a loved one, a job, or an illness, you want to know that one day your life will return to (what we call) normal. The dichotomy though, is that as we move through the stages of our lives, we're always being transformed because we undergo a process of change. We may not even be aware of it when it's occurring because growth sometimes happens in silence.

I believe one key to happiness is accepting that we do change, that people change, and that circumstances change. Yet, there is that within us which is changeless. It has been referred to as your spirit. Whether you are in your physical body or not, your spirit is consistent. It is after all, the essence of who you are. While your rational mind may have difficulty believing this, how do you explain the unexplainable? You most probably have experienced feelings of déjà vu, that sense of already knowing people and places in a very intimate way in a short amount of time. All throughout our lives we create, act, suffer, enjoy, excel, and encounter many conditions through our thinking. Some believe that prayer is a mental approach to accepting reality. Others view counseling as the same thing. The one question is how do you define reality? Is it the sum of our experiences and what we think about them? A dictionary definition of reality is thus: "the quality or state of being real; a real event, entity, or state of affairs, or the totality of real things and events."Your experience defines your reality. For example, someone who suffers from an addictive personality would experience a different sense of reality than a non-addicted person.

The point is, that in order to experience peace of mind, you must be willing to relinquish those situations, people, and anything else that takes away from it. I often think of the saying in the New Testament of the Bible "To be in the world, but not of it." Why? What would this saying suggest to you? I have always interpreted it to mean that since we are only passing through here, we don't need to get so bent out of shape by all these things in the outer, for in the long run, how significant are they? I further believe that we are born to learn lessons and to make a difference. If not, then I can understand

The Art of Making Peace With Your Life

why so many people are overwhelmed by life and try to control other people or circumstances, thinking that will take away their emptiness. Emptiness is not a bad thing, for it suggests that you can fill the space with something valuable. You always have a choice.

It seems that whenever we have situations that we don't understand or cause us distress, we turn to the spiritual side of our thinking. Some call it religion, I refer to it as taking comfort in or from your spiritual beliefs. If you don't have any, what sustains you in times of crisis? Where do you put your faith, and what does faith have to do with psychology? Faith is both creative and having great conviction. Does your faith help you or hinder you? When we demonstrate faith, it is the belief that we can live the way we'd like to. Fear is having faith in what you don't want to happen; in the belief that things won't work out. However, what is meant by "not working out?" Does it mean that things don't go the way you want? Sometimes, they don't. Life is both a cause and effect process. I have come to learn and believe that when things don't work out the way I want them to, it's because something else is supposed to happen. In Judaism, this is called "Ba'shert." In other religions or philosophies, it is known as karma, following the Tao, fate, destiny, or the unseen hand of guidance.

We can take charge of our experiences by what we learn from them. However, our challenge is to work through our problems. It may help to view your experiences as a messenger. As your attitude improves, it is reflected in your ongoing experience. You may notice that you attract new friends and interests. When you shift your attitude, those around you will either do the same or they may move out of your life. Most of your growth is determined by the way you think and the way you think is influenced by your growth process. It is sometimes very hard to have faith in what we don't understand. Moreover, we can't even begin to fathom why certain things happen. Yet, we are reminded by those who have gone through difficult times that at some point we must ask ourselves not why something happened, but what we can do about the situation. Stressful events are anything but peaceful. Sometimes we draw comfort from those who've gone through similar circumstances and gain strength by the way they have dealt with the situation.

Soulful Love : The Search for the Self

While some of our wishes do come true, they don't always last forever. What does, on this earthly plane? What causes you to believe what you do? Have you ever noticed a difference in how you feel when you're being productive? You usually feel better about yourself and your life when you're involved in it. There are times for rest, and times for action. Finding the balance adds to your peace of mind. Believing in your abilities and knowing that you're capable of achieving what you want all contributes to a healthy self-esteem. If you don't know what you want, the universe has a way of giving you what you don't want. In this way, we're assisted to get your answers through elimination. It is deductive thinking at it's best.

Throughout life, you may fall off, yet you get back up again. When you mess up, clean up! We are always in a process of movement, from one place to another; if not physically, then mentally. Allow life to happen by moving in the direction that it's going. For example, you readily give up disease to be healthy. You give up discomfort to experience comfort. You give up frustration to be at peace. we need to let go of something in order to accept something different. It's helpful to become less resistant.

In Robert Fritz's book <u>The Path of Least Resistance: Learning to Become the Creative Force in Your Own Life</u> he states,

"…You got to where you are in your life right now by moving along the path of least resistance…energy moves where it is easiest for it to go…You can learn to recognize the structures at play in your life and change them so that you can create what you really want to create.

"Creating what you want is not a revelatory process, nor is it what you want something to be discovered…What do I want? The answer to this question is known, either rationally or intuitively, by those who are actively involved in creating.

Creative people know they make up what they create."

What does all of this have to do with peace of mind? Everything. Millions of people go through life frustrated by their potential, never having the chance nor taking one to discover what they're capable of. This comes from a fear of taking risks. However, taking risks is a part of life. When you know what your goals are, your desires motivate you. Your power is only a short distance from your

The Art of Making Peace With Your Life

thoughts and everything you seek is within. You can choose to surround yourself with positive energy which emanates from both within and without. Some would say that we are also influenced by negative energy; however, once again, your experience is determined by what you believe. Doesn't it make more sense to surround yourself by that which is positive? If you follow your desires, you will most probably feel settled. When you don't pursue your goals, you usually feel the opposite. When you are at peace, outer circumstances affect you less because you choose to see situations differently.

Whenever you feel frustrated, hopeless, or fearful, determine to do something about it rather than give way to those feelings. The mind responds by corresponding to that which is expected. What do you expect? The mind is like a laboratory. It experiments. For example, you may say "I feel scared or lonely." These feelings are real and need not be dismissed. However, to move through them, you must become aware of what has caused you to feel this way. Once you identify those factors, you can begin to deal with it. Rather than buying into adversity, you can choose to see the experience as a blessing in disguise, but it takes practice. Looking within is helpful when dealing with these situations. It is one reason why meditation has become so popular.

More people realize the value in taking time out of their busy schedules to quiet their minds. When you put yourself in a peaceful environment by lighting a candle, listening to relaxing music or practicing yoga, you automatically reduce your stress level. All of these rituals are designed with that purpose in mind. While meditation is important, so is making time to talk with and listen to others. Everything is a balance. We all want to be heard. Meditation is crucial to the mind. The mind is the master and the body is the servant. If our inner house is not in order, nothing in the outer will be. A meditator looks after his or her own mind. What do you give your attention to?

Have you ever given yourself permission to experience good feelings for an extended period of time? It is possible, however, we have to give ourselves time to heal from those experiences which caused us to feel anything but peaceful. Having the freedom to make

Soulful Love : The Search for the Self

choices is a wonderful gift. It requires honesty and the ability to ask important questions. Honesty helps us to move out of negativity by creating more openness in our lives. When we let go of outcomes, the people we're in conflict with are usually changed to some degree.

When you face difficulty, try to understand it from a more spiritual perspective by asking what you're learning here. Accept that you will know the truth about the situation. The only thing we need to heal is our own confusion, memories and our thinking. We do this by letting go of negativity, which is very hard to do. But once again, like with any other accomplishment, it takes practice and persistence. We can't instruct others unless we've gone through the experience. Think of what you wish to demonstrate. Again, stop thinking about what you don't want. Belief is half the battle. Being unaware might invite more random experiences into your life. However, this is not to say that being aware will prevent situations that you don't understand from showing up. Learning to see people in a different light really changes our experience of them. It may not change them, however.

Imagination plays a key role in moving your life forward. Much has been said about the use of visualization to create what we desire. Through imaging and using creative awareness, you prepare yourself for these experiences. Be extremely careful with what you allow yourself to think about. You always have the power to rethink any situation and create a new condition. When you know what makes you upset, you can do something about it. Wanting has two parts to it – the form and the experience. Sometimes, your experience is different from what you want or thought you wanted. Yet, all it takes is a willingness to work with what is. When you're dealing with others, it requires both parties to be creative.

Listen to your inner voice. Practice saying, "I want to experience _____ because I'm ready to feel _____." The more you do this, it will happen. Beware however, that while you may get something, it may be only temporary. For example, every time you're ready for a change, recognize that when the change comes, you never know how long it will last. I am reminded of a woman's story. She was moved to another state by her company. Two years later, the company changed owners, and she was out of a job. She then had the choice to

The Art of Making Peace With Your Life

stay where she was, move back to her original home, or go some place else.

Another way that the law of visualization works is through the use of affirmations. For example, if you want to take a trip and you don't have the funds or time to do it, eventually, the only way it will happen is if you create the space and the time to make the journey. Part of that creativity includes becoming resourceful to obtain the necessary funding. In this case, you might create an affirmation that goes something like this; "I am open and receptive to do what I have to in order to make this journey. The way opens easily." To some, this exercise may seem foolish, however, I would suggest as I have to many others that you create an experiment for at least one to three weeks and then judge for yourself by the results.

Learn to be an observer in your life. It's almost as if you can step back and pretend that you're watching the events in your life unfold as if you are behind a video camera. Observation takes practice and is extremely useful in learning to be less judgmental. It can remove negative emotions such as the need to be defensive, jealous, threatening, or inappropriately angry. Being the observer helps to clear away negativity. How do you observe people and their opinions? We all have a script. Most of it is learned and unconscious.

As <u>Soulful Love</u> has pointed out throughout the different chapters, becoming aware is a critical key to creating purpose and peace of mind. What you view as hard to give up becomes easier because you see a benefit in freeing yourself from what binds you. Look at all of the possibilities that life is showing you. How do you use the power you've been given? The kind of power I refer to is self-empowerment — the ability of your mind to produce desired results. It is the same idea that Einstein referred to when he said that we use a very small percentage of our brain power. That is because most have never been taught how to access and unleash that power.

Think of what you give and receive in any relationship. Is there a balance? It is important to know how to receive if you've always been a giver and conversely, the opposite is also true. You have to learn how to give unconditionally if you've always been a receiver. It is an interesting truth that very often what we give to others returns

Soulful Love : The Search for theSelf

to us by different people. Whoopi Goldberg states, "When you are kind to someone in trouble, you hope they'll remember and be kind to someone else."

Everything starts with giving. People are struggling or tired of trying to get things. Many build expectations around others, rather than themselves, which creates stress. Therefore, think of what you can give in any relationship. Truly successful people always help others and they're not afraid that their good will be withheld from them. There's a universal principle of goodness which operates in the world, especially when people are in crisis. What is unfortunate is that many people wait for emergencies before they help others. When you develop a conviction to be helpful, harmonious, and loving, chances are you will receive the same.

Many people expect rejection based on the past. You must be willing to let go of the past mindset which created those conditions and afford others the same opportunity. We must get into the habit of empowering others to know that they are special and unique. We all have days when we feel inadequate and we need to remind each other that we're not alone. Ernest Holmes, the founder of Religious Science/The Science of Mind stated, "Never look at that which you don't wish to experience. Don't accept it." If you dwell upon those things or stay angry, you create more of the same. Therefore, you don't have to convince yourself of what you don't want to feel anymore. Stay with an idea until it becomes a tangible reality, an accomplished fact. Have a quiet expectancy and a calm confidence. Although it is really hard to not be disturbed by things, doing so will allow you to demonstrate something different over conditions. The use of your creative power does not need to be forced or urged into action. The law of attraction is set into motion because the movement begins in your mind.

Patience has been defined as a quality of tranquil waiting. It also serves a purpose in reminding us that everything unfolds in its right time, which may not be your time. Consider the famous song based on Ecclesiastes, "To everything turn, turn, turn, there is a season, turn, turn, turn and a time to every purpose under heaven." Faith is an important ingredient in waiting. Being open and honest is the best way to go. You can learn to move the energy contained in a problem

The Art of Making Peace With Your Life

by brainstorming creative ideas. Engage in some form of activity to generate a new dynamic. A new thought solves old problems. This is what happens in a think tank; people engaging their minds together to create something out of nothing.

What influences your thinking today? Many people look at their lives and believe they must accept their fate. Yet, the truth is that everything is fluid. Consider that ice, which is water in a frozen form, becomes liquid when melted. The activity of the heat upon the ice creates the new form, the same way the water being acted upon by the cold creates the other form. Consider those individuals who have been struck by adversity and yet overcome it. We have many examples, Helen Keller, Job, Nelson Mandela, Lance Armstrong, and Mark Mathabane, to name a few. If you don't know who these people are, find out. Perhaps you know a few heroes of your own.

Make a personal inventory of what you like and dislike about yourself. Do the same for the people in your life who you want or need to forgive. You may be surprised to find some qualities are the same. Maybe, that's why we attract certain experiences. Either there's an element of what we don't like about the other person within ourselves, or we are being given the opportunity to affect the other person in some positive way. If that doesn't work, evacuate! In all things, maintain a sense of humor because if you don't, you might just crack up! Seriously, we can all watch a sitcom and laugh at it, but when it comes to our own lives, we get mired down in the muck instead of making a change. Are you aware of the changes you've made in yourself up until this point? This is your present work. We are partly responsible for what we create. Very often, after time has passed, we can look back at those situations which we thought would break us and see how they made us. We even laugh at them.

Some people believe in prayer. Prayer has been essential to the well-being of a soul that understands itself. Prayer is not to change a situation as much as it is about changing our thinking about the situation. For example, you might pray for someone you love who is ill to be healed. However, who are we to say what form the healing should take?

I recall when my father was being kept alive by a respirator for three weeks in intensive care. After the first week and a half of praying for his ability to breathe on his own to be restored, I finally had to let go. What was comforting when I finally told my Dad that it was okay for him to leave because it was such a struggle for him, my prayers changed to whatever was in his best interests. A week and a half later he passed away peacefully and I was fortunate to have been with him that very afternoon, brushing his hair, kissing his forehead, and telling him how much I appreciated him for having been such a wonderful father.

The same is true of my Mother's passing because while I prayed for her desire to want to live, I had to accept her decision of not wanting to be here anymore so that she could be with my Father. What was wonderful however, was being able to be with her throughout her illness and have the opportunity to become so close and finally accept each other. I recall her saying when she was at home with Hospice care, "If you love me, pray God takes me." What more could I do for her so that she no longer had to suffer for every breath? I am grateful that they are both at peace now.

How have you personally recovered from your prayers and/or wishes which weren't fulfilled? Were you able to truly believe that everything happened for the best and move on with your life? It takes a lot of practice, time, understanding and awareness to think this way. The alternative doesn't provide you with much mental health. Perhaps, that is why the saying, "Let go and let God," came about. There are many other spiritual and philosophical statements which mirror the aforementioned, such as, "not my will, but thy will be done," "go with the flow," and "when in doubt, do without." I particularly like Gracie Allen's saying, "Never place a period, where God placed a comma." Nothing is ever really taken away from us. Letting go doesn't mean losing, it means something better is on the way or here now. When something ends, it is really changing. As you release the change and move your thinking forward to the experience you want to have, you'll know what to do, how to say it and release any blockages.

All of this being said and done, another component of making peace with our lives, is being aware of how others perceive the limitations they have about themselves. Do you expect limitation in your own life? Just as you can't force people to be where they are not, the same is true for ourselves. The best we can do is mentally support them, and let's not forget to seek out support when we need it. Mental support is usually for our own peace of mind. To be able to recognize another's limitation doesn't mean that we have to limit our own thinking. Observe what has been a pattern in your life and know that it will change as your thinking does. Be willing to receive and express affection, especially in difficult times. Confusing issues is one obstacle that surfaces in intimate relationships. Healing personal relationships is done on a daily basis. If you don't continue to heal from hurtful experiences, both before and while you are living through them, you may re-experience the same emotions. Your emotions are dictated in part by your belief system. Hurtful experiences within relationships are a reminder for you to maintain your mental equilibrium. You can't think that "I'll be alright when —————— does ————," because this kind of thinking puts us in bondage to others, requiring them to change. The more you know about a problem, the more you'll be at peace, even while you're working through it.

Think about what creates peace of mind. When you're at peace, you feel good about your relationships. Sometimes, this state of mind is so healing that anyone you're involved with picks up on it. Your own ability to accept, adapt, and adjust to situations that you can't change has a positive effect. What you think about radiates a current and you can observe what's going on by seeing what shows up in your life. Dr. Brian Weiss recommends that we know our own thoughts and assumptions. He states, "Experience is much stronger than belief. Learn from your experiences. <u>What helps without harming is valuable</u>. Discard outdated beliefs and thoughts."

Of course, it takes a lot of work to discard outdated beliefs and thoughts because whether or not you realize it, every day provides new opportunities to choose which path you'll take. Letting go of the old, which no longer works for you, means that you're creating a new dynamic, expecting different results versus buying into fears that recreate the same scenario. We must give up that which causes us to be negative. At the same time, you can reframe a situation in a way that helps you to assess whether or not you contribute to any negativity as well.

If a situation is difficult, there is obviously still more to learn. Our emotions influence our thinking. When we cry, a certain chemical is released through our tears which is why we usually feel better afterwards. As the tears recede, your thoughts become more clear. As a river doesn't stay in one place, so is your understanding of your life. Our human existence requires that we meet and reconcile with those people we consider important in our lives. If not, then we never have closure. In those circumstances where the other person is not willing to communicate with you, you must mentally reconcile so that you are no longer haunted by unfinished business. In this way you make your own peace, realizing that you have done your best and allow nature to take its course. Everything unfolds to its purpose.

Life is about balance. Be aware of what causes you to get off center and keep a log of it. If you believe that the situation in question is working out, then you have to be willing to watch it unfold without being too controlling. Keep affirming what you wish to demonstrate because there is no such thing as a failure. Everything works itself out and usually it is for a larger purpose that we are not even aware of. Our daily dramas contribute to this purpose. If you are preoccupied with the past, you don't believe that there are no accidents! While we do have control about the way we think, we have to remember that we're really not in control of anything else.

Part of our life's work is really believing that possibilities are limitless. Growth, change, and awareness are all part of this process. When you observe the process of change, something always happens; we make a change or get pushed out of the way. On some level, we ready ourselves for what we experience. Not all change has to be heart wrenching, it can be done with more ease and adjustment in certain situations. Renowned author, Maryann Williamson writes, "Don't ever underestimate the power of a nervous breakdown!" A breakdown can actually lead to a breakthrough. Rather than wishing things were otherwise, look at them differently by realizing they are that way for a reason.

A helpful exercise is to think of and record five ways in which you are successful each day. Be aware of how you define success. Is it attainment, accomplishment, mastery, fruition and victory? See what interests you. Redecorate your mind. If you don't know what's in your mind, look at what's in your life. Getting along with others is an important part of life. As such, change is something that we will experience throughout our lifetime. Our thoughts set definite forces in motion. We all desire to have soulful experiences where we feel the interchange, presence and expression of love. Nature does not wait for us; it keeps operating even as we move through our emotions. When you feel bad, seek comfort. Believing that there is a presence operative in your life which knows better than you do what is in your best interests is very comforting. This kind of thinking has helped many to cope and surmount the most difficult situations. Eric Butterworth admonishes us to do the following:

"Why not pick the most difficult thing facing you right now and say, I know that this is the best thing that could happen to me; for I know that in the happening there is revealed a new lesson to learn and some new growth experience…and this is my opportunity to begin to give birth to new ideas, new strength, and a new vision. I accept the reality of the difficulty but not its permanence."

As long as we continue to see any situation as difficult, it will remain so, until you switch your mindset about it. Facts are only relative. Do you limit your own ideas? As stated earlier, prayer and affirmative thinking deals with the potential of any situation. When you trust yourself and know that you're right where you need to be, your experiences will reconfirm this for you as well. Life is an inner agreement. You create the conditions of your experiences. If you don't like what is going on, change it. No one can withhold your good from you.

Listen to your words when you speak. Love is a transformative experience and you know what it feels like to be really loved. It is said that our life externalizes at the level of our thinking. Thus it is that we can assess our past, present and glimpse what is yet to be. We all know what is true and what isn't. Truth is very often explainable, meaning that we interpret the truth by our feelings, intuition, intellect and our experience. We no longer need to lie to ourselves. *First the truth makes you miserable and then it sets you free.* Our struggle is accepting the truth in any situation and the dichotomy is that life is not meant to be a struggle, all be it a growth experience. This is what is meant by free will. Our search for the meaning and purpose of our lives can create or destroy the peace of mind and sanity we seek. Knowing that you're okay where you are reminds you to be gentle with yourself. While it's not easy to build a mental equivalent of happiness, new thoughts replace old, outworn ideas. Get interested in something and you will be successful. You have to learn for yourself how to think positively. Practice saying to yourself, "This is what I have, now, what do I want?" Be a part of the solution. As problems present themselves, be flexible in your thinking as needed. Remember that problems are really opportunities in disguise and force us to grow. Put some emotional distance between yourself and the problem. Contemplate what is useful and build on that. When you are drawn into a trauma or difficult situation, your goal is to remain centered and know the truth. Consider the wisdom in this Chinese proverb, "So you've fallen down, how long are you going to lay there?" Stop expecting other people to change because it is you who makes the changes. When that happens, the situation becomes different.

Do you believe that life is an exciting journey? I wonder what would happen, if upon awakening, we all thought that something wonderful would happen to us today. Faith and fear don't work together. Withdraw from any thinking about how something will happen and allow it to unfold. By doing this, you won't have to get stuck in an old story. You won't even want to rewind the tape, you'll want to change it. It requires discipline to work through blocks. Change produces new experiences and your consciousness has to develop enough to clear up false beliefs such as, "I don't deserve to be happy." Working with your thoughts and feelings helps you to feel a sense of wholeness. Most of us are still struggling with the belief that we need something or someone to feel whole. This is why many relationships don't work out; people are expecting the other person to fulfill all their dreams and make them whole. Yet we know this is unrealistic. When you do something out of love, truth, and integrity, you're not seeking to inflict harm on another. This is noble and hurts no one. Thus, we don't get trapped in any experience. We are free to think as we want to.

Imagine what your life would be like if you knew that you never made a mistake nor would you make any in the future. It has been said that there are really no mistakes, only different paths. What are your expectations? While we know that mistakes help us grow, we can choose to learn in a new way. The art of making peace with your life suggests that you first quiet the mind and then go within and trust your intuition. A good example of a mistake is when you take someone else's advice over your own. Too often, we seek answers from others because we don't trust ourselves. However, the more you believe that others have your answers only delays your ability to trust yourself. This is not to negate that the help we receive from others can be of value, but it does suggest that we must become our own best friend.

When you can trust yourself, then you won't be mad at anyone else. Practice saying, "If I quiet my mind, I'll know what to do and when and how to do it." In this way, you have no one to blame for the results of your choices. It is helpful to put closure on each day. You can do this by releasing and forgiving whatever you need to and give thanks for each experience. Write them down. This practice is a sound philosophy because it allows life to evolve without your need to force any issues. Forgiving yourself and others is true forgiveness. You can choose to give up pain and confusion by right thinking. Take control of your mind, thinking, and actions. Know that your answers are present and believe that there is a solution to every problem, even if it is only acceptance. What doesn't belong in your life falls away naturally, even if you thought it was there to stay. In reality, the "It" represents an experience you've had which was there for your growth and learning.

In the previous chapter, "Prescriptions for Living," I offered some affirmations to help you create what you want. There is a process known as A Seven Day Mental Diet which is basically fasting from negative thinking. It's a real discipline. What happens when you stop resisting? Can you allow your mind to rest? If you continually hold on to problems, they only resurface and you'll still have to deal with them. This usually happens when we give our power over to another person. When you clear away thinking which says, "I won't be happy unless" or "I will only be happy if...", you are disciplining your mind to be aware of not giving your power away. All problems need space. You assist the process of resolution when you affirm that everything is unfolding in the right time and place. Take action when needed, but be mindful of how you get involved. Do your actions help or hinder a situation?

Nothing in life is certain. Eric Butterworth reminds us that the most secure individual is a life term convict in a penitentiary, because almost all of his needs are met. But, what kind of price is that to pay for security? If our lives are an expression of growth and expansion, then how we view security is determined by what we believe is possible.

The word "secure" comes from two Latin words, "se" which means without, and "cure," meaning care. The essence of being secure is not having any cares; a freedom from anxiety. As Butterworth suggests,

"Your security is in the wings of your faith, your intuitive relationship with the divine is a process that flows from within. Your ideas are the coins of the kingdom out of which you mold and fashion your good. In Hebrew, the word for security is a word that literally means "Worthy." True security is in worthiness and not in worth.

You have to discover a philosophy that works for you. How you define security makes all the difference in how you make peace with your life. You've been given many ideas to ponder. Our lives are ongoing and discovery is a gradual process. No one can tell you how or what to think. They may try, however, in the final analysis, you are the one who inhabits your body. You know full well when you are out of kilter, and you also know what it feels like to be at peace. If you experience more mental and emotional stability, seek less drama, and know what's important to you, then you've enhanced your ability to live a more peaceful existence. The choice is up to you. As with any other art form, you are required to continue practicing, otherwise you can grow stale.

EPILOGUE

"Only in growth, reform, and change, paradoxically enough, is true security to be found." I can't recall where or when I read this statement, however, it had a strong impact on me. In reflecting back on the years it has taken me to complete Soulful Love, I can honestly say that I've learned to accept these words rather than fight against them. If the only thing in life that is secure is change, then it is up to us how we choose to move through both the predictable and unexpected times of transition as best we can. It has been a hard road for me to learn how to "go with the flow." In retrospect, it has been a mixture of awareness, growth, and knowledge, along with learning how to trust myself and my guidance. I have discovered how important it is to rely upon one's own faculties, and when in times of confusion, if you don't know who to ask for help and where to go, find out!

I believe that Soulful Love can assist you in finding a balance between your spiritual belief's and how you apply them on a daily basis in all of your relationships. If you don't heal the circumstances of your life which have caused you pain, then you allow yourself to be oppressed by them. As we all move forward into this century, we'll have to learn new ways of communicating; ways that don't promote heartache, despair, sadness, and/or suicide. Unfortunately, these are the adjectives that we have accepted far too long in describing loving relationships, and I don't think that we were destined to live our lives in emotional turmoil.

It is possible to diminish the amount of destructive negativity you subject yourself too. You have to learn to channel your energy into different, healthy alternatives. This is what I have chosen to do over the years, and it is my hope that I will continue to practice what I preach. It's interesting to note that over a year later, when the book was first published, the epilogue had never been printed due its being lost in electronic transmission. Having had to return to the task a year later and be able to pick up from where I left off was impossible! Why? Precisely for the same reason I began the Epilogue with…**"Only in growth, reform, and change, paradoxically enough, is true security to be found."** May your search never be in vain. I thank you for reading the book and look forward to an ongoing dialogue. Please contact me at Dr.Deri@aol.com .

Bibliography

Chapter One

Adams, Kenneth M.   Silently Seduced, When Parents Make Their Children Partners – Understanding Covert Incest, Health Communications, Inc., Deerfield Beach, FL, 1991.

Beattie, Melody J.   Journey to the Heart, Daily Meditations on the Path to Freeing Your Soul, Harper San Francisco, San Francisco, CA, 1996, pp. 236-237.

Dunion, Paul   "A Village Beyond The Lie," The Peace Exchange, Vol. VI, Issue IV, Dec. 1999, Swarthmore, PA, pp. 1-2.

Frankl, Victor Emil   Man's Search for Meaning, An Introduction to Logotherapy, Simon & Schuster, New York, NY,

Gibran, Kahlil   The Prophet, Alfred A. Knopf, Inc., New York, NY, 1923, pp. 17-18.

Kimmel, Michael S   Changing Men: New Directions in Research on Men and Masculinity, Sage Publications, Inc., Newbury Park, CA, 1987, pp. 9 – 11.

Moore, Thomas   Soul Mates – Honoring the Mysteries of Love and Relationship, Harper Collins Publishers, Inc., New York, NY, 1994, pp. 28 – 29.

Vanzant, Iyanla   In The Meantime – Finding Yourself and the Love You Want, Simon & Schuster, New York, NY, 1998, pp. 306 – 307.

Chapter Two

"The Double Standard – A Parable of Ages," The Suffragist Magazine, January 10, 1914, p. 4.

DuNann-Winter, D   "Peace From An Ecofeminist Perspective: Boys Will Be Boys…Unless…," The Peace Psychology Bulletin, Vol. 3, No. 3, p. 12, November 1994, Division 48 of The American Psychological Association.

Engleberg, H.   "Lancet Low Serum Cholesterol and Suicide," 339 (8795): 727-9, 1992 March 21. Department of Medicine, Cedars-Sinai Medical Center, Los Angeles, CA.

Faizi, Gloria   The Baha'i Faith, An Introduction, Baha'i Publishing Trust, New Delhi, INDIA, 1992.

Gelles, Richard J. & Cornell, Claire Pedrick — "Intimate Violence in Families," Text Series Two, Sage Publications, Inc., Newbury Park, CA, 1990, p. 41.

Herman, Judith Lewis — Trauma and Recovery, Basic Books, Inc., New York, NY, 1997.

Kaiden, Larry — "Social Responsibility." The Peace Exchange, Vol. II, Issue IV, Swarthmore, PA, Men's International Peace Exchange, 1994, p. 4.

Kushner, Harold — When Bad Things Happen to Good People, Simon & Schuster, New York, NY, 1986.

Labowitz, Shoni — God, Sex and Women of the Bible, Simon & Schuster, New York, NY, 1998, p. 67.

Lorber, Judith — Gender and Society (Official Publication of Sociologists for Women in Society – Special Issue: Violence Against Women), Vol. 3, No. 4, Sage Publications, Inc., Newbury Park, CA, 1989, p. 547.

Men Against Racism and Sexism Austin, TX, (512) 326-9686.

Mindell, Arnold — Sitting in the Fire, Lao-Tse Press, Portland, OR,

Peay, Pythia S. — Common Boundary Magazine, July/August 1994.

Ronis, Deri — "Transforming Destructive Conflict: Healing the Oppression of Patriarchy", Canadian Peace Research Journal, Vol. 29, No. 1, February 1997, pp. 13 – 24.

Schlissel, Steve — Director of Mean Time Ministries, Internet, 1999.

Sharp, Gene — Gandhi as a Political Strategist, Porter Sargent Publishers, Inc., Boston, MA, 1979.

Shervin, Judith & — "Love is More Than a Fairy Tale." WN/Chicago Tribune, reprinted in Today's Boca Woman News Magazine, Vol. 4, No. 6, p. 7, 1995, Boca Raton, FL.

Tobach, E. — Commentary on: "Peace From An Ecofeminist Perspective." The Peace Psychology Bulletin, Vol. 3, No. 3, p. 16, November, 1994, Division 48 of the American Psychological Association.

Trotter, Wilfred — Instincts of the Herd in Peace and War, Omnigraphics, Inc., Detroit, MI, 1916, reprinted 1990.

Webster's II New Riverside Dictionary, Houghton Mifflin Company, Boston, MA, 1984.

Chapter Three

Belenky, M. "et al"   Women's Ways of Knowing: The Development of Self, Voice, and Mind, Basic Books, New York, NY,

Boulding, K.   Three Faces of Power, Sage Publications, Inc., Newbury Park, CA, 1989.

Bryant, D.   Ella Price's Journal, The Feminist Press, The City University of New York, NY, 1997

Engelberg, H.   Lancet Low Serum Cholesterol and Suicide, 339 (8794): 727-9, Dept. of Medicine, Cedars-Sinai Medical Center, Los Angeles, CA 1992 Mar 21.

Faizi, Gloria.   The Baha'i Faith, An Introduction, Baha'I Publishing Trust, New Delhi, India, 1992.

Fillmore, Charles   The Revealing Word, Unity School of Christianity, Lee's Summit, MO 1959

Gray, J.   What Your Mother Couldn't' Tell You and Your Father Didn't Know, Harper Collins, New York, NY, 1994.

Harman, W.   The Scientific Exploration of Consciousness: Towards An Adequate Epistemology, Journal of Consciousness Studies I, No. 1, Imprint Academic, Thorverton, Exeter, UK: Summer, 1994.

Kaiden, L.   Social Responsibility, *The Peace Exchange*, Vol. II, Issue IV, Men's International Peace Exchange, Swarthmore, PA.

Muller, Robert   Most Of All They Taught Me Happiness, Doubleday Company, Garden City, NY, 1978.

Reibstein, Janet,   Sexual Arrangements Marriage and the Temptation of Infidelity, Charles Scribner's Sons, New York, 1993

Sharp, Gene   Gandhi As A Political Strategist, Porter Sargent Publishers, Inc., Boston, MA, 1979.

Shervin, J. & Sniechowski, J   Love is More Than a Fairy Tale, WN/Chicago Tribune, 1995, reprinted in *Today's Boca Woman News Magazine,* Vol. 4, No. 6, Boca Raton, FL.

Tobach, E.   Commentary on "Peace From An Ecofeminist Perspective" *The Peace Psychology Bulletin,* Vol. 3, No. 3, November 1994. Division 48 of the APA.

Trotter, W.   Instincts of the Herd in Peace and War, Omnigraphics, Inc., Detroit, MI (1916; 1990 reprint).

Webster   Webster's II New Riverside Dictionary, Houghton Mifflin Company, Boston, MA, 1984.

Vanzant, Iyanla   Acts of Faith, Simon & Schuster, New York, 1993

Winter, D. Peace From an Ecofeminist Perspective: Boys Will Be Boys... Unless... The Peace Psychology Bulletin, Vol. 3, No. 3, November 1994. Division 48 of the APA.

Chapter Four

Cohen, Alan Happily Even After: Can You Be Friends After Lovers?, Hay House, Inc. Carlsbad, CA., 1999

Kaslow, Florence W. The Dynamics of Divorce: A Life Cycle Perspective, Brunner/Mazel, Inc. New York, NY, 1987

Phillippe, Melissa Heal it Presence Productions, San Rafael, CA,

Chapter Five

Adams, Kenneth M. Silently Seduced: When Parents Make Their Children Partners: Understanding Covert Incest, Health Communications Inc. Deerfield Beach, Florida, 1991

Blanton, Brad Radical Honesty: How to Transform Your Life By Telling The Truth, Bantam Doubleday Dell Publishing Group, Inc. New York, New York, 1996

Bradshaw, John Healing the Shame That Binds You, Health Communications, Deerfield Beach, Florida, 1998 The Family: A Revolutionary Way of Self-Discovery, Health Communications, Inc. Deerfield Beach, Florida, 1988

Butterworth, Eric Spiritual Economics: The Prosperity Process, Unity School of Christianity, Unity Village, Missouri,

Cohen, Alan The Heart of Parting, The Happy Times Monthly, Boca Raton, Florida, June 2000, p.6

Dreamer, Oriah M. The Invitation, Harper, San Francisco, 1999

Gray, John Ph.D. What Your Mother Couldn't Tell You And Your Father Didn't Know, Harper Collins, San Francisco, CA Nov. 1994

Hendrix, Harville Getting the Love You Want, Harper Perennial, New York, NY. Feb. 1990 (reissue)

Keyes, Ken, Jr. A Conscious Person's Guide to Relationships, Living Love Publications, 1979

Muller, Robert Most of All They Taught Me Happiness, Out of Print

Norden, Michael J. Beyond Prozac, Regan Books, Harper Collins Publishers, New York, 1995

Redfield, James — The Celestine Prophecy, Warner Books, New York, New York, 1993

Schaeffer, Brenda — Is It Love Or Is It Addiction, Harper Collins Publishers, San Francisco, 1987

Toufexis, Anastasia — The Right Chemistry, p. 49, Time Magazine, February 15, 1993

Wanio, Paul — I Love You I Think; When Sex Disguises Itself as Love, NightStar Press, Delray Beach, Florida, 1995

Zweig, Connie — Romancing the Shadow A Guide to Soul Work for a Vital, Authentic Life, Ballantyne Publishing Group, New York, 1997

Chapter Six

Goldsmith, Joel — The Gift of Love

Holliwell, Raymond — Working With The Law, Church and School of Christian Philosophy, Phoenix, AZ, 1992

Holmes, Ernest — The Science Of Mind, G.P. Putnam's Sons, New York, New York, 1938

Peck, Scott, M.,. — The Road Less Traveled, Simon and Schuster, Inc. New York, New York, 1978

Ram Dass — Be Here Now

Ronis, Diane, — Brain Compatible Assessments, Skylight Professional Development, Arlington Heights, IL.,

Yogananda, Paramahansa — Inner Peace, Self-Realization Fellowship, Los Angeles, CA 1999

Chapter Seven

Fritz, Robert — The Path of Least Resistance, Fawcett, Columbine/Ballantine Books, New York, NY, 1984

Weiss, Brian, M.D. — Messages From the Masters: Tapping into the Power of Love, Warner Books, New York, NY,

Index

A Conscious Person's Guide to Loving150
a passion for life157
A spiritual life is reality212
ability to accept endings166
accept suicide136
Against Racism and Sexism67
Agape 150
alcoholic or violent family26
anger103
Anger is energy115
assistance of a counselor140
attack the problem103
authentic207
awareness 149
B
balanced love relationship83
Be gentle with yourself 219
Be Here Now217
become aware91
become the right person 127
becoming aware150
Being romantic71
beloved within myself78
beyond selfishness62
boredom 101
borrowed time88
breaking up is hard to do205
C
can't survive without someone 128
casual sex.151
causes of conflict amongst couples114
Celestine Prophecy27
Challenges and Suggestions:99
change will benefit65
chemical brain imbalances58
co- dependency31
Co-Dependent86
commitment123,152
commitment-phobic 159

complacency 101
Confusing 241
controlling behavior131
Covert Incest191
Creative Force 234
cultural attitudes62
Cumulative stresses 153
D
define lazy102
define love82
Denial225
describe masculine71
Desire 224
detachment brings joy112
Discover The Power Within You100
Divorce or separation95
domestic violence75,170
don't get overly enmeshed 136
E
experiment219
F
face your worst fears121
family responsibilities138
feel love in a spiritual context163
Feminist and women's studies74
Flow of Life101
Forgiveness 225
Freedom 220
functions of serotonin62
G
game playing89
get rid of this negativity109
get what you wanted70
H
Healing is a process111
healing oppression58
Healing the heart107
healing the inner child131
Healing the Shame 87

Healing the Shame That Binds You 207
hormonal drives 97
how your brain functions 153

I
If I quiet my mind 245
if we don't heal ourselves 148
Imagination 236
In the Flow of Life 101
increase the serotonin 153
incredible transformative experiences 163
Indifference 101
Inhibited Sexual Desire 102
Inner peace 227
Intimate relationships 177
Introspection 231
Is It Love Or Is It Addiction 166
Is It Love or Is It Addiction? 98

K
know thyself 148
knowing thyself 115

L
Law of Attraction 213
Learn the art of surrender 215
learning and truth 156
learning to heal 61
Least Resistance 234
lets agree to disagree 104
Letting go 211
levels of sharing 100
life is difficult. 29
Listening 98
lives of quiet desperation 128
love and accept who you are 157
Lying kills people 175

M
magical results 219
make peace with yourself 157
Man's Search for Meaning 30
marriage 77
Maslow 148
mental health support groups 64
mindset 70

N
nagging 99
Namasté 212
Necessary Losses 187
need for revenge 108
nervous breakdown 242
no guarantees 25

O
observance 226
oppression breeds violence 62
Overcoming Family Violence 152

P
passion 78
Patience 238
patriarchy 73
peace of mind 147
Peace of Mind 23
peaceful lifestyle 71
perception of death 79
Personal growth and change 95
Power Within You 100
Powerful words 228
psychic contradiction 89
purpose 87
purpose in life 28

R
Radical Honesty 94, 121
Reconciliation 131
reframe 103
Regression Therapy 126
Relaxing Yang Way 164
release your anger and stress 81
Remain open 174
re-marriage 193
repressed anger 115
respect their limits and needs 124
Revenge 63
Romancing the Shadow 161
romantic and platonic love 149

S
Science of Mind 215
search for the beloved 78
Search for the Beloved 80

Seeing Beyond – Loving Practice 201
Self-actualization 112
Self-respect 118
Sex is not a game 155
Sexual Arrangements 95, 122
sexuality 151
sit with each other and listen 135
Soul searching 23
spaces in your togetherness 100
spiritual awakening 32
stay together 96
Stop creating obstacles 214
substance 227
surrender the ego 160
T
taking social action 64
The Dance of Intimacy 161
The Dynamics of Divorce 130
The Path to Love 186
The Path To Love 148
The Right Chemistry 189
The Search for the Self 211
The unexamined life 68
There Are No Condoms For The Heart 151
There's no judgment 200
tools available for healing 117
Trust your intuition 165
truth 229
Truth 243
U
unconditional love 98
unhealthy behavior 120
unleash that power 237
unresolved anger 127
until death do us part 97
W
What constitutes normal 85
When Bad Things Happen to Good People 122, 197
When the student is ready 69
Wipe the slate clean 214
work with a therapist 116
Worthy 246
Y
You have to befriend yourself 123
you'll survive 134

Kima Global Publishers

If you enjoyed this book (and naturally we hope that you did) we recommend the following titles for your further reading enjoyment.

Why not also visit our website: http//www.kimaglobal.co.za

You can not only see all our titles but can also safely order on line anywhere in the world.

Holographic Psychology

Maria de Rocha Chevalley Psy.D.

This book explains how our mind-body works Holographically and that the brain is a Hologram, interpreting a Holographic universe.

Maria shares how our fears reflect in the vicious circles the law of cause and effect. The book establishes that we must heal beliefs in separation from wholeness in order to move from depression to creativity through bridging the Mind Holograms.

Maria was born and brought up in Brazil, but moved to Switzerland to bring her work to a wider audience.

I SBN:0-9584493-2-5

Suggested retail price on request. Available from our online Bookstore.

Realizing the Self Within

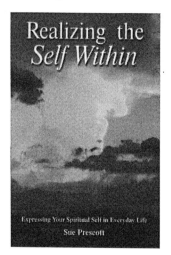

Sue Prescott

Expressing your Spiritual Self in Everyday Life. Tells you

- why your everyday self gets in the way of expressing you spiritual Higher Self.
- what it means to be Self-Realize and how to develop that potential.
- How to use your Spiritual Self to solve problems and make your life more fulfilled.

ISBN 0-9584261-6-3

Suggested retail price on request. Available from our online Bookstore.

Healing Habits

We all have habits and the author has, over years of study, established the esoteric and emotional causes of the habits we indulge in. She gives methods and techniques of how to heal the underlying causes, which will release the habit. Over 100 habits are covered including some unusual ones. It makes fascinating reading, but one should avoid pointing out other people's habits if we want to remain popular!

ISBN: 0-9584493-5-X

By Ann Gadd